THE GAMER'S GUIDE

TO THE

KINGDOM OF

GOD

By Michael King

Edited by Sunshine L Brown King

The Gamer's Guide to the Kingdom of God

© Copyright 2015

This book and other titles by Michael King can be found at TheKingsofEden.com, and is made available through Amazon.com and select retail outlets.

ISBN-13: 978-0692576151

ISBN-10: 0692576150

Kings of Eden Publishing

Printed in the USA

TABLE OF CONTENTS

DEDICATION

I dedicate this book to my beautiful wife who also doubles professionally as my talented editor, Sunshine L. King. You have heard me prattle on about this topic so many times over the years, it is a wonder you persevered through the first edit, much less the completion of the book. Thank you for your time, effort, and above all your patience and encouragement. I love you and our life together, and I am excited and blessed that I get to share it with you, my very best friend.

ACKNOWLEDGMENTS

What began in 2009 as a series of Facebook notes eventually grew into something much more: a deeper revelation of the Kingdom of Heaven with a unique gaming-twist that I have never seen before in other books or messages.

I first want to thank God--Father, Son, and Holy Spirit--without you this book has no purpose. May these written words release light into spiritual darkness and bring life to everyone who reads them.

I want to thank my beautiful wife who also doubles professionally as my talented editor, Sunshine L. King. You have heard me prattle on about this topic so many times over the years, it is a wonder you persevered through the first edit, much less several. Thank you for your time, effort, and above all your patience and encouragement. I love you and our life together.

Thank you to my parents, James and Dale Cirillo. You have taught me from a young age to love Jesus with all my heart, and I believe that this book, as many to come, is a testament to not only you teaching me to follow Christ, but to pursue writing as well, which you have always fostered in me. You have encouraged and tried to instill in me an ethic to not give up and drop out early, and I am glad to say that unlike the piano lessons, I stuck this through to the end.

A special thank you to Denise Hayes of Denise Hayes Studios for the amazing cover art. Your work, as always, is fantastic!

A major thank you to Praying Medic and Praying Medic's Wife at Inkity Press for your time and energy to help me get in the publishing world. Your knowledge and experience has been extremely valuable, but even more than, that I value your close friendship.

Thanks to the Watch of the Lord Team--you were a part of the most spiritually formative years of my life.

To Diane Burke, Watch leader, you have been a dear friend over the years. From healing, deliverance, the prophetic, prayer, and the deep Christ-like character in your life I have absorbed over the years, I would not be who or how I am today without your tireless effort, prayers, and friendship. I am forever grateful.

Jerry Brancefield, thank you for being an older brother, encouraging me and sharing your wisdom, your prayers, and even your struggles as you have watched and helped me through my own. You are an amazing man of God with a heart of gold. Blessings to you and your family always.

Geoffrey Pitman, brother, you rock. I have many fond memories of us living and praying together, and I treasure you in my heart. You were a blessing to walk alongside while we both were in State College amidst many others who didn't understand where God was taking me. I have been truly blessed by the times we lived together, prayed together, cried together, and generally made a glorious mess of things.

Jen Yeisley, you have been a great friend and prayer partner, but more than that, you have been a sister in the Lord. You are an awesome woman of God, and God has many miracles, signs, and wonders planned for you. Mark my words, God will raise you up as a prophetess in these times where revelation of God's goodness is so desperately needed.

I also want to give special acknowledgement to those in my Facebook Community. There are far too many of you to name, but you made a significant impact on the formation of this book--from those who participated in the original Facebook Notes to those who have cheered me on in the final stages. I am grateful for all of your influence on my life and the formation of this book. I love you all.

Introduction:

For the Noob

There are two kinds of people in this world--gamers and noobs (newbies who are just starting to be gamers). If you're a gamer, this section will be a bit of a review. To the noobs, this chapter will help you follow along with the rest of the book. While I will explain things as we go and there is a glossary at the back of the book, this section will reduce the risk of you being overwhelmed by new content later on.

The most common method of gaming at this time is online gaming due to the prevalence of computers and high-quality computer games. *Final Fantasy I* started in 1987 and it has been very popular--with a *Final Fantasy XV* scheduled for release in 2016. *World Of Warcraft* has been on the electronic-game market for 10 years. Other well-known titles include the *Diablo* series, *Runequest*, *Skyrim*, and *Guild Wars*, but these are just a few of literally hundreds of role-play games (RPGs) on the market. *Dungeons and Dragons* is probably the best-known RPG overall and simultaneously has a very bad reputation in most Christian circles. While it falls into the paper-

and-pen category, most gamers recognize that paper-pen RPGs are the origins of the online games people play today, and as such, the same principles that apply to one, apply to the other.

What makes a gamer a gamer? At the risk of stating the obvious, it is the enjoyment of and regular playing of video games. Video games can be divided into multiple categories based on their genre, and those who play them often gravitate toward one or two genres of preference, such as 1st-person shooter, strategy, RPG, etc. However, many games have similar characteristics that create a certain measure of crossover. This book focuses on RPG-gaming and will address the subject of the Kingdom of God from that perspective.

Since this book is about the Kingdom, it is important to know what is meant by that reference. The Kingdom referred to in this book is that of the domain of the God of the Bible. Other names for God include Holy Spirit, Jesus Christ, Yahweh, and Jehovah. This Kingdom exists both on the earth and in other spiritual realms known collectively as "Heaven," which is both a physical place where people go after they die and a current spiritual reality that coexists with ours—like an overlapping dimension.

Due to the major influence Heaven exerts on our world, it is important to understand how it functions and how to work with Heaven to change our reality. More than that, it is necessary to understand how to get the most out of life here as what we do impacts both now and the afterlife. We are far more influential than we understand and need to make the most of that power.

Prior RPG experience is helpful for understanding the contents of this book, but it was written in such a way that almost all of the information will make sense without it. The basic premise of RPG games is that a player's character is developed at the start of the game with a few choices. First, the player chooses the character's race which automatically affects certain attributes such as the amount of strength, intelligence, or natural immunity to poisons that the character may have. All of these influence gameplay later on. There are usually multiple classes to choose from, with a class being synonymous with a profession. This too will influence gameplay. After those are decided and the game is started, the character will essentially do quests and gain experience to increase his level. Increasing his level allows the player to use better weapons and kill stronger bad guys, thereby allowing him to "level up," again, using better weapons to kill stronger bad guys so he can level up and kill stronger bad guys so he can . . . I'm sure you can see where this is going.

While seemingly redundant, there are actually broad variations in the ways an RPG can be played, and different people can play the same game with different goals in mind. For instance, one can have a goal to be the strongest with the best equipment, while another simply wants a way to have fun with his friends. These goals, and the variety of methods used to accomplish them, create far more variety in gameplay than at first glance.

Each game has a background story that creates the environment and a context for the current characters. In other words, the game may give history on what brought the player to the present state. Sometimes the history given is global in scope, while other times it is local. There is often a second ongoing storyline being developed as the game continues, which helps flesh out the events surrounding the player's actions during the game.

To answer the question that often comes next, no, there generally is not an "end" to the game. "What is the point of a game that has no ending?" RPGs emulate life, albeit a fantasy-world life without the same level of emotional involvement as Real Life since Real Life doesn't just "end" once a series of plot points have been developed and resolved. Rather, once one set of challenges or experiences end, another set takes their place. RPGs are really no different, and as such, they provide a realistic backdrop to discuss how to engage spiritual pursuits in our lives, which then overflow into all that we do.

In each chapter we begin by looking at an aspect of RPG games, and from there we extend that concept into the Kingdom and how it impacts our lives. As you read this book, take time to think about how the tenets discussed herein can be applied to your life. I am confident that if you let yourself, you can learn a lot and gain new perspectives on many aspects of being a follower of Jesus—including how to engage spirit beings, how to let the power of God flow in and through your life, and how to position yourself for new and fruitful spiritual experiences.

Ding! A system message appears in front of you.

Turn the page.

CHAPTER 1

INITIAL SETUP PHASE

The initial setup process of an RPG game, from initial design to first-time players forming their characters, provides a fantastic backdrop to discuss some formative spiritual concepts and realities. There has to be a process of game-creation as well as one for character setup before players can begin playing a game, and these closely parallel our lives here on earth. In addition to game creation, another element must be included: a backstory that explains the battle against evil and which provides a solution to fight it. After all, what is the point of playing a game if it can't be won? First, we will look at the game creation process and review Earth's backstory, then look at the character setup process and how the player has to begin the game so he or she can win.

Let's begin by imagining that a designer is making a computer game. First, he has to create the setting for the game to take place, which means he designs the heavens where the deities will reside as well as the earth-like land where his players will play the game. All of this creation will take place prior to designing the characters since the characters themselves have no place to live until the world itself has been fabricated.

As the world is being designed, it will also require a background story to be written--a reason why the players came to this world and interact on it. This storyline will address some basic questions about the world: Why do the adventurers need to come and fight on behalf of that world? What turmoil in the realm of the Gods brings chaos to the people of the land? Is there a solution to the evil that is spreading across the land? Can the taint of creation from dark forces be stopped? All of these questions are similar to the questions that have plagued mankind for centuries, and this world-creation on the part of the game designer can reasonably be likened to the Biblical creation story—the story where God and Man came from—where the original struggle between good and evil began. After all, isn't that what all RPG games are really about, and isn't that where the idea ultimately came from? The theme of almost any RPG game could aptly be described as "An epic saga of good versus evil digitally mastered in 3-D with high-definition graphics, heroic characters, and compelling storylines, complete with scores of powerful weapons, varied classes, and unique quests." In other words, most RPGs are a fantastical rehashing of our human experience and our attempt to overcome the darkness within us and in the world around us, just personified through a computer screen.

Once the background story is complete, the setting must be reviewed, which in this case is Heaven, a vast place. As discussed in the introduction, Heaven is spiritual in nature but by no means is it limited to the spirit realm. Genesis 1:1-2 says, "In the beginning God created the heavens and the earth. Now the earth was formless and empty, darkness was over the surface of the deep, and the Spirit of God was hovering over the waters." This passage says both little and very much all at once. First, God created the heavens and the earth at the same time, which suggests that they are meant to parallel one another. We have gotten used to an earth-only experience but this was never God's design. Second, this passage notes that earth was without form and was empty, but it says nothing about heaven having a similar state which suggests that the heavens were not in such disarray.

The heavenly realms—including what is known as *Paradise*—are the place people go when they die. Paradise is what usually comes to mind when people refer to Heaven (or a bunch of white clouds and angels with harps) but the totality of the Heavens is far more vast than our universe. In the book of Revelation, chapters 2 and 22 it becomes clear that the Tree of Life is located in Paradise. This isn't just a single tree, but rather a species of tree that grows on both sides of the River of Life—a river that flows out from God's throne in the Throne Room of Heaven. Paradise is one of many places in the vast lands of heaven and is the place the apostle Paul spoke of in 2 Corinthians 12. As a place, Heaven itself is so vibrant that it is overwhelms the physical senses, and Paul was shown various mysteries that not only was he not permitted to share, but they were so awe-inspiring that he would have had difficulty expressing them anyway. Many men and women throughout time have been taken to Heaven through out-of-body experiences and mystical visions and have brought back new perspectives and insight into spiritual reality, many of which have direct and significant impact on earthly realities. Some people have even been shown inventions and other physical objects while in heaven and have been able to re-create those devices here, benefitting humanity.

The Kingdom of God is literally the *domain of God the King*. It is both the place people go after they die as well as a spiritual reality that overlays ours, much like tracing paper over an art design. It is not only made up of the heavens, but the Kingdom of God also ɛsides within the hearts of mankind, and as we choose to extend that domain into the world around us, the Kin; ʾom expands into our outer world as well. Genesis 1 tells the story of God forming all of creation. In verses 26-28 we see Him giving mankind authority over all of the earth:

Then God said, 'Let us make mankind in our image, in our likeness, so that they may rule over the fish in the sea and the birds in the sky, over the livestock and all the wild animals, and over all the creatures that move along the ground.' So God created mankind in his own image, in the image of God he created them; male and female he created them. God blessed them and said to them, 'Be fruitful and increase in number; fill the earth and subdue it. Rule over the fish in the sea and the birds in the sky and over every living creature that moves on the ground.'

Literal ruling authority was given to mankind at that time, but there was a task we were given at that time as well. Where God said, "Subdue it," referring to the earth, that word is the Hebrew word *radah* which means to subjugate, rule, and have dominion over. As mentioned earlier, the earth was empty and formless after God created it, but it is suggestive that something had happened to the earth to bring it into disarray before the time of man. There are a great many theories about this. Many people believe in a literal seven-day creation story, and that is one possible version, but I want to suggest another version that I feel also fits well with the understanding we have of both science and spirituality. While the goal of this book isn't to definitively prove a certain creation-model, I will attempt to paint a sensible picture of what I believe that could look like.

First, the world was created. I believe this creation is measured in interpretive periods referred to as "days" but not meaning literal days, it was on day four where God created time and the passage of time and seasons. In other words, if time literally didn't exist for the first three days of creation, I find it unlikely that they were 24-hour periods and the entire process could be likened to epochs or ages similar to what prehistoric science has uncovered. As this creative process was happening during these periods, complete with dinosaurs roaming the earth and everything, Lucifer, God's right-hand angel, rebelled and was cast down from heaven to earth. As related in Revelation 12: 7-9 it says:

Then war broke out in heaven. Michael and his angels fought against the dragon, and the dragon and his angels fought back. But he was not strong enough, and they lost their place in heaven. The great dragon was hurled down--that ancient serpent called the devil, or Satan, who leads the whole world astray. He was hurled to the earth, and his angels with him.

What it seems like happened to me is that this war that Lucifer and his angels waged against the Angel Armies of God created mass destruction in the universe, and the Earth sustained significant damage as a result. This war took place during the first five day-periods of the creation story, but is in reality an ongoing war that continues to this day. In the midst of that destruction and disarray, God created mankind to *subdue* the earth to bring it under their rule and thus functionally return it to being under God's dominion. In other words, from the very beginning man was tasked with literally bringing the Kingdom of God to earth. The means by which this would happen is that man was to take the design and overall blueprints for Earth found in Heaven and make the Earth mirror the Heavens once more. In fact, Romans 8:21 references the bondage to decay that the earth has been under and how it is waiting for the children of God to free it from its chains. This whole process as shared above is akin to the RPG backstory—the events which happened before we, the players, enter the game. As a result, all of

manity has been given the task of returning creation to God's
—first spiritually then physically—as we become players in the
he of global and even cosmic transformation.

In RPGs, there is a process called Character Setup where the
yer designs the avatar or in-game character and defines certain
arting attributes, including but not limited to: physical appearance
and characteristics such as intelligence, strength, and dexterity, all of
which are influenced by the player's race (most games give options
similar to those found in *The Lord of the Rings* series by JRR Tolkien--
dwarf, elf, human, orc, etc.), a choice of class or profession, and
finally the character's talents and skills. Only when all of these things
have occurred can the game truly begin.

Light. You are floating in endless light in a timeless space. Light as a
feather, you are bathed in warmth and love as you slowly open your eyes.

Ding! A system message pops up in front of you:

Welcome. System records indicate you are an unregistered
user. Please choose your username and starting location.

. . .

. . .

Thank you. Your Race has been determined.
Please prepare for departure.

After reading that message, you lose the feeling of weightlessness and start to
speed downwards, out of the endless light and into starry space. Faster and
faster, you speed past stars and nebulae, meteors and stardust as you close in on

a tiny blue planet. Entering its atmosphere you spiral downwards into a house and dive into a woman's abdomen into another space which is dark, but still warm and full of love, and you feel light as a feather once again.

In the same way that characters are created by the player pre-gameplay, our lives are no different. The dominant belief for centuries has been that we have no choice in being born. We simply "happen" to be born to our parents in our family system by pure chance and live our lives as a result of that. Much like the world was once viewed as flat and is now known to be a sphere, this view is being challenged by a perspective that I believe more accurately reflects reality—that of pre-destination. To explain, I am not referring to the Calvinist version of predestination having to do with God destining some for salvation and others for eternal damnation, but something else entirely. Predestination by definition literally means to have chosen an end-result *before* something occurs--to have pre-defined a destination! Whenever I have heard people talk about their "destiny," they speak of how they feel they are here on earth to accomplish something. This "feeling" is not simply an emotion. It's an innate *knowing* and this perception of a deep sense of purpose transcends religious and cultural barriers. Deep down we all recognize that we are here on earth for a reason and we are not simply the product of random chance on a spinning ball of rock in the midst of empty space, surrounded by other larger, glowing, spinning balls of mass. No, I suggest each of us *chose* to be here on the earth, in this time and in our family setting. Some may find this hard to accept, but bear with me as I explain further.

Every time the DNA--the sperm and egg--of two humans collide, a new life forms, and at that moment of union a spirit enters into that new body. Regardless of how that union occurs, whether organically or through artificial insemination, there *will be* a new life created and tually a baby will be born. The combined DNA will decide the ical attributes, race, and gender of that new life, but what is om taken into account is that in the same way that any number perm could have collided with that egg, there are a great number pirits in heaven waiting for bodies so they can be born, and *which* rit inhabits that body is not decided on earth, but rather in heaven. he physical begets the physical, but the spiritual chooses the spiritual.

Eternity operates outside of the realm of time, and as such is not bound by our human understanding of time. God and each human spirit have decided together when in history we will be born and to what set of parents. Before conception, we are shown in heaven what our life will be like on earth, including the problems we will face physically, emotionally, and even spiritually. As hard as this is for some to believe, it is possible that each of us chose to be here in this time and place. We did not create the physical circumstances, but we did pre-know and willingly choose to enter the body that would accompany those traits.

Numerous verses in the Bible point to this reality of predestination or pre-choice. Jeremiah 1:4-5 says, "Now the word of the Lord came to me saying, 'Before I formed you in the womb I knew you, before you were born I set you apart; I appointed you as a prophet to the nations.'" This says God had already chosen Jeremiah to be a prophet long before Jeremiah was born, but that's not all it says. This passage suggests Jeremiah and God had a discussion about it. To know someone is an active and ongoing process, not simply a momentary absorption of knowledge. According to *Strong's Concordance* the word *know* in this passage is the Hebrew word *yada*, which is not just a factual head-knowledge, but a perception, discernment, and understanding of a person or thing by experience and acquaintance. Simply put, God said he knew

Jeremiah because he didn't just know *about* him, but that God and he knew each other relationally before Jeremiah came to earth as a baby. Thus, Jeremiah had pre-existed in Heaven. Furthermore, the word *appointed* in the above passage is the Hebrew word *nathan* which means to appoint, consecrate, bestow upon or put onto. The very nature of that definition suggests that God didn't just have an idea in his head but actually held a ceremony of some kind in heaven to consecrate Jeremiah and bestowed that office upon him.

Psalm 139:16 says, "Your eyes saw my unformed body; all the days ordained for me were written in your book before one of them came to be." Simply put, David recognizes here that God actually wrote a book about David before David was even born. Both this passage and the passage from Jeremiah point to the reality of our pre-existence. Here, David recognizes and has some memory or revelation of the fact that his destiny—the choices he pre-determined to make before coming to earth—were decided and recorded in heaven before he became a living being.

These are two Biblical examples, but many people throughout history and in the present-day have reported similar experiences. I have a close friend named Hope who for years understood that she pre-existed with God before coming to earth. She and another friend both have actual memories of being in heaven prior to being born. There are many others who have had similar experiences. In fact, I once wrote a post on my social networks asking for others to share their experiences and understanding about this topic, and in less than 24 hours I had no less than ten different stories of people who had either had their own experience of pre-existence or knew of someone else who had one.

One of these examples is that of my wife's friend who we will call "Katy," who once had a dream where she was talking to an infant girl planning on coming to earth. Katy told her it wasn't the right time to do so, and shortly after this dream she had an early first-trimester miscarriage—early enough that she hadn't even known she was pregnant until the miscarriage occurred.

A second example is that of Kat Kerr, a prophetess who travels and speaks to various churches about her revelation on heaven and who has taken multiple trips to heaven herself. She speaks in a number of her messages, including at meetings I have attended, that we are all spirits that exist in heaven with God beforehand and how we choose to come down to earth, knowing our parents and families and the trials and difficulties we will face. This falls very much in line with God's nature as a collaborator, namely that He wants to both make decisions and walk *with* us through life, not simply be the Divine Dictator who bosses us around.

The well-known minister Jesse DuPlantis was taken into a heavenly visitation which he recounts in the video and audio recording titled *Close Encounters of the God Kind.* In this message, he shares that he saw in heaven a great many spirits going up to the throne where God was seated and these spirits clamored excitedly, asking God to send them to be human spirits here on earth. As Jesse watched, he saw God take a deep breath and as he exhaled those spirits were sent from heaven into bodies here on earth, much like in Genesis 2:7 where it says that God breathed spirit into Adam and he became alive.

The reason for sharing this is that like RPG character creation, there is a process we go through prior to starting this "game" of life where we determine what our life will be like, and then we have to make choices in-game that move us in the direction of the destiny we pre-chose with God in heaven. Once we understand that the Earth, the "game world" has been created and we, too, have undergone our own character creation, we finally have to look at how to begin the game in such a way as to win.

It is pointless to try to bring Heavenly reality to earth if we don't have authority or ability to do so. Because the goal of this life-game is to bring the Kingdom to earth, we need to be positioned properly to make that happen. In Genesis, as mentioned earlier, God gave man both a mandate and authority to subdue the earth. Man made a poor decision and chose to eat of the fruit of the tree of the Knowledge of Good and Evil, of which he was commanded not to eat, and in doing so handed significant authority over the earth realm to Lucifer, now known as Satan. The solution to this loss of authority, as well as to the whole problem of defeating evil, is found in the person of Jesus. While the person of Jesus may not seem like a solution to some, let me explain why and how this is so.

Jesus did not come to the earth simply as an avatar embodying the presence of divine, or a good teacher with sound spiritual principles to demonstrate how to live. He was a good teacher, he did demonstrate how to live life, and he did carry the divine presence, (also known as the Holy Spirit) with him, but one defining characteristic sets him apart from all other teachers and religious leaders including Mohammed, Buddha, Joseph Smith, Bodhidarma, Lao-tzu, and other well-known founders of spiritual tenets. Jesus demonstrated publicly before thousands of witnesses many unbelievable miracles including his own death and literal resurrection from the dead. He also taught these same miracles to his disciples and in doing so, altered forever the spiritual playing field by which we are able to exist and have dominion over this earth realm.

Jesus, through his death and resurrection, fulfilled certain spiritual requirements, legal conditions that were written into the fabric of the Universe at its creation. One law in particular, albeit a strange one, says that blood contains both power and life. Furthermore, as sin requires a life as payment, blood sacrifice is required for all sin and only a *perfect* blood sacrifice will suffice. To explain this spiritual law further, it must be included that because the spiritual consequence and judicial ruling for sin is a death sentence, all men and women have died throughout all of time with a *very* few exceptions, and those only due to fulfilling other special conditions. All deaths occur as a direct result of the existence of sin within us. All humans who were procreated of a human father carry the "genes" for sin as it is bound and woven into the paternal DNA. Jesus alone was created with divine genetic material on the paternal side, which meant that he didn't carry the genetic material for sin and was inherently perfect in all his thoughts and actions. This made him eligible to be the perfect sacrifice to atone and forgive all sin for all time, but Jesus didn't stop there with forgiving sin; he went beyond that and restored *all* that was lost.

The Bible says in Romans 3:23 that, "The wages of sin is death," which means Death only has the right to claim those who have sin within them, and because Jesus had none within him, Death itself (as a very real spiritual force and entity, not simply an idea) broke basic spiritual laws upon killing Jesus, and thus came under heavenly judgment. The end result of the judicial ruling against Death was that Jesus took control over the power of Death, Hell, and the Grave--all of Death's domain. Where sin had been able to infiltrate and take dominion over Man's domain through the consequences of one man's actions, Jesus reversed that ruling and permanently cancelled all rights of death and destruction that affect the whole cosmos. Then he rose from the dead and delegated authority to his followers to reverse death, loss, and destruction wherever it may be found.

While this is a fascinating story and a perspective that is not often taught, how does this relate to the subject of RPGs, and what does it have to do with this book? If we do not accept this spiritual truth for what it is, we are inherently crippled in this life and unable to adequately participate in the Real-Life Game. The notion of fighting works of darkness is an absolute joke so long as spiritual darkness has free reign within us and we have not surrendered our hearts to the Light. While there are many people out there who have some grasp of this Light in various forms, God revealed himself to all of humanity in bodily form as the person Jesus, who in John 8:12 said, "I am the light of the world. Whoever follows me will not walk in darkness, but will have the light of life." Through what Jesus purchased for us by his death and resurrection, which cannot be duplicated by another, he made it possible for us to come into perfect alignment with God's plans and purposes and he daily empowers us to be His direct emissaries on this earth to destroy the works of darkness and restore light to all things.

An emissary is not just a representative from one country to another, but has the authority to make *binding decisions* on behalf of the nation he represents. When a ruler sends an emissary in his stead, he is saying, "This person has all of the knowledge and ability to make decisions and rulings in the same way that I would do it, and I back them with the full authority of my Kingdom in the carrying out of those decisions." For this reason, Kings do not choose emissaries lightly. Yet, God has seen fit through Jesus to make us His emissaries in the earth, with legally binding spiritual right(s) and ability to forever alter the physical and spiritual landscape around us. The signup is easy and free yet simultaneously costs us everything.

It is free because we didn't have to become a sacrifice and die in order to make this reality possible and receive this gift of forgiveness of sin. We don't have to do anything to earn it or "be good enough" to obtain it; no amount of being a "good person" will give us access to this right or the righteousness that comes with it. We get to have it simply because we get to have it. Yet there is a responsibility that comes with it. Jesus said in Matthew 10:8b, "Freely you have received, freely give." Because we have freely been given a sacrifice of Jesus' life to purchase life abundantly for all humanity for all Time and Eternity, we are responsible to freely give of our own lives to destroy works of darkness and to put evil under the dominion of Jesus not just in theory but in action everywhere we go. As we are all in this together and we do not stand alone, this is far more possible than one might imagine. For as we engage our spiritual might to combat darkness, we link arms together with those around the planet who are doing the same.

The Book of Romans explains some of what happens when we decide to not just accept that Jesus is God, but the reality of the fullness of what he did. He died as a perfect sacrifice, destroyed the power of Death, then rose again and went to Heaven with God the Father to prepare a place for us to coexist in Eternity with Him as we subdue evil on the earth with the Holy Spirit--the Divine Spirit Guide that He places within us. As this happens, there is a spiritual circumcision that takes place. When anyone decides to follow Jesus, the sin nature is irrevocably removed, qualifying him to be Jesus' emissary in the earth. Contrary to some Christian teachings, once this sin nature is removed there is no way to get it back. It is dead, gone, cut off, removed, severed, unattached, disconnected, isolated, eliminated, confiscated, deleted, amputated, subtracted, and detached. This is seen in the practice of circumcision. And while circumcision of males or females in the natural world is a highly barbaric and sexually mutilatory practice, it provides a clear image of what happens to our inner darkness--our inner sin nature that pulls us constantly toward outer expressions of that evil and corruption within. When a foreskin is cut off, it is a separate entity from the physical body, no longer attached or linked in any way. This tissue, now 100% separated, dies on its own, never to return to the original owner. One cannot, five or ten months later, decide to have the now-dead skin reattached to his body. Jesus removed the sin nature once and for all, and as his disciples, we no longer possess this internal characteristic that binds us to evil and darkness.

The actual act of "becoming a disciple" is quite easy and is as simple as an internal decision to follow Jesus as his disciple. The *only* thing we have to do is *believe* although sometimes people feel like they need to say or do something for that to be the case. While not required, I have included a short prayer for those who find one helpful. The exact wording isn't important, but the act of confessing it verbally, making a declaration to the Universe that we are disciples and emissaries of God and are now legally bound with the rights and responsibilities afforded therein, has some value.

One last reminder: Jesus is *the* Perfect Being of Love who has never caused or intended any harm towards us and has only ever worked for our benefit and well-being to bring love, life, and light to us. Anything we have ever experienced that was not of love, life, and light was performed by those in the Kingdom of darkness, for darkness is nothing like Jesus. We are only agreeing to serve the Most Beautiful One who has cared for and about us far more than we can ever comprehend, and as we get to know Him more and more we will come to recognize how true it is.

The Prayer

I choose as an act of my will to become a disciple of Jesus. I acknowledge that Jesus lived on this earth as a human, died as a perfect man, and destroyed death, rising from the dead three days later. From there, he went on into Heaven to prepare a place for me to join him. I accept the to follow His teachings and those of the Holy Spirit within me, and I open myself up to be filled and baptized with Holy Spirit as the empowerment God has sent me to be successful as His emissary in the earth from this day forward. I acknowledge this is a permanent and binding decision to follow the Perfect Being of Love, Jesus the Christ of Nazareth. And so it is (Amen).

If this is something that is new to you, I encourage you to go find others who are like-minded. Not all will understand the RPG references I have made in this book, but the underlying realities we have explored remain the same wherever you go. God will connect you with others (and probably already has) who can live out this journey with you. I'm not even telling you to go to church, as there are many in churches who don't understand the depths of Goodness that God has for you, but ask God to lead and guide you to other like-minded disciples of Jesus, and He will do just that.

A series of system messages appear in front of you. Ding!

You have now chosen your primary profession: Emissary of Light. Your name has been listed in the Lamb's Book of Life.

You have received "Holy Spirit": Holy Spirit is a spirit guide who is also the God of the Universe. He is listed in your inventory. He cannot be dropped or discarded, and is permanently bound to your character.

You have completed the Initial Setup Phase. You may now login. Enjoy your experience!

CHAPTER 2

THE COSMIC GM

Before there can be any role-playing in a game, there must be a Game Master (GM) present to oversee the game. All RPGs have them, and without a GM, the game itself is literally unable to function. The GM is responsible for developing and creating the storyline, as well as giving the players in-game choices. While this analogy holds more true with tabletop RPGs, the GM functions as the central intelligence behind all computer-based games, making any software updates and solving in-game player problems as the arise. As with RPGs, Real Life has a GM as well; his name is Holy Spirit, one aspect of the Person of God. John 16:12-15 explains the work of Holy Spirit, saying:

> I have much more to say to you, more than you can
> now bear. But when he, The Spirit of truth, comes, he will
> guide you into all truth. He will not speak on his own; he will
> speak only what he hears, and he will tell you what is yet to
> come. He will bring glory to me by taking from what is mine,
> and making it known to you. All that belongs to the Father is

mine. That is why I said the Spirit will take from what is mine and make it known to you.

Holy Spirit is the ultimate Spirit-guide who directs us on the earth much in the same way a GM directs the characters in RPGs. He has ultimate wisdom and understanding and has the solution to every problem one might encounter in life, but is also the ultimate Teacher, possessing all knowledge as well.

Holy Spirit is our Cosmic GM who directs the play of the Game. He even tells us things that are going to happen in our futures and advises us on how to address them. All cultures and religions have a belief about people who hear from God. They are called seers, prophets, holy ones, and oracles, who nowadays are sometimes referred to as psychics, prophets, or similar, but all of them have the quality of hearing God speak to them for direction and future guidance. The Holy Spirit, like a GM, keeps track of the information that regular game players don't know. He knows every intimate detail about every aspect of life, including our own abilities and destinies that we aren't even aware of yet. In contrast, we the Players have extremely limited knowledge that is confined to our experiences or what we can learn directly from others. Holy Spirit is always available as an in-game tutor and help-desk worker, so when we have questions we can ask Him to tell us the details about what is happening next. He brings glory to God the Father, another aspect of His being, by walking us through this game so we can play and win.

Without the GM, we would be powerless. After Jesus died and rose again, he spent 40 days with his disciples, continuing to teach and train them for the things that were to take place after he left and ascended to heaven. He gave very specific instructions in Acts 1:4-5, "Do not leave Jerusalem, but wait for the gift my Father promised, which you have heard me speak about. For John baptized with water, but in a few days you will be baptized with the Holy Spirit." Jesus was very clear that in order to start playing, they needed to have the GM oversee their gameplay. Jesus knew that in order to be successful, it was imperative that they received the GM as a helper through every step of the game. In the same way that the disciples received Holy Spirit GM's help to begin the work of sharing Jesus with the world, we too have been gifted with this same Spirit.

In order to walk this out, it presupposes that there is some sort of external communication that we can engage in with God. In reality, it's like having one's own special helpdesk that is available at any time and not just ready, but willing and able to help and guide us at any moment. Let me first give you a practical example: God will help you take tests in school.

I was in an Old Testament Studies class in college and the professor always gave essay questions as part of his tests. Instead of just one essay question though, he would offer three essays questions and tell the class what they were so they could prepare for all three. On the test each student would get one of them at random. During both the midterm and the final I had prepared all three essays to some extent, but with each test I had only one essay I knew well (these were not open-book and had to be written from memory). As anyone would, I wanted to get the essay I knew best. At midterm, I was riding in on the bus and the Holy Spirit said to me, "Move one seat to the left," referring to the seat in class where I always sat. On entering the classroom I did this, and I got the essay I wanted. I aced that entire test except for two points off for spelling a prophet's name wrong. At the final, I had a vision where I saw a blueprint of the classroom desk setup and the one I needed to sit in was highlighted in blue. I forgot about this on test day until after everyone was already seated. I looked around in a panic until I realized I was already sitting in the right seat. Again, I got the essay I wanted again and performed well once more.

Holy Spirit is not just able but He is more than willing to help us on a daily basis, providing direction on even the smallest matters in life. He told me to slow down once while driving on an unfamiliar road with a heavy trailer behind my truck. As I slowed I came upon the road I needed to turn on next and made the turn. If he hadn't, I would have missed the road, and turning around with that trailer on a two-lane road in the country would have been impossible, and I probably would have gotten lost. The Christian term for this is *prophesy*, but at its root prophesy is simply a two-way conversation with God. In game terms it's like chatting with someone through private message although this private message can come in picture, audio, or text format.

There is another aspect to the GM-status that holds an important correlation to the real world. Jesus in Matthew 28:18-20 says, "All authority in heaven and on earth has been given to me. Therefore go and make disciples of all nations, baptizing them in the name of the Father and of the Son and of the Holy Spirit, and teaching them to obey everything I have commanded you. And surely I am with you always, to the very end of the age."

Jesus, the Holy Spirit, and the Father are one, so if Holy Spirit is the GM, so are the other two. Jesus acknowledged that he has been given *all* authority in heaven and on earth, as any GM would have-- total authority over the game. Mark 16:15 says something similar, but with a slightly different emphasis, "Go into all the world and preach the gospel to all creation." Here the emphasis is on all creation, not all nations of people. Jesus didn't just commission the disciples to preach the gospel, but to transform all of creation *through* the power of the gospel--the good news of Jesus's death and resurrection. Giving them a commission is the same as giving them the authority to accomplish that commission. This means that we too have been given authority over all of creation to manifest God's goodness on a GM-power level. To do this, however, we will need to increase the level of authority and power we operate at, and we must train our skills and stats. The next chapter will discuss levels and effective ways to start leveling up, and a few chapters later we will discuss skills-training and stat development.

CHAPTER 3

LEVEL UP!

The main goal of any Role Play game is to grow stronger, to increase in level, and to gain more abilities. While not the *only* purpose of a game, it is one of the most prominent aspects of any RPG, and rare is the game that doesn't involve level-based play. As a player plays, he gains experience through his actions, whether killing evil creatures, completing quests, or by ingesting certain magical or God-blessed items. This experience-gathering in turn causes him to reach points of critical mass, upon which he levels up.

The results of leveling up can vary from game to game, but all games of this type have in common this trait--the player advances in some way. Regardless of how that advancement happens, whether the person becomes wiser, stronger, more spiritual, more skilled with weapons or a craft, or all of the above, increase happens. The next time he meets a bad guy it takes less time and effort to vanquish him than it did before the player had leveled up. The more bad guys (known as mobs) the player defeats, the easier and faster a new enemy can be killed. More enemies beaten means faster experience gain which means increased battle-speed. This again translates back to increased experience gain…and it continues from there.

An example of this is that in the beginning of the game, the player might fight a fox and defeat it but with great difficulty. As he is a Level 1 player and has very low skills and strength, his attacks are very weak. As the game progresses and he gets stronger, reaching Level 15 or 16, he is able to fight a brown bear with ease, and then eventually around Level 30, he can defeat an entire group of armed bandits by himself with minimal injury.

Level increases are mathematical and come after a predetermined amount of experiences has been obtained. Experience (exp.) is usually obtained by killing mobs, but there are usually other ways exp. can be earned, such as quests or player killing (which is a major no-no). For example, the fox might give anywhere from 2-10 experience points (exp.) when killed, the goblin 22-30 exp., the ogre about 150-160 exp., the wyvern 370-380 exp., and so on. The way to level up in-game is to kill lots of mobs and complete quests. The new levels allow the player to get new skills and weapons, which lets him kill mobs faster and easier and kill harder mobs of higher level. This is in actuality a lot like compounding interest, where the investment profits increase the size of the principal investment, ultimately increasing the profit yield, which in turn adds to the principal, and so on.

One of the most enjoyable parts of an RPG is the regular increase in level and upgrading to new enemies, new weapons, and new areas to explore, but even amidst the enjoyment, monotony hits. Higher levels don't just allow the player to kill mobs faster and gain more exp, but they require the player to obtain a larger quantity of exp. in order to advance further. For example, a Level 1 player might need 100 exp. to reach Level 2, but he might need 1,400 exp. to go from Level 5 to Level 6 and 10,100 to go from Level 14 to Level 15. While it is easier and faster to obtain exp. at a higher level, the experience-requirement increase means one thing and one thing only: It's time to grind. Grinding is where the game goes from being for-play-only and becomes a combination of work and play. When a player grinds, he has to kill mobs repetitively until he finally gets enough exp. to reach the next level.

Sometimes players grind out of a need for gold or other resources instead of levels, but either way, the process can get tedious. The player is stuck killing mobs over and over as he very slowly watches his exp. bar (which measures the percent of exp./100 and tells the player how close he is to the next level) rise. There are some computer programs and/or game commands that do this sort of thing automatically, allowing the player to camp out in one place and kill continuously even if away from the keyboard (afk). By doing this he can make dinner, go pick up his kids from school, take a shower, and even go to sleep while his character does the work. There are risks associated with going afk, as his character can run out of stamina or spiritual power and lose the ability to fight. Under the right circumstances this can lead to death, requiring the character to be resurrected when the player returns to the computer, and if he leaves the computer overnight, his character could be dead for hours before he returns to fix the problem.

This "level-up" concept is actually found in the Bible, where in 2 Corinthians 3:18 it says, "And we, who with unveiled faces all reflect the Lord's glory, are being transformed into his likeness with ever-increasing glory, which comes from the Lord, who is the Spirit." While that might not sound very much like leveling up, there are other translations which express it a bit differently. The *KJV* and *NASB* say "from glory to glory" and the *ESV* and *NET* say "from one degree of glory to another." Expanding a bit further on the actual meaning of the passage based on the original Greek, it says that as we behold the Lord we "undergo metamorphosis into God's likeness, separating ourselves entirely from one level of exalted splendor and departing into another level of exalted splendor." This passage literally means that we level up!

Experience and even simple observation show us that as believers our spiritual journey works exactly like this--with progression in levels of glory. The Bible talks about how as beginners, we crave pure spiritual milk--the easy stuff, just like in the early levels of an RPG. At Level 1 a player would be extremely lucky if he could one-shot-kill a rabbit or fox, but as he trains, learns, and grows, he becomes stronger. Likewise in the Kingdom of God, a new believer is likely to have difficulty overcoming basic spiritual problems, but as a believer continues to forgive and get inner healing, grow in relationship with God, have God's transforming fire purge the negative things out of his life, and learn how to operate in Kingdom authority, he also advances in level. He goes from Level 1, the "I don't know much about following God, but I really love Jesus" stage and progresses a few levels. As he forgives those who have wronged him, repents (which means to change ones beliefs, not feel bad about things) from old ways of thinking and starts believing what God says about him, and grows closer still in relationship with God he advances even further.

Water Baptism, a process where one is immersed in water (or sprinkled with it in some denominations) and comes back up for air is an act of identification with Jesus' death and subsequent resurrection, whereby Jesus stripped away our sin nature and removed it from us. This is a full level increase all on its own. Something about water baptism, performing a physical act that identifies with a spiritual act, causes an internal change in our souls. Baptism in the Holy Spirit, another level-up where the Holy Spirit releases a new measure of power and divine gifts upon the believer, comes with additional divine affinity as well. One moment he is not baptized, the next moment he is. It is a definable moment when more divine power is accessed or attained--a total shift in level.

This level-up concept is *highly* relevant to Kingdom life if for no other reason than because it's how normal, natural life operates. The concept of compounding interest does not just apply to RPGs, as many things in Real Life increase on an exponential curve. The more of any renewable resource someone has, given a fixed period of time, the faster he is able to accrue more of it in a second fixed block of time.

Plants and bees are good examples of this natural function. When a farmer plants a plant, it produces seeds--not one, but many seeds per plant. For simplicity let us say each plant produces 20 seeds. If a farmer plants those seeds and they all bear fruit, he will harvest 400 seeds. If he plants those seeds and all of them bear fruit at the next harvest, he will harvest 8,000 seeds, then 160,000 seeds, and so on. At some point he will either start eating or selling the seeds or he will buy larger fields to be able to plant the vast quantity of seeds he has obtained.

Bees multiply a bit differently, but still have the ability to increase exponentially. A queen bee lays eggs and some of them turn into new queen bees. The queen then makes a "swarm" which is a portion of the bees from that hive, leaving the new queen behind. This makes two smaller hives where there was previously only one. As each queen lays more eggs, the hive sizes increase. The queens lay more queen eggs, form new swarms, and split the hive again. Doing simple math on hive-splitting, the first split makes 2 hives in place of one. The seconds split makes 4 hives, then 8, then 16, then 32 hives and so on.

Jesus spoke of this kind of multiplication in some of his parables, noting, as with the examples above, that the ways of nature mirror the ways of the Kingdom. He explained it quite simply when he said in Matthew 25:29, "For whoever has will be given more, and they will have an abundance. Whoever does not have, even what they have will be taken from them." Compounding interest works in both directions, whether in your favor or against you.

To illustrate this, let me tell you a story about a woman I once knew who loved cats. She took in strays and fed them, but she didn't have the money to get them fixed. Invariably the cats bred and produced new litters--which meant she had to spend more money on cat food and supplies. As she didn't have money to get them fixed in the first place and then was scrounging money for cat food, she ended up having those cats breed and birth even *more* cats. Once I helped her move out of her house and at that time, she had more cats than I can recall--more than thirty of them in the house, not including the ones that randomly roamed the property. It all started with just a few cats, but because she did not pay proper attention to the law of exponential increase she paid a hefty price for it in the long run.

Likewise, for some reason many believers largely miss this fact in the ways we manage our spirituality. As with the farmer, if he only sowed one seed each year, he would reap the same harvest. If he wanted to increase the size of his harvest he would have to sow more seeds, and to expect anything more from a single seed is somewhat idiotic. If we want to get more than we have currently, we will have to do more now than we did before, or engage it at a higher level than we did prior. Whether in prayer, reading our Bibles, helping the poor, or whatever the action we are engaging, we cannot expect a greater level of change and transformation if we do not enhance, increase, or deepen the work we are doing. While this certainly could appear at first to promote a works-based method of following Jesus, this is not about earning our way into heaven by our efforts. Heaven-when-you-die salvation is a once-and-done deal and comes by faith, requiring no effort; rather, we are working to manifest Heaven here on the earth. Many have prayed for revival or renewal, but what if the steps to get there have been in front of us this whole time? What if we need to get purposeful about our multiplication processes --that it's not about waiting for external revival but an internal leveling-up in Real Life that needs to take place. After all, the Kingdom is first and foremost *within us*.

As mentioned earlier there is a way to play RPGs on autopilot, and there is a way to do this in one aspect of Real Life as well. Praying in tongues, also called a prayer language, praying in the spirit, or in academic circles *glossolalia*, is a spiritual gift that allows the believer to bypass his mental understanding during prayer. Holy Spirit gives words to his spirit to say which he intuits internally and then prays out loud in what usually sounds like nonsense, but which at times can be in other earthly languages that the believer has never learned. First Corinthians 14 explains that the basic purpose of tongues is to edify and strengthen one's self. This can be done throughout the day even while doing other activities. It takes minimal mental effort and as such requires very little of the conscious mind, so other tasks can be performed while praying in tongues without extensive mental interruption. Praying in tongues is the equivalent of a cheat-code, connecting the believer's spirit to God's spirit without conscious involvement. This allows him to energize and strengthen his spirit even though his conscious mind in the realm of the soul is uninvolved and does not generally grow or change as a result of the interaction. The benefit of this is that in most other spiritual disciplines for the spirit to be energized requires the conscious mind to connect as well. While other prayer disciplines have their own benefits, not discussed here, this type of prayer has the bonus of bypassing that mechanism entirely.

I have personally used this ability while driving, walking around during work, and while doing things that are more manual than mental in nature. I find that when I pray in tongues for ten or fifteen minutes straight while driving to work in the morning I am much more likely to do it randomly throughout the day as well. Essentially, when I activate the "cheat code" by praying in tongues for that time in the morning, I set myself up to continue running that "cheat" throughout the rest of that day. Even when interrupted I tend to pick back up praying a short while later. What I have effectively done in those times are built a temporary habit that lasts no longer than a day, but is still a beneficial habit. Over time these one-day habits build into a lifestyle of regular prayer which contributes to gaining new levels in the spirit. My one caveat here is that praying in tongues can be difficult to do if high-level critical thinking is required as it has the ability to distract when heavy focus and concentration are needed, but even this varies from person to person.

Praying in tongues is not the only "afk-grinding" method available. Good habits, especially habits directly relating to spiritual disciplines (such as prayer, fasting, service, worship, reflection, meditation, Bible-reading, etc.), can work in a similar manner although they require a bit more effort. If we purposefully practice any habit, we can change patterns of thought and activity. When we practice enough we will find we automatically start doing or thinking in the way we have trained, even if we weren't doing it consciously. Sports, martial arts, and dance all train the body to engage muscle memory, which essentially is making the body form a habit--where the muscles and neurons get used to performing an action a certain way. If trained appropriately, when a situation comes up the body will automatically operate how it was trained without conscious thought involved. There are actual nerve roots and nervous system pathways the body uses to react faster than normal in these situations.

From a habit-building perspective in my own life I have found that I automatically start driving toward my workplace when I drive on certain roads, even if it is my day off. I have built a subconscious habit to the point that my wife will have to ask me "where are you going?" when I am getting ready to make a turn toward my workplace instead of heading toward our intended destination. Likewise, when we get in the habit of reading the Bible upon waking, praying before bed or meals, or praying in tongues while driving, even if we are tired we will tend to automatically engage in these actions. This habit-building serves us well when we want to maintain momentum in a particular spiritual discipline but lack focus.

As mentioned earlier, grinding in-game can get tedious and a player can only kill so many of a mob until he is bored and ready for something else. As the main point of the game is to kill mobs to get better levels and items to kill other mobs, the player is kind of stuck doing it over and over anyway. In spite of the occasional boredom, there is a highly redemptive value to this concept of grinding. The more we engage in spiritual disciplines where we connect with God, the more we become like Him. With this transformation we step into higher levels of power and authority and become more loving and mature as the fruit of the Spirit, our inner character, grows on the inside. The best part of this is that unlike in RPGs which at times make use of redemptive violence, we don't kill people to level up-- doing that would actually cause us to incur penalties which we will discuss in a later chapter.

This leads to a question--if killing stuff won't level us up as it does in-game, what else in the Kingdom *does*? While not an exhaustive list, we will review six more things in the rest of this chapter that contribute to new levels: deliverance/exorcism, worship/soaking/ contemplative prayer, hearing and reading the Bible, impartation-style prayer, intercessory prayer, and receiving new revelation.

Deliverance/Exorcism

Demons really do exist although the vast majority of them don't do the stuff depicted in horror movies, as most aim for subtlety over grand displays of power. Not that some couldn't display power more overtly than they do, but when you're a demon and you start chucking objects across a room, your host or a passerby is likely to take notice, and one of them just might make you leave. No, subtlety is the most common play in a demon's handbook, and if demons can make a person think they don't exist or make that person believe they are not being influenced by demons when they do exist, the demons are steps ahead. The main goal of any demon is described in John 10:10, "The thief comes to steal and to kill and to destroy. . ." Most demons have a limited sphere of influence, but that doesn't stop tens, hundreds, or in some cases even thousands of them from taking up residence within a person. The more demons, the more weighed-down the person will be and the more struggles he will have in life.

Demons often operate by suggesting thoughts or ideas into our minds, making the thoughts appear as our own. They can also influence behaviors, agitating, saddening, or angering us in situations that don't call for that level of emotional response. Even when we realize what is happening it can be very difficult to overcome the emotions that are swirling inside us to change our behavior in that moment.

As such, the Bible gives this admonition in Hebrews 12:1b: "Let us throw off everything that hinders and the sin that so easily entangles, and let us run with perseverance the race marked out for us." Removal of demonic hindrances allows us to move forward and to do it faster. It not only helps us increase in level, but allows us to accelerate the process. A visual for this is that of someone pulling a cart full of both provisions and dead bodies; the provisions represent life-giving things and the dead people represent demons. When the person pulling the cart stops and hauls a dead body off, dropping it at the side of the road, the cart becomes much lighter and therefore easier to continue pulling forward. Once the cart is emptied of all the dead bodies, the person should be able to run forward without the internal baggage holding him back, armed with nothing but provisions for the journey ahead. While demons are not the only kind of internal hindrance, they are a significant and often-ignored stumbling-block. As a result many churches and believers don't know how to cast them out or otherwise deal with them, to the point that some groups have highly developed theological systems to "prove" that believers are somehow immune to this internal hindrance when they aren't, which conveniently puts those groups in a position to not have to learn anything about casting out demons. This subject will be covered in more detail in the chapter titled "Combat," and is inextricably linked to the topic of Inner Healing, which is addressed in the "Healing" chapter, both toward the end of the book.

WORSHIP/SOAKING/CONTEMPLATIVE PRAYER

Worship, soaking, and contemplative prayer are all somewhat different in the way they are carried out, but the main similarity is that they all are designed to connect on a personal level with the Person of God, not simply learn information about God. Worship is typically overt, involving singing songs and often including physical movement, dance, etc. It can be done quietly, but most often is associated with words, songs, and movement. The second, soaking, involves sitting or lying comfortably, welcoming the manifested presence of God into the room, and then simply resting in and enjoying God's presence. This can be done silently but is often done with instrumental or worship music to set the mood and help engage focus on God. The third is largely a silent meditation of scripture, leading the person into a deeper connection with God using the doorway of scripture meditation. I have put all three in the same category as all three essentially focus on the same goal--being in God's presence.

The Bible says in Psalm 16:11b that "in your presence there is fullness of joy; at your right hand are pleasures forevermore" (*ESV*). It says in Exodus 33:14 that "My Presence will go with you, and I will give you rest." When Moses asked God to reveal His glory, God caused His *goodness* to pass before him. The Bible says that God's presence contains light, fire, lightning, clouds, and hailstones. There is righteous judgment there as well as shelter and protection. In God's presence blessings are handed out and secret sins are revealed. Even the earth itself shakes in the midst of God's presence. All of these things are given on behalf of those who love God, not against them. Any judgments that are released are against everything that hinders love, and any fire from Him directed at us is only to burn away all that holds us back in life.

In the same way that deliverance sets people free from darkness, soaking, worship, and contemplation can do the same, but from a completely different angle. In fact, these disciplines couple quite well with casting out demons for a reason. Exorcising demons removes dark spirits, but true internal transformation requires a combination of three things: removal of demons, healing of inner hurts, and transformation of mindsets. Even if a demon is cast out, if the other areas are not dealt with there is little preventing that spirit from returning. These disciplines of soaking, worship, and contemplative prayer direct the light of God to our inner hurts, bringing His healing touch to bear on those dark places within us. As we do this Holy Spirit cleanses our souls of everything that is pain or darkness, even those things we are ashamed of and try to hide from His light.

These disciplines accomplish more than just removal of darkness or increase of Heaven's light within us. As we engage God in worship we undergo subtle transformation. In the same way that a master musician tunes his instrument, when we worship God He tunes our hearts to more closely match his. Soaking is more restful than worship in that we are not actively pushing toward anything. When we soak we become more relaxed as the stresses of life fall away, and we gain mental clarity and spiritual strength from our times of rest in God. Contemplative prayer accomplishes these to some extent, but tends to require a bit more mental focus than soaking and has a more subdued atmosphere than worship. The exact method we use, whether soaking, contemplating, worshipping, or a combination of the three, in and of itself is not the most important thing. The part that is truly life-changing is that as we do these things we delve deeper into the Person of God.

THE BIBLE

Reading the Bible has great benefit although on any given day the effects may not be overt. This is because a long-term effect is mental transformation, and the effects of Bible-reading are cumulative over time. When I read or listen to the Bible in the morning before work it shifts my focus heavenward. As I do it consistently, my days have a subtle positive tone to them, which is often only recognized after I get out of the habit and I observe its absence. Reading the Bible in the morning positions the heart to be more receptive and focused on God throughout the day. This focus-shift means that we approach all situations with a more heavenly perspective and mindset, often causing us to think, speak, and act in a manner that is life-giving when otherwise we might not have. This internal shift is not always easy to recognize, so it is important to trust and step out in faith and do it whether we see immediate results or not. The transformation takes place daily, bit by bit. After all, Jesus said in Matthew 4:4, "Man cannot live on bread alone but by every word that proceeds from the mouth of God," and again in Matthew 6:11, "Give us this day our daily bread." Though this daily word is not limited to scripture-reading only, is a fantastic way to activate the provision of God each day in our hearts and lives.

Reading the Bible is not the only means to obtain this effect-- hearing it is another. I have the Bible on CD and have ripped the audio to my laptop as well. Back in the day before smart phones, I used to keep the physical CDs in my car which allowed me to listen while driving, and when at home I would play it via my laptop while doing chores or whatever else. Nowadays I have the entire New Testament on my smart phone and I typically cycle through the whole thing in 5-chapter increments. I have found that for me five chapters daily is an achievable goal which usually takes anywhere from 15-30 minutes of listening.

I am largely an auditory and visual learner, so while both reading and hearing are great ways for me to absorb information, there are benefits to hearing scripture aside from reading it. First off, I am not a morning person even though I get up early each morning to go to work. When I have tried to sit and read that early, I simply found myself getting sleepy and gaining very little from the activity. Listening does not have that same effect on me, and I am able to listen with headphones while eating breakfast and getting ready for work in the morning and this works well for me. Romans 10:17 says, "Faith comes by hearing, and hearing by the word of Christ." Another benefit of hearing the Bible is that our faith is cultivated. I think part of the reason for this is that when read aloud, my mind is not focused on the act of reading but rather on the information itself. There are times that by hearing it I encounter a scripture in a new way, think of an application I had never thought of before, and stumble on new revelation or find new questions to ask God about. These new ideas may cause me to reconsider my current beliefs and perspectives based on what I have just heard.

This re-evaluation of beliefs is part of the transformation process that comes through hearing or reading the Bible, and as our beliefs transform, so do we. Ultimately, regardless of what method works for each individual, whether a specific time of day, daily chapter goal, Bible-reading plan, hearing versus reading, etc. the ultimate goal of this discipline is to have regular, even daily encounters with the written words of God which can help lead us to encounters with the Person who is the Living Word that cause us to become more like Him. To be fair, I am not always consistent in this task. I, like everyone else, am human, and I tend to do things in phases. For a few months I will diligently engage in this discipline and then for whatever reason it will drop off for a while. This is a normal part of life, and while all of these disciplines listed here are beneficial, it is also important to recognize the times and seasons in our lives and not mentally beat ourselves up when we fail to follow through on our goals. There will be some seasons where a discipline is held to steadfastly with great gains, and other seasons where God may be doing something different, and different practices evolve out of that, and that's okay too.

IMPARTATION-PRAYER

Impartation is a term describing the release of spiritual virtue from one person to another. In 2 Timothy 1:6 Paul wrote to his disciple Timothy and he stated, "For this reason I remind you to fan into flame the gift of God, which is in you through the laying on of my hands." In this passage, Paul described a particular spiritual gift that he gave to Timothy through the process of laying hands on him and releasing that spiritual virtue (It is assumed that Timothy was aware of what this gift was although Paul did not explicitly state it in the text). When Paul put his hands on Timothy's body and prayed for him, he transferred spiritual substance from his life to Timothy's. A good comparison is that of a magnetic card reader commonly used in stores that transfer funds from a debit card to a merchant's account. When the card connects with the reader a nontangible transaction takes place, but even though the transaction itself is invisible and takes place in hyperspace, funds are still transferred. Impartation works in the same way.

Many spiritual belief systems have similar practices for impartation, though the exact name and actions may vary. Some have elaborate ceremonies and others are very simplistic, but it is a very real thing. A similar event is mentioned in Numbers 11:17-18 in the Old Testament, where Moses is overwhelmed by the level of responsibility that he is bearing by himself over an entire nation. He prays to God to help him and God's reply is this:

> The Lord said to Moses: 'Bring me seventy of Israel's elders who are known to you as leaders and officials among the people. Have them come to the tent of meeting, that they may stand there with you. I will come down and speak with you there, and I will take some of the power of the Spirit that is on you and put it on them. They will share the burden of the people with you so that you will not have to carry it alone.'

God instructed Moses to take a portion of the spiritual access that he had on his own life and transfer it to others so they might all share the burden of ruling the nation together.

When someone else releases God's virtue into our lives, there is an instant power boost. Get enough of these boosts and maintain them, and were on our way to new levels in the spirit, new gifts, and new experiences. I personally use almost any excuse to have others lay hands on me and pray for me to receive spiritual virtue. This is not, however, the only way to make use of this ability. I have also discovered that doing the same to others provides increase as well. After all, the scriptural principle of sowing and reaping applies to every area of life. Luke 6:38 says, "Give and it will be given to you. A good measure, pressed down, shaken together and running over, will be poured into your lap. For with the measure you use, it will be measured to you." Whether I'm praying for others or having them pray for me, I still win because to receive prayer is to receive a spiritual blessing, and to lay hands on another and pray for them is to sow out spiritually, and I know that if I sow spiritual blessings, gifts, and power then I will also reap in like kind.

In spite of my can-do attitude and willingness to pray for people at a moment's notice, laying hands on others is not without its risks and this is important to be aware of early on. First Timothy 5:22 expresses a warning about laying hands on people: "Do not be hasty in the laying on of hands, and do not share in the sins of others. Keep yourself pure." There is a bit of debate in Christian circles as to the exact meaning of this verse although the chapter mostly discusses leadership-related instructions and therefore in context would seem to refer to commissioning someone for a position of authority.

In spite of what it first appears to say, the warning to be slow to lay hands on others has at least two applications, and the leadership-instruction is the first. The second has more to do with not laying hands hastily on others in prayer. There have been times where I have had an internal sense that I specifically needed to *not* lay hands on someone or have them touch me, and in those cases while I did not understand the details as to why I was able to ascertain there was something spiritually amiss with that individual and there was a risk of something of their spiritual baggage being shared with me. It is probably for that reason why the verse in 1 Timothy 5:22 states ". . . and do not share in the sins of others." Spiritual energy is transferrable regardless of whether that energy is holy or dark, and in those cases it is best to avoid the risk of being spiritually "slimed."

In contrast to myself, where I will let almost anyone pray for me, my wife is very choosy about who prays for her and especially about who touches her. We are both aware of the passage discussed above, but we approach it very differently. She waits for a leading from God *to* have people lay hands on her whereas I expect that God will warn me in the situations where I need them to *not* touch me and I assume the rest of the time everyone is fair game. Her approach is that she only wants to be led and guided by Holy Spirit, which means she doesn't want to move to action when she does not sense an internal leading from God. While I also want to be led and guided by the same Spirit, I have a different approach for a reason. Luke 11:13 says, "If you then, though you are evil, know how to give good gifts to your children, how much more will your Father in heaven give the Holy Spirit to those who ask him!" My expectation is that because I'm asking for good things in prayer, I will only receive things that are from God who is perfect Goodness. My faith, in this case, is highly protective, and as I like to point out from time to time, Titus 1:15a says, "To the pure, all things are pure." I simply don't believe in receiving darkness through prayer, and as a result I don't generally end up with it. Neither approach is wrong as long as one is open to changing his approach in the moment if God leads otherwise.

As mentioned before, impartation is a useful method to level up, but the downside of this method is that when receiving impartation we usually only receive a small *portion* of that which another person carries, so it often takes a *lot* of impartation to notice major change. One key to understand here is that impartation is much like planting a spiritual seed, but that seed is renewable. By this I mean that when we impart to others we do not *lose* spiritual virtue but rather pass it in as a renewable resource. Using RPGs as a backdrop for this, it is much like a player giving 1% of their total mana (their spiritual power in-game) to another player. Instead of losing those mana points, their mana simply regenerates as it always does. As there is no limit to mana regeneration, likewise there is no limit to the amount of virtue one can impart to others, but giving 1% at a time will still take a while to have noticeable effects.

To explain further how this works in Real Life, we will look at it using math and some arbitrary percentages I have assigned to give a general picture of what typically happens. If a person operates at a level of 100% and he imparts to another, usually only 1% of his virtue is passed on in seed form (meaning the recipient must grow and develop what they have received for it to be potent and effective). If he imparts to 100 people, doing earthly math he would have no more spiritual virtue to pass on, but thankfully that isn't how it works. When we give away, we do not end up with less than we started with. Spiritual virtue flows through us much like a river that collects in a reservoir. When we impart to someone else the reservoir level drops slightly, but is soon refilled by the river that is still feeding it. Practically speaking this means there is a limitless supply of God-energy available to us in any and every situation; the goal is to enlarge our reservoir so more can flow through us in any moment. Even if the percentage remains the same, 1% of 100 gallons is far less than 1% of 100,000 gallons and our spirits are the same. During impartation this means that as our reservoir enlarges, we are able to impart more virtue to others.

It is important to realize that receiving impartation from a great many people is helpful, but it is not some magical process by which we can force God into doing things our way and on our timetable. Receiving prayer from a thousand people with no actual engagement of that which has been imparted on our part accomplishes little to nothing. This doesn't mean that impartation is useless, but rather we must understand how to make this impartation effective and engage it for it to be of use to us.

Imagine that our spirit is like a bucket of oil and impartation fills that already-full bucket with more oil. When we receive impartation, the bucket is temporarily expanded beyond its normal capacity for a period of time. If there is adequate engagement with God in the time period after that expansion, (usually the next few days to a week, but there is no set period of time), then the vessel more permanently expands. If not utilized, the vessel will usually shrink back down to size and the impartation is essentially of no effect. More is not always better, especially if we collect it with a sieve. It's about gathering *and* maintaining, not just collecting for the sake of collecting--we're not spiritual hoarders. In-game this could look like farming materials from a certain mob but never actually using that material for anything. If used properly that material might be used to produce a valuable weapon or expensive piece of clothing or jewelry, but just collecting the material for the sake of collecting it never translates into something useful for the player.

INTERCESSORY PRAYER

Intercessory prayer is a very good way to grind and an excellent habit to develop. It is a guarantee that if we spend time in intercession, especially lengthy times of prayer, that it *will* provide level ups, as the act of praying exercises our spirit. Paul wrote to Timothy about this very thing when he said in 1 Timothy 4:7b-8, "Train yourself to be godly. For physical training is of some value, but godliness has value for all things, holding promise for both the present life and the life to come." Paul was not just referring to living a righteous lifestyle, but engaging in actual spiritual training. After all, he wrote the following to the church in Corinth in 1 Corinthians 9:24-25, "Do you not know that in a race all the runners run, but only one gets the prize? Run in such a way as to get the prize. Everyone who competes in the games goes into strict training. They do it to get a crown that will not last, but we do it to get a crown that will last forever." Paul was speaking here of the importance of spiritual training.

In the same way we can get "in shape"' and "out of shape," it is possible to disengage spiritually to a point where we atrophy our spiritual muscles. The good news is that if we have trained our spirit and soul to have a larger capacity, it doesn't matter how much time has passed--stepping back into the things we did before will be easier and will likely not exhaust us as much as it did before. Physical exercise works the same way as spiritual exercise--when we have been in shape for some time, even if we lapse and our muscles have atrophied, they strengthen and respond faster the next time around when exercising again.

In 2004 to 2006 I lived in State College, PA, and used to pray at church every other Friday night for six hours with some friends using Mahesh Chavda's *Watch of the Lord* format. This was my favorite time of week as God always showed up in new ways. The evening before the 2004 Presidential Elections, a Monday night, I held an all-night personal prayer vigil at God's instruction, spending over twelve hours praying for God's hand to lead and guide both the elections and the nation. When I wasn't praying, I was worshipping or soaking. The last three hours I was joined by my Watch partners.

Five nights later on that Friday, we held the Watch as we normally did, but this time something unique happened to me. Shortly into the night I felt completely spiritually drained. I had no internal compulsion or energy to pray, worship, or really do anything at all. I wasn't physically tired, but I laid down on the ground to soak as I had nothing to give at that time. My friend Diane came and waved a flag over me and prayed for God's fire to come upon me as I lay there. I remember one moment when I observed how drained I felt, looked up at her waving her flag, then looked down again and in that second the Lord had renewed my spirit--I went from spiritually empty to spiritually full in the blink of an eye!

As I pondered this later, I realized that my soul was used to praying for six hours every *other* week, but not twelve hours at the beginning of a week and another six at its end. Compared to physical exercise it would be like running a mile once a day, but then one day deciding to run three miles in the morning and another two miles that afternoon. In simple terms, I had overtaxed my soul and I was wiped out.

As for the results of that experience, I can say this--sometime shortly after that Election Week, our Watch Leader felt the Lord urging her to make the Watch a weekly event instead of biweekly and all of us were on board. I never felt that kind of tiredness again, even after we went to weekly meetings. I also started holding my own personal six-to-nine-hour prayer sessions early each week for a few months. I spent a *lot* of time praying in that period in my life but I was never that drained again (and yes, I was single so I had a lot of available time). Like a weight lifter, from that point on I was able to handle a greater measure of sustained spiritual activity; I had exercised my spiritual muscles. While this did not seem like a new level to me at the time, in hindsight it had to be. Though I did not know it, this was not the only level-up experience that God had in store for me through the Watch.

During another Watch, I was asking God why not much change was taking place in our church. Since the four of us prayed weekly, and the Sunday service was (to us) notably different on the weeks we prayed versus the weeks we hadn't (back when the Watch was biweekly), we expected far more than we saw taking place. I personally was a bit disappointed as it didn't feel like our prayers "took," so to speak. I realize now that God changing hearts is an internal thing, and it was presumptuous and somewhat naïve of me to question whether our prayers were being answered since God responds to every single prayer we pray. I was looking at what I could observe, not taking into account that God often works on things which are clearly not visible. With that said, as a group we expected supernatural displays of power such as healings and miracles, but at minimum were looking for a few people getting slain in the spirit now and again (where God's power touches someone in such a way that they seem to pass out). We all felt some disappointment at the lack of visible displays of power. Our team didn't sense much spiritual momentum moving us forward as a church in spite of our dedicated intercession.

In response to this, God gave me the following vision one night during the Watch: I saw a faerie man, a lot like a leprechaun cobbler, sitting at a wooden bench tapping away at something. I couldn't see what he was tapping at, but as he did this he produced a red, glittery, sparkly dust. While I observed him making this dust, I also saw a red octagonal gem nearby that seemed to represent a sort of pie chart. It had eight "pie pieces" to it, and over half of them were a glowing red, while three were still dim. As the faerie tapped and made this red dust, one of the dim red slices became a glowing red and the gem seemed to power up even more.

In this vision the faerie then spread the red dust all over our church sanctuary--on the pews, aisles, stage, etc. I saw people sit in the pews on Sunday morning, and in doing so, soaked up the power in the dust before they left for the week. This faerie would then go back to work again, making red dust all week and sowing it in the church building on the weekends. When the red gem glowed all the way around, it was evident in the vision that the faerie had reached a new level. The dust he now made was larger and brighter even though he put the same amount of time and energy into it as he had before. When he sowed it around the church, people absorbed not just enough to keep them where they were, but enough that they began to move forward and change.

This vision was profound to me then and remains so even today. It clearly demonstrated to me that as we obtain new levels in the spirit, we have a greater capacity to cause change in the lives of those around us. The faerie represented both myself and the rest of the Watch team, and the red dust was akin to the glory or anointing--the power of God. I understood that God was encouraging us to continue our spiritual practices during the week. Continuing these practices and coming together on weekends, we regularly released God's power all over the sanctuary. As we did this, the rest of the congregation and even visitors were able to step into greater measures of freedom in their lives. Our forward momentum and actively moving into new levels caused the amount of God-life released each week to increase, bringing greater change with it. While we did not necessarily witness some of the visible displays we were seeking, we could eventually tell that our prayers were having ripple effects in our church. As more people stepped into greater freedom, it accelerated further and set off change in those around them too. This ultimately meant that the Watch team stepping into new levels pushed the church into a deeper and more powerful walk with God as a whole--and all this from walking out our spiritual lives daily, then coming together and praying each week.

That vision and experience also demonstrated to me something that I have learned over time about the effect of prayer with other people. Jesus said in Matthew 18:20, "For where two or three are gathered together in my name, there am I in the midst of them" (ASV). I once had an experience in my living room back when I had college roommates where I felt the presence of God change in some way each time an additional person entered the room to join in worship with us. There is something synergistic about a group of people who pray together, and if we want to level up faster, we would be wise to find others who want to grow spiritually and join with them in prayer.

NEW REVELATION

I was praying once and asked God how I could accelerate and increase my effectiveness in healing ministry, and He told me this: "At this time you have two options--pray for a lot of sick people, or get new revelation." Praying for a lot of sick people is the equivalent of grinding. The more people we pray for, the odds are that some of them will get healed, and any increase in results encourages continued action and increased faith, which eventually results in leveling-up in the healing ministry. The more we pray for, the more we sow healing, and as mentioned before, we will eventually reap healing as a result. On the other hand, getting new revelation is the equivalent of some kind of permanent stat increase or cheat-code. New revelation creates internal transformation. Revelation isn't just a new idea that helps us think about something differently--it causes literal change in our beliefs and understanding and may alter how we approach and respond to situations. When that change takes place, we advance.

Receiving new revelation is not something we can make happen at will. Desiring new revelation can certainly influence the speed at which we receive it, but it is not generally as fast as flipping a switch. My personal recommendation is that if we desire new and deeper revelation do two things--first, ask God for it; second, start looking for it in our daily lives, for whoever asks will receive and whoever seeks will find. It is not necessary to obsess about it, but we must keep our eyes and ears open as we interacts with others. We might try reading a new book by an author who is not well-known, or maybe by reading a book by someone he has been told all his life is heretical. There's a chance the heresy-writer might actually hold the key we are searching for.

I have found that when I desire new revelation, invariably within the next few months (sometimes sooner), a friend will tell me about stunning new teachings they have been listening to or a minister with a really different perspective on the Kingdom of God. While teachings from others are not the only way to receive new revelation, I have found that often in my own life when I hunger for something new in the Kingdom, God usually brings new teachings to me. I also receive direct downloads from Heaven, where Holy Spirit shares things with me that I have not heard from a man or read in a book. Overall the action of receiving revelation is something that is God-directed. What I mean by this is that I can listen to people talk about things I have never heard before, and as a result I will gain knowledge--new *information*. But something must take place on a spiritual level within me for that information to become *revelation*.

It is a difficult feeling to describe, but it is possible to actually feel the effects of revelation taking place within us. There is a sort of inner expansion that takes place--a quickening of our spirit being. It usually is accompanied by an *Aha!* moment mentally, where an idea clicks into place. Oftentimes, after hearing it, the revelation seems so obvious that we don't know why we didn't understand or realize that particular concept before.

One method I find helpful when I listen to revelatory audio teachings is that I listen to them at least twice. The first time I receive the revelation, my soul and spirit are stirred to believe and accept that which I am hearing. The second time around helps me mentally process the information so that I understand it better with my conscious mind and help the revelation sink deeper. This is important because receiving new revelation means I have the seed of change within me, but more often than not it takes time to fully manifest. I often listen to it several times to deeply root within me that which God is revealing to me.

As I mentioned earlier in this chapter, God's virtue within us often manifests in seed form--starting small and growing with time and tending. Pastor Peter Tan in his free eBook *The Spiritual World* has the following to say on this matter:

> The reason why it takes time for the outward manifestation of an inward reception and impartation is because the inward transformation is incomplete. Even though sometimes individuals think (mentally), and convince themselves that they already have it, in their true selves, they haven't got it fully until it is an automatic, subconscious and habitual part of their daily lives. . . . When one first receives a truth or a new impartation and understanding of life, they do not have it until it is within their subconscious, in their actions and is a part of their daily habit of life. It is not just when we think and believe about something that we have it, but it is when we are practicing the truth that we truly have it. It is when we are not thinking about it and yet it forms part of our substance of life-consciousness that we truly have absorbed it into us. (38-39)

Hearing someone else teach something is not the only way to receive new revelation. It is possible to obtain new revelation when teaching others although it is infrequent. I'm not suggesting we hijack other people's time and make them listen to us chatter on in hopes that we will come up with something new, but I believe it is important to know that teaching others can give us access to new revelation. It is not just that a body of knowledge grows when more people understand an idea, but at times when teaching we might find ourselves saying something we have never heard or thought before.

As we are speaking it, we hear it for the first time and learn it while we are talking to others. In spite of not-knowing how or where that information came from, that same revelation-feeling touches us. The times that has happened to me I have inadvertently paused as I take a moment and let my own brain absorb what I just said. As an author, I find that any time I set out to write a book, the information and revelation I need starts to filter my way. While at the beginning of writing a book I may not have everything I need to complete it, by the time I reach the end I have often added entire chapters based off of new revelation and ideas that filtered my way during the writing process. This book is actually four chapters longer than I expected it to be, as the Lord gave me new chapter after new chapter when I thought I had completed the manuscript.

In the same way that praying in tongues accesses the spirit but bypasses the mind, I believe that uncovering new revelation via teaching is a manifestation of the Holy Spirit speaking through the spirit and giving understanding that our conscious minds have not yet laid ahold of. As this happens we receive it consciously along with our hearers (or at times our readers). One thing to keep in mind is that the revelation itself is often in response to a need on behalf of members of the audience. In a more interactive teaching setting, the student may have just asked a question which the teacher is trying to answer, and as the teacher is answering, the new revelation comes forth. This is a manifestation of the gift of teaching, and the Holy Spirit is gracious to answer the student's question even if the teacher didn't know the answer in advance. From a gaming perspective this is a lot like exploring a well-known dungeon only to discover a secret door with valuable treasure in a room on the other side. The act of teaching brings the revelation much in the same way that searching an old dungeon reveals new rooms and new treasures.

The level-up concept has many more parallels and applications than I have named, but this is enough to get us started on our own journey to expand in our experience of the Kingdom of God. To sum it up, the bottom line is this: As we exercise our spirits, we get stronger. There are many ways to do this, and like any RPG, we can't rely too closely on only one type of method as everything has its strengths and weaknesses. With that said, as we get [spiritually] stronger, we are able to do more, pray more, experience more than we used to, as well as reap all the benefits that come with that increased capacity.

Remember that any prayer-filled, God-filled lifestyle will cause us to reach new heights in God. Prayer sessions don't have to be hours long, and there is no length of time that guarantees a higher "level" of spirituality, although length of time certainly can help. A word to the wise is that it can be easy after looking at all the things that help us level up to get so "doing-oriented" that we forget that God also wants a relationship with us, and at times wants us to be much more "being-oriented." Holy Spirit will continue to lead and guide us as we seek to live out that relationship, and we can get instant answers from Him. As we engage this process our Heavenly GM will bestow upon us new levels and new gifts, new powers to defeat new enemies, and will cause us to invite new players to join the Game. As always, when we do these things the darkness before us recedes even faster. After all, the Kingdom of God is always advancing and increasing, and new levels is just the beginning!

CHAPTER 4

THE PURPOSE OF PARTIES

In RPG games it is both faster and easier to level up when fighting mobs in a party than it is to level up on one's own because more difficult mobs can be taken on and defeated faster with less hardship on all involved through teamwork. A party is a mechanism in-game whereby the system allows multiple players to work together in a team system with certain benefits. It is possible for any players to fight a mob at the same time outside of a party, but whoever either deals the most damage or deals the final damage gets the experience points and loot (called drops) that come from the mob and the other players are left in the cold. The party system equalizes things so each player shares in the experience regardless of who deals the final blow, and the drops are shared somewhat evenly. One of the benefits of this party-system is that each player can see the health and mana power (the power that allows them to use skills and spells) levels of the other players. This insider-information tells the healers when to heal, and lets other players know who is in trouble and needs help. Each player can see the others' class and level as well, which tells them a bit more information about their teammates and allows them to function better as a team.

A party has a party leader who is ultimately in charge, able to add and remove players from the team and to change how the drops and experience are shared. This player may have more experience than everyone else, or may simply be the best one at leading among that team. However, there is no prerequisite to being the leader of a party other than the group recognizing that person as such.

The Kingdom is the same way. For example, most believers are part of a church, whether via an organized religion system or as an informal group of like-minded Jesus followers who live and relate with one another. In the same way that the makeup of members in any in-game party (also known as a party-build) has its benefits and drawbacks, there are upsides and downsides to each. In the end all church-groups share the same party-like traits although the comparison between churches and parties is most applicable to a small group.

When playing in a party in-game, there is a lot of sharing that takes place, and this too is how the Christian experience is designed as shown in Acts 2:42-47:

> They devoted themselves to the apostles' teaching and to fellowship, to the breaking of bread and to prayer. Everyone was filled with awe at the many wonders and signs performed by the apostles. All the believers were together and had everything in common. They sold property and possessions to give to anyone who had need. Every day they continued to meet together in the temple courts. They broke bread in their homes and ate together with glad and sincere hearts, praising God and enjoying the favor of all the people. And the Lord added to their number daily those who were being saved.

In a party, any loot (called drops) that are gained through fighting mobs and the subsequent experience are usually automatically divided, and even though one player may take the frontline as a tank (damage-taker that acts like a shield to the rest of the party), as a whole the damage is shared as almost no player remains unscathed in a fight. The Christian experience as demonstrated from the verses above is meant to be like this too. Paul instructed believers in Romans 12:15 to "Rejoice with those who rejoice; mourn with those who mourn" because life is meant to be a shared experience. In the same way that a boss-monster cannot be taken on by one person alone, we cannot take on life and its hazards by ourselves. As believers if we want to live overcoming lives, we will have to form parties.

Another benefit of partying is that even when we *leave* a party, having gained considerable experience and ability, the strengths we have acquired remain with us; as a result, when it comes time to join a new party, the new party will get the benefit of our growth from our last party's efforts. At the end of the day, more mobs beaten means more experience and more leveling, and more leveling means faster kill-time for mobs, etc.

The vision about the faerie cobbler in the last chapter revealed the effects of one individual purposefully engaging spiritually to influence a community. However, the practical application of that individual leveling was actually put to use in a party-setting. The Watch team was a dedicated group of 4-5 people with a number of others who came and went, and our team carried out the knowledge and wisdom of that vision together. In reality, the sowing of the "red dust" would have been far less effective if it had been only one person doing it. Not only that, but in the example where I was spiritually exhausted from having over-prayed, it took a team-member praying over me to restore me back to "full health." In-game, this is the equivalent of a party member whose stamina is exhausted or who is almost out of HP (health points) and then a priest-class party member comes along and heals or restores whatever has been lost. The restoration of that which was lost allows the party member to continue and the team to move forward more effectively.

A few years back a friend gave me another example about the practical importance of partying and purposeful leveling up. The story was related to me is as follows: The church in the Olympic Peninsula in Washington State recently had a victory over the whooping cough (pertussis) when an outbreak was starting in their region. A group of the churches in that area banded together, fasting and prayer to tackle the problem. The result: no more whooping cough.

There is an upside and a downside to that story, both of which need to be acknowledged. The obvious upside is that the problem was solved, and in the process some people may have learned something about the value of teamwork and partying together. The downside is a bit less obvious but is critical to understand from a perspective of practical spiritual growth. While the story does relate a victory, and one that should be celebrated, a couple questions must be asked. How many people did it take and with how many hours of prayer to obtain that result? What if instead it could be done with two people instead of a group of churches? As the story goes, when there was a major plague epidemic in Africa, it only took two men-- John G. Lake and his intercessor friend, to drive the plague from the country. We need to be thankful and appreciative of any victory, but we can't settle on just having more massive-group events as the solution. While this may seem oddly placed in a chapter about parties, we need to grow to a place where we are able to solve large-scale problems with a small-scale party or even alone. Parties are fantastic, and they're a really wise thing to do, but unfortunately we will not always be able to form a party whenever we want, so we need to make strategic use of parties when we can to promote personal growth as well as regional change so when problem arise we are prepared to deal with them even alone if necessary.

There is actually a mathematical equation that addresses this issue of accelerating change. Author Gregg Braden explains in his book *The Divine Matrix* that it takes only the square root of 1% of a population to start the process of effecting change. This means that in a population of 1 million, it will only take 100 people to start effecting change (Braden, *The Divine Matrix, 115-116*). If we figure the world is increasing in population and is around 7.25 billion people then the approximate number of people required to internally hold that change in their hearts to begin to see positive external change in the world would be 8,515 people. Any more people than that simply accelerates the process. Essentially, the ripple effects of individuals have actually been quantified. And Gregg Braden is not the only one to speak on this ripple effect that groups of people have on the earth.

Pastor Peter Tan in his book *The Spiritual World* explains the matter of spiritual corporate activity in this way:

> From time to time, where a community, society or city yield themselves to evil, it looks like a volcanic eruption in the spirit world when momentarily the dark fires and lava of Hades flows onto the surface of the earth subjugating the human society until spiritual light is once again restored through human vessels who yield themselves to the divine light of Christ; and the evil spirits retreat into their dark abyss. (28)

The choices we make corporately decide whether we will serve the Prince of Darkness with our actions and energy or whether we will advance the Kingdom of Light. Instead of waiting for an entire city or society to yield itself to evil and then restore spiritual light through the sacrifices of human vessels of the light of Christ, we need to cause a massive eruption of light in our communities, cities, and societies and let the light of God flow out onto the earth. We cannot afford to wait for another external "revival" to happen. Rather, we need to lay down our own lives to cause purposeful internal transformation and thereby releasing positive change in our world using the principles and spiritual laws of Heaven.

Depending on how we look at things, it could be said that as followers of Jesus we fight an ongoing losing battle, in that the wars, natural disasters, corruption, and disease that riddle this world have massive negative impact. However, this negative worldview is not entirely accurate and doesn't paint the whole picture as there are great victories that people all over the earth are making in their families and communities, even nationally and internationally. In spite of the headway we are making, and in light of the defeats we experience, I am still convinced our current level of God-experience cannot possibly be the "head not the tail" and "above not beneath" experience that the Bible talks about. There is a great deal more we have yet to access in the Kingdom of God.

We must come to a place in our "leveling up" process that instead of just defeating one disease only to be faced with another two taking its place that we actually are *gaining* ground against darkness. Essentially we have to start beating real-life mobs faster than the cosmic computer program can spawn new ones. Even in a party, we can't keep having only small victories such as a reduced crime rate in our section of the city only to have a drug cartel make the entire city its new home base. We cannot effect a cessation of a local gang war only to have a civil war break out in our entire country. The above examples are more like barely-reduced defeats than actual victories. Oftentimes it feels like we as believers are engaged more in damage control--keeping things from getting too much worse--than we are actually making things noticeably better.

It is times like these when we must continue to grind, be patient, and do what we know is right. We must do our best to keep moving forward, but at times even that won't work, and what should we do then? Ephesians 6:13 states, "Therefore put on the full armor of God, so that when the day of evil comes, you may be able to stand your ground, and after you have done everything, to stand." There may be times when all we can do is stand our ground, but even this will be done best in a party because are all stronger in a team. As we continue to watch, stand, and wait, the moment will open and we will be able to advance once more, obtaining new vision, new wisdom, and new strength, and reaching new levels and deeper relationship with God.

Over the years my wife has had a recurring vision of a small, select group of people who work together in the spirit realm and accomplish great deeds; she refers to them as spiritual mercenaries. The key to note here is that the vision has always involved a group, not one person individually. I had a dream once that illustrates this shift from the single-person focus to a party.

In the dream I was greeting people at a combination wedding-and-coronation. One of the people I greeted was the main character from the movie *Superstar* which came out in 1999. I never referred to her by her name, but called her Superstar during the entire dream. Two very short girls in their twenties were also present, both wearing high heels. As they removed their heels, they become roughly dwarf-height but with normal body proportions. One girl dropped into the background of the dream, but the other one remained in the foreground, and I became aware that she had back pain associated with an injury.

I turned back to Superstar, who was suddenly *morbidly* obese--all of that weight was put on in-between the time I greeted her and then was with the little people. She also had back pain and the same kind of injury. Both she and the little woman needed prayer for their backs, but I only prayed for the little woman. She falls over slain in the spirit, and her back is instantly healed. In the dream I know that God is touching her and not Superstar at that time, so I don't even try to pray for Superstar.

This dream makes a comparison within the body of Christ between those who are seen as "Superstars" and everyone else--the "Little People." In the dream, the Little People really are quite small, but try to make themselves appear bigger than they are, presumably because they're trying to "measure up" to the Superstar. However, when they stop trying to measure up and in humility step down from their posturing, choosing to be themselves over a fabricated image they were projecting, they step into the blessings from heaven that God is releasing. The Superstar has become obese which is suggestive of both a level of spiritual laziness as well as a poor internal state setting up the conditions for the obesity. She isn't just obese, but morbidly obese, which suggests that the Superstars are a "dying breed" so to speak. Unlike in the movie, Superstar is older, whereas the Little People are in their twenties, at a normal "fertile" age to reproduce.

What God is saying in this dream is that the day of the superstars is coming to a close as the old breed dies out in favor of the new. The once-unknown "Little People" are being positioned to stop emulating popular opinion of the spiritual order of the day and instead to uniquely receive and manifest God's grace as they humble themselves and get real with those around them. It is the time where they are being linked even more deeply with Christ and are rising into authority as mature sons and daughters of God. In other words, partying among the "Little People" is the new thing.

In game-terms, it's no longer about trying to dual-class as a high Damage-per-second (DPS) warrior as well as a specialized healing priest-class with some area-of-effect (AOE) skills as well. In a party each person can specialize and function in his own capacity, and when no one is busy trying to be a superstar everyone can improve and be successful together. In the dream, once the short girl stops trying to measure up, the conditions to cause the back problem (the weight of her over-extreme expectations) are no longer present, and healing manifests.

This group-of-Little-People theme is important to understand, but needs some clarification. The above dream is referring not just to people of little power or of minimal spiritual influence, but speaks to the lack of celebrity status in Christianity. Many spiritually powerful people are hidden and not well-known by human standards, yet while their names may never be listed as keynote conference speakers these giants of faith are taking the spirit realm by storm. And in truth, it is necessary for this to occur. After all, an analogy of little-people only travels so far. One low-level player will be unable to succeed alone against the vast majority of in-game enemies. As time goes on and the game becomes more challenging, low-level won't cut it anymore, regardless of whether that player is in a party or not. As we have already discussed, one of our goals is to level up so at some point we won't be weak anymore, even if we are unknown. There's nothing wrong with being powerful, and the truth is that only high-level characters can effectively take on high-level bosses. As we all reach a place of greater spiritual maturity we will be great examples to those around us, and instead of having a precious few superstars to look up to, the Body of Christ will be full of good examples of godly living, where each of us can say as Paul did in 1 Corinthians

11:1, "Follow my example, as I follow the example of Christ." After all, the original purpose of superstars was only to show everyone else what is possible to attain to, not to elevate them above all others.

There is one final RPG element that applies to the subject of partying–and that is "power-leveling." This is an in-game tactic where a high level player parties with a low-level player and tackles mobs that would be suicide for the noob player to fight alone. The low level character adds almost no value to the party whatsoever (also known in-game as a leech), but advances far faster than he would have been able to on his own. It closely relates to a phrase that has becoming increasingly popular in certain charismatic-Christian circles--"We'll make our ceiling their floor." While the phrase is annoyingly cliché and grossly overused, right up there with "viral" and "epic," the underlying concept has some useful elements to it. The idea is that those who are mature in the faith make room in the spiritual realm and on earth for newer believers to rapidly advance in all things Kingdom.

This is a method we can use that will require a sacrifice of our own time and energy, but will help advance the Kingdom of God on earth. We can each find those who are young in the Lord (this can be a person of any age) and who are spiritually hungry, and walk alongside them, modeling our behavior, authority, wisdom, and experience to them, teaching them what we can and imparting what we carry. In so doing, they will advance spiritually far beyond their own capabilities in a shorter period of time, and the Kingdom as a whole advances. We will also find that as we propel others forward that we share in the experiences and revelation they gain, adding to and enhancing our own. This is a secondary benefit to helping others grow, much like how a master craftsman is able to benefit from the work that his apprentices produce. As it is a team effort, the time and energy we spend with others will end up helping us in the long run.

Power-leveling as a gaming practice is actually more common than some might think, to the point that there are actually people who do it for a living, as well as those who do it for free for their guild members, friends, etc. I find it significant from a prophetic perspective that people are willing to pay real-life money to gain in-game levels. This signifies that leveling up is a valuable life-practice for us as believers. Jesus told a parable about finding the pearl of great price and selling all we have to obtain it, and this pursuit of power-leveling could be compared with that parable. The good news is that this isn't just an in-game concept. In Real Life there are ways to power-level, and I did much of my power-leveling at the Watch of the Lord many years ago. That is not the only way this can be accomplished, however. There are ministry schools in the U.S.A and all over the world that are a sort of "Charismatic Ministry Training," whose basic purpose is to train believers for supernatural ministry, essentially creating a power-leveling training-school for those who attend. The most common at this time use a curriculum from Bethel Church in Redding, CA, but there are many schools that have developed their own curriculum. These ministry schools are another effective way we can partner with others to help teach and train believers in a party-setting to help change the world.

CHAPTER 5

STATS AND SKILL TREES

No RPG character would be complete without a Skill Tree--an intricate set of skills that layer on top of each other to develop their fighting, healing, and crafting abilities. These skills enhance game play by enabling the player to unlock powerful items and enhancements to strengthen him, his parties, and even his guild.

Before we can discuss skill trees, we must mention Stats--basic mathematical attributes that the Game System uses to decide a player's skills and abilities. Now I'll be honest, there is no deep mystical correlation that I could find on stats, but it is important to understand how stats work and how they influence both game play and Real Life before continuing further.

While appearing quite complex at first glance, the table on the following page is actually pretty simple. A stat is a value that denotes a level of ability. A normal player's starting strength ranges from about 6-18, as do all of the other main stats--strength, agility, stamina, wisdom, intellect, luck, and vitality. Other stats such as leadership, art, charisma, etc. can often be gained in-game but usually are not included in the beginning. All stats are used in-game to decide gameplay. The higher the Strength, the more damage the player's attack will do. The higher the Vitality, the more health the player will have. Higher Agility (or Dexterity in some games) will decide how often the player manages to evade other attacks as well as how often they are able to deal extra damage when attacking, known as a Critical Strike.

Sample Stat Table:

Name: Evan		Alignment: Neutral	
Level:	2	Class: None	
Title:	None	Gender:	Male
Fame	0	Infamy	0
Health (HP)	120	Mana(MP)	160
Strength	11	Wisdom	16
Agility	8	Intellect	11
Stamina	9	Vitality	12
Luck	0	Leadership	0
Attack	3	Defense	1

When a player levels up, he is usually given a number of free stat points to allocate to the various skills, but it is also possible in some games to increase stat points through actions. For example, doing a lot of reading in-game could yield additional points to Intelligence and Wisdom, whereas leading other players in a party or raid group could increase Leadership points.

These stats and subsequent stat gains influence every aspect of gameplay. Different classes of character require larger amounts of certain stats, varying from class to class. A wizard or priest will need higher Intelligence and Wisdom, and the priest may even have a Faith stat as well. A warrior will need high strength and vitality, and a thief, rogue, or assassin will need high agility and luck. The level of these stats, and the level of these stats compared to the level of the enemy, will dictate probability of success in combat as well as other in-game activities.

A Real-Life correlation to stats is our inborn human abilities. For example, my IQ and that of everyone in my family is above average. Both of my brothers and I are all very intelligent, and I personally have a very quick mental processing speed. I enjoy reading books but I am able to flip through them at a rapid pace and my retention of details is high. I did very little scholastic studying until college because up to that point I learned almost everything simply by paying attention during class and taking notes. This ability comes in handy as a nurse when I have an emergency situation that I need to problem-solve through. I am able to assess the patient and situation and usually come up with a plan of action in a very minimal timeframe. On the other hand, it has the ability to drive my wife (and others) batty at times. Since I think quickly and have high retention, I get *very* bored with slow-paced movies and I don't like to watch the same movie more than twice (read that as "maximum of twice") as I am utterly bored then too. This has also contributed to my overall lack of patience as well.

On the other hand, my physical build is more slender than that of either of my brothers. I am not petite by any means, but each of my brothers has a broader shoulder and pelvis than I do, and I would be willing to guess that my older brother probably has overall slightly larger bones than I do, and at 6'6" he is a big guy. I am not weak, but with the same amount of effort both my brothers can probably build more muscle mass in the same amount of time as I can, but when we are all in shape, my endurance is probably a bit higher than theirs and I am a better runner. All of these things can be translated into stats in-game. I would have comparatively higher agility and lower strength by a few points each and my brothers would have higher strength and slightly lower agility in contrast.

In Real Life there is no official stat-measurer (although it might be nice if there were), but we have other methods of measuring ability that tell us what we need to know. IQ, physical strength, time it takes to run a mile, speed of completing tasks, all of these are ways we measure abilities in the Real World, and like in-game, these have direct influence on our ability to perform other tasks.

Now that we have a better grasp of stats, we can continue to discuss skills and Skill Trees. While RPGs use a variety of skill trees and methods of leveling each individual skill, I will use the level-progression model similar to the one the player uses to level up. Each skill is designated a level at the beginning of the game, usually Level 1 at 0%. As the player uses the skill, whether in or out of combat, the skill increases in experience and after reaching 100% it becomes Level 2. This continues on to Level 3, 4, and so on. The player typically starts with a certain set of skills when choosing a profession during game setup, but under the right circumstances new skills can be learned in-game.

One last point about in-game skills, before discussing the Kingdom at some length, is that some in-game skills have sub-skills as well--a set of skills that make up the larger skill. The Blacksmithing skill is a perfect example of this. It is impossible to do any blacksmithing without having the Repair skill, Heating and Cooling skill, Polishing, and Grinding, all of which fall under the overall Blacksmithing skill set. Cooking could be considered similarly although no game maker ever divides the cooking skill up, but reasonably it could be subdivided with a Baking skill, Food Preparation (dicing and slicing, etc.), Food Seasoning, and more. Whether regular or sub-skills, all have a correlation to Kingdom realities.

As we grow in our spiritual walk and if we spend any amount of time with other believers, it is easy to observe notable differences from person to person in skill level as well as general areas of talent or proficiency. One person may have significant ability when casting out demons, seeing many delivered of Satanic Ritual Abuse and Dissociative Identity Disorders, but having poor healing ability, barely managing to get minor headaches to go away 50% of the time--and that 50% only when the headache is caused by a demon. A second believer may have highly accurate words of knowledge and moderate results in healing, but is completely dominated when dealing with the demonic. He may have a lot of revelation and can heal chronic diseases, broken bones, and an occasional cancer, but when demons start manifesting, he starts looking for someone else to deal with it. In this example, both individuals operate in the same skills but at entirely different levels of proficiency.

In Real Life, when someone turns to Jesus in salvation, he is given the deposit of the Holy Spirit, a guarantee of what is to come. Not only does he receive a deposit, but in John 3:34 it states that, "God gives the Spirit without limit." If Holy Spirit is given without limit, and Holy Spirit is the GM, the Skill Creator, then that means that each and every skill actually already resides within each believer. And if that is so, then it stands to reason that each person should be able to operate in every skill, which the Bible refers to as "gifts." This means every believer has the skills of healing, words of knowledge, and all the other gifts listed in Romans 12 and 1 Corinthians 12. This goes even further--every single ability available to mankind--both powers of the past and present and even powers of the Age to come are presently within each believer due to the presence of Holy Spirit, who is given without limit. People have their own predispositions and interests toward different areas, but we all have access to all the gifts.

There are many more skills than any of us are aware of--including skills some might only dream of--levitation, teleportation (also known as translocation), and even bilocation. These are a few of the "uncommon" or "rare" skills, but other skills could be considered "'hidden"--ones that almost no one has heard of. I once met a man who became able to play guitar literally overnight, having had no skill or ability on that instrument the day before. There are people who have memorized the entire Bible complete with verse addresses, and have instant recall, retaining and recalling it by the power of God, but even these are only scratching the surface.

If all skills, including rare and even hidden ones, are given by Holy Spirit without any limits placed on them, why is it that so few people seem to be flying or teleporting these days, even among those in the Christian community? Certainly there is more happening than at first glance. Many are afraid to talk about their experiences for fear of ostracism, and this is a very real fear. I have personally been on the receiving end of unpleasant treatment from others on numerous occasions because I dared to share my own uncommon spiritual encounters. In spite of some hiding their experiences, it seems the vast majority of believers simply are not having them and that is probably a greater reason behind why this phenomenon is not showing up on the nighttime news stations. That leaves us with a deeper question--why do so few seem to be exhibiting these skills if they are given without limit? I can at least partially account for this disconnect between what we've been given and what we experience.

Imagine that each person has a "Skill Garden" where each spiritual skill is represented by a plant. Because the Spirit is given without limit, each person will have one of *every kind* of plant in existence in his garden. What will *not* be the same, however, is the size and shape of each plant. If it's the same Spirit and the same skills, then why would the plants look different from garden to garden? First Corinthians 12:4-6 says, "There are different kinds of gifts, but the same Spirit distributes them. There are different kinds of service, but the same Lord. There are different kinds of working, but in all of them and in everyone it is the same God at work."

Even though all the gifts themselves are given by the same Spirit, they work differently from person to person. This could be compared to the difference in plant shape in the above analogy. An example of this is two people who operate in the gift of prophecy but one only ever has visions and the other never has visions but hears God's voice speaking inside his head. Both will be able to prophesy, but the way that gift operates is a bit different. Plant size, however, has to do with the level of the skill. A Level 1 skill would be represented by a plant that is maybe only an inch or two tall, whereas a high level skill would be better represented by a full-grown fruit-bearing plant. 1 Corinthians 12:11 states, "All these are the work of one and the same Spirit, and he distributes them to each one, just as he determines." The "distributes to each one, just as he determines" doesn't mean we don't have the ability to access certain gifts but can be considered a designation of starting skill level as each skill is available to each of us.

Unlike RPGs, Real Life does not guarantee each skill we are given starts at Level 1. One person might have a Levitation skill at Level 1 but start out with a Prophecy skill at Level 3. There is no guarantee that being a noob-believer means you will start out with all noob-level skills. Certainly, each noob will invariably have a great number of Level 1 skills, but that doesn't mean all of them will start that way. Even if a skill starts out low, it isn't a limitation but rather an opportunity for learning and growth. Sometimes a skill starting out at a low-level can be part of God's protective plan for us. If someone who is spiritually immature begins with a rare high-level skill, it is possible he would become very destructive in his behaviors, falling prey to pride and other significant character flaws. Mind you, being a higher-level believer doesn't necessarily protect him from those pitfalls either, but the hope is that as he grows in the Lord that his character will grow along with him.

In any RPG the player's development is actually part of the joy of the game. It's rather fulfilling to realize the weak, pathetic player who at the beginning could barely take on a fox by himself and was never able to pull multiple mobs without a handful of healing potions or a cleric on hand is able to decimate scores of much higher-level mobs in the same amount of time it used to take to kill that single fox. While in Real Life the rewards are not always as obvious, due to spiritual drops being invisible to us, it remains that a spiritual rewards system does exist, which I will address in a future chapter. Additionally, it is possible to look at our own lives and see our development spiritually, professionally, even economically, and we get to enjoy the fruits of that development as well.

On the other hand, if a believer is not able to look back on his life even a year prior and see growth, he is probably doing something *very* wrong and needs to contact the GM (Holy Spirit) via private message (prayer) and get some things fixed. The good news is that if for any reason he does fall behind, there is grace and mercy to cover it, fix it, and catch him back up. God truly *does* give experience bonuses to restore what has been lost! Additionally, where death in an RPG causes loss of exp. and skill proficiency, Real Life does not have those penalties, continuing with our spiritual growth from the Eternity-side of things. As a result, at no point in time does the Kingdom ever move backwards, decrease, or in any way lessen. The first part of Isaiah 9:7 says, "Of the increase of His government and peace there shall be no end" (KJV). At times there will even be a Resurrection skill used to bring the person back out of Eternity to the Earth-side to keep things going from the physical realm. The one key to note here is that while there is no experience-loss this side of Eternity, I have heard many different testimonies of people who have shared that the *type* of experience gained here on earth is different than there, and that it should be our goal to mature as much here as we are able. The reason for this is that Heaven contains no conflict and adversity, so the character built here among conflict and trials is of immense value.

In-game skills improve in the way one might expect--through constant use. It is possible to start a new RPG only to see other players randomly standing around jumping. Before understanding the skill-leveling system, the first thought that would have gone through my head is "What on earth is he doing?" Most likely that player is leveling his "jump" skill through constant (ok, maybe incessant) use. Just like with in-game skills, spiritual skills only grow in experience and cannot be down-leveled or deleted, as Romans 11:29 says, "For God's gifts and his call are *irrevocable* (emphasis mine)."

This begs the question of how Real-Life skills are improved and leveled up, and it is the same as in-game. Hebrews 5:14 states, "But solid food is for the mature, who by constant use have trained themselves to distinguish good from evil." The name of the game here is "constant use." If we want to get good at prophecy, we must find ways to regularly prophesy. If we want to get good at healing the sick, we must find sick people and pray for them often. If we want to . . . well, you get the point. In the same way that it is nearly impossible to become skilled at playing an instrument without ever touching one, it is nearly impossible to grow in spiritual gifts/skills while never actually using them. It is possible to use these skills infrequently and still grow, but the speed of growth will be greatly reduced compared to someone who regularly exercises them.

In my own life I made use of this fact when I was learning about prophesy. I didn't know much about it, and I was loaned a number of books from a mentor--I read all of them and then searched for more. Not knowing it was a skill that could be used at any time, and at the time believing it was reserved for the "special few" instead of everyone, I prayed regularly that God would give me the ability to obtain this skill. It turns out I already had it, as does everyone else, but in order to train this skill once I realized I had obtained it, I took advantage of almost every opportunity and even made some of my own! For example, every so often the church I was at would have baptisms for new believers or for people who felt they needed a "spiritual renewal" of some kind. Right after the person was baptized, the pastor opened up the floor for anyone who was there to speak words of encouragement and to prophesy over the individual. I would fast and pray for days before these baptisms in order to position myself to receive prophetic words for these people, practically begging God at some points. You see, I didn't know that this skill could be practiced more frequently, and I didn't realize that I didn't need to beg God for it, so I worked really hard to take advantage of all of the opportunities presented to me in order to train that skill. While I might not have needed to work so hard, I still gained a lot from this purposeful practice.

After a few baptisms, I also started going to the Watch meetings where there were a great many opportunities to grind this skill due to the way we prayed which made regular use of it. At the time of writing this, while I can't provide a number of my Prophecy skill level, I can say conclusively that taking those opportunities to practice at that time were very effective, and the method of constant-use continues to be effective for me to this day. At times I have even posted on social media and offered free prophetic words to anyone who wanted them. This gave me new opportunities to not only hone my skill, but I have found the types of prophecies I have been hearing for people begin to branch out as my skill has refined over time. In fact, these days it is possible for me to have prophetic experiences without even looking or asking for it when in the beginning that never happened. While most of the time God is sharing simple messages with me instead of earth-shattering mystical apocalyptic messages, that doesn't matter, and there is nothing less-important about the simple messages than the obscure and esoteric ones. The point is that through constant use I was able to step into new levels, resulting in the ability to use the skill quite comfortably and access it at any time I choose.

In fact, I can recall multiple new levels in just that skill alone. During one span over a few weeks I encountered several angels, and from that point on, I have had a deeper interaction with the angelic realms than I had before. I had no conscious angelic interactions prior; it was a clear delineation of a level-change in my operation in the gift of prophecy--I was now starting to see in the spirit realm. When this happened, I yet again took the opportunity to be purposeful about it. Over those few weeks I listened to sermon messages on the topic and spent time in prayer about it; in general, I sought out opportunities to level this new aspect of the skill while it was presenting itself, knowing that those opportunities were not always actively thrusting themselves at me--a "strike while the iron is hot" sort of approach.

That shift from prophecy to angelic experiences could also be a representation of Skill Tree advancement. A Skill Tree is an in-game concept map that shows a player's skills and denotes a predetermined pathway of skill progression. Skill Trees are somewhat logical in how they progress, where basic skills come before complex ones. If someone is building a skill tree in-game for a cleric, the Tree might start with "Basic Healing" then "Moderate Healing." At "Moderate

Healing" it will branch off in two direction, adding "Resurrect" on one branch and "Massive Heal" on the other. At an advanced level, after "Massive Heal" the skill "Party Heal" might appear, with the ability to heal a whole party of people at the same time. Each of these skills have a certain amount of Skill Points (SP, or Mana Points, MP depending on the game) required to use them, and certain stats decide how much SP each character possesses. If one runs out of SP, he will have to wait for a short period for the SP to regenerate enough to use the skill again.

My Prophecy Skill Tree looks a bit like this:

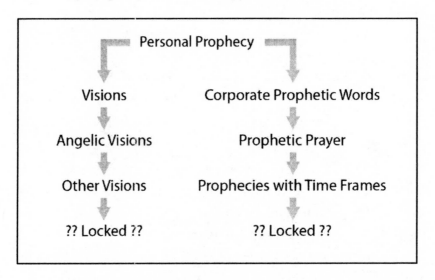

(*Disclaimer: The above Tree does not represent exactly how it will be for everyone-- this just shows my own experience.)

With the ability to level up one's skills comes a measure of responsibility. Skills are given by Holy Spirit not just for personal gain, but for the good of everyone. As mentioned before, Paul wrote in 2 Timothy 1:6, "For this reason I remind you to fan into flame the gift of God, which is in you through the laying on of my hands." We have a responsibility to grind and level up our current skills as well as expand our active skill lists to become more functional in the

Kingdom.   Paul also exhorted Timothy in this area, saying in 1 Timothy 4:7b-8, ". . . train yourself to be godly. For physical training is of some value, both godliness has value for all things, holding promise for both the present life and the life to come."

Each of us is a vital part of the Body of Christ, and each is needed in order for everyone to function and fit properly. Paul wrote and explained this concept to the Corinthian church. In 1 Corinthians 12: 12-14, 21-26 he states:

> Just as a body, though one, has many parts, but all its many parts form one body, so it is with Christ. For we were all baptized by one Spirit so as to form one body—whether Jews or Gentiles, slave or free—and we were all given the one Spirit to drink. Even so the body is not made up of one part but of many. The eye cannot say to the hand, "I don't need you!" And the head cannot say to the feet, "I don't need you!" On the contrary, those parts of the body that seem to be weaker are indispensable, and the parts that we think are less honorable we treat with special honor. And the parts that are unpresentable are treated with special modesty, while our presentable parts need no special treatment. But God has put the body together, giving greater honor to the parts that lacked it, so that there should be no division in the body, but that its parts should have equal concern for each other. If one part suffers, every part suffers with it; if one part is honored, every part rejoices with it.

While the same skills exist within each of us, different people perform different functions. In the same way that in-game race and class differences influence each player's strengths and weaknesses, our personalities, propensities, and even emotional disposition play a part in deciding our role. Each person's role will vary in the same way that a party or guild cannot function properly without various members taking on different roles.

It is necessary to note here a common misconception some have held about spiritual gifts. I was told by a family member once that "No one can have all the spiritual gifts or else they won't need anyone else, and God wouldn't do that." As explained above, each of us has the Holy Spirit within us which means we have access to *all* of God's gifts. It's not like I get the portion of Holy Spirit that allows me to prophesy, but somehow that same God-of-the-Universe in me is unable to heal when that selfsame God is able to heal people through a brother in Christ. The notion that we don't all have all the gifts is somewhat absurd. The opposite idea, that having access to all of the gifts of the spirit means we would stop needing others is equally absurd. Ecclesiastes 4:9-10 says it this way, "Two are better than one, because they have a good return for their labor: If either of them falls down, one can help the other up. But pity anyone who falls and has no one to help them up." I challenge a single person on the planet to have a successful overcoming life in Christ without a single other person around them to help them when they are in trouble, having emotional difficulty, encounter physical pain or trials, or are being bombarded by the enemy. The fact is that unless we are forcibly stranded on a deserted island somewhere and it is impossible for us to connect with other believers, then we would be both foolish and in serious pride to believe otherwise, regardless of how many spiritual gifts we possess. Gifts are not the same thing as good character, also known as the Fruit of the Spirit (found in Gal. 5:22-23). Even *if* we were stranded on a deserted island, most likely God would send angels and saints in the cloud of witnesses to help us to grow as He has done countless times with people in countries undergoing heavy persecution for being disciples of Jesus.

I believe it is important that we as the Body are able to understand how to use our skills to the fullest. While there is a basic system of Real-Life spiritual skills that operate with a mostly-definable set of rules and ways that we can enhance our abilities, there is one more thing to keep in mind. At the end of the day, God is God and we are not. There are going to be experiences and abilities that manifest that do not fit inside the easily definable "skill lists" we may be used to. We must remember that what I share here is not a perfect representation of how everything will *always* work, but is a solid representation of how they *usually* work, and as such the precepts and observations explained here will serve well when learned and applied, but there will be exceptions to the rule.

As I just stated, not everything will fit in the "normal" box of skills, and this causes problems for some. I have had countless conversations with other believers who cannot seem to wrap their heads around the concept in Ephesians 3:20, that when God says he is able to do, "Exceedingly abundantly more than you can ask or think" that He actually means it. I hear statements like "where is that in the Bible?" as though somehow being written down or not written down in the thousand-plus pages of the Bible limits God and his ability to perform that miracle or other skill. The fact is that God can do anything He likes, any way He likes, and for any reason He likes. This is the God who one day just invented all of the elements found in the Periodic Table then created entire universes out of them simply because He wanted to--I am fairly certain that "all things are possible with God" actually means what it sounds like. If God wants to completely ruin this entire chapter by doing something crazy in someone's life that doesn't match a single thing I've written here, He can, and he doesn't have to ask my permission to do so.

The sad reality is most of the people who ask questions like that already put God into a box of limitations many years ago, and have a highly developed system of what He can and cannot or will and will not do, complete with reasons why and Scripture verses to back them up. Clearly they are forgetting the many things God has said about his limitless power and methods. One example is Isaiah 55:8-9, "'For my thoughts are not your thoughts, neither are your ways my ways,' declares the Lord. 'As the heavens are higher than the earth, so are my ways higher than your ways and my thoughts than your thoughts.'" Taking it one step further, the Bible states that Jesus did more miracles in the three years he was in ministry on the earth than the books of the world could contain, so I'm guessing that four small gospel books, half of the contents of which are parables and recounting his crucifixion, doesn't come anywhere close to enumerating the different miracles Jesus performed. A particular miracle being found in the scriptures is honestly pretty irrelevant, and arguing about it because it isn't explicitly written is not only juvenile from an earthly perspective but it demonstrates how poorly one understands the nature of our Creator-God who *loves* to do new things. I also point out that the "gift of miraculous powers" is plural, meaning more than one miraculous power. Like blacksmithing in-game, the gift of miracles in Real Life is simply a skill with multiples of sub-skills--to the point that there may be manifestations and applications of that skill that are to-date completely undiscovered!

Some of the skills in the Bible have far more sub-skills than we have realized, and I encourage every reader to take the opportunity to search out his own skills, acquire new ones, and put them into action. The most straightforward way to start leveling skills is to start using them, and if unable to figure out how to use them, it is best to start reading books, asking others, and praying for revelation on how to make that happen. As each of us does this, and continues to develop his skills, he will most certainly be rewarded.

CHAPTER 6

BUFFS AND ENHANCEMENTS

I have previously touched on the topic of growth-acceleration and how this is reflected in both RPGs and Real Life, but the "how-to" of acceleration bears a more in-depth look. Acceleration can be accomplished in a number of ways, two of which were discussed in the previous chapter—Parties and Power-leveling, but the methods do not stop there. Buffs, which are skills that supernaturally enhance a player's abilities, are yet another means by which we can speed up our spiritual growth, whereas their counterpart, debuffs, slow it down.

BUFFS AND DEBUFFS

In-game, buffs come from a variety of sources. Various potions can buff a character, and some items are enchanted to provide a buff to various stats and skills as well. The most common character-based buffs are usually a skill of the more magical variety. Ultimately the point of any buff is to augment a skill or stat the character has in order to temporarily increase his abilities. Buffs can typically be used an unlimited number of times, so when one buff ends, it can be activated again although sometimes there is a cool-down period --a short length of time that must pass before it can be used again. A single type of buff does not change from character to character, but that particular buff will always affect the same specific skills or stats regardless of who is on the receiving end.

Buffs are used most commonly in a party setting. The most common type of party buff is that of a priest-type class whose buff increases the health points or health regeneration of all party members. While magic users--shamans, priests and mages usually are the only ones to have buffs, some games allow each class of player to have an available buff, which increases the potential for a stronger party. One in-game example of this is where a priest uses a buff that increases everyone's health points (HP) and a mage uses a buff that increases magic attacks. While everyone benefits from the increased HP, the downside is that when a mage uses a magic-attack buff on a warrior who uses non-magical attacks, the warrior gains no benefit from the buff. Likewise, a warrior-based buff that increases strength or physical attack power will not benefit any of the mages or priests who use non-physical attacks.

Buffs that are part of items (such as a sword that increases both the player's strength and attack-speed while equipped) are part of the in-game experience but do not have a clear Real-Life counterpart. The closest analogue of an in-game potion buff to a Real-Life example would be a potion that increases the Intellect stat by 5 for 30 minutes compared to drinking a caffeinated beverage prior to a test for increased clarity of mind. While other comparisons like this one can be made with in-game and Real-Life items, they are not really the main thrust of this chapter; instead, I want to focus on the character-based buffs.

I have a friend Beth who has identified that she steps into an increased prophetic flow every time she gets around another mutual friend, Hope. Whether Beth hears more about her own life, has more spiritual experiences, hears more about world activities that need prayer, or even just has God talk to her directly more often, there is an increase when she and Hope are together. Something about being around Hope creates a buff where Beth is more in tune with hearing God and engaging the supernatural. Another man I know regularly has gemstones appear from heaven. When others get around him, they invariably start finding gems too, and sometimes the gems continue to appear long after he is no longer present.

One example from my own life took place at an annual Christian Conference hosted by *Global Awakening*, a ministry founded and run by Randy Clark. At the conference, "Voice of the Apostles," in one particular session that year a prophet named Larry Randolph spoke. The thrust of his session was personal prophecy; Larry looked out over the crowd, heard what God was showing him, and then shared it with the individual or group that it was directed towards. At the end, the Lord instructed Larry to pray for me to receive an impartation of his prophetic gift, and he laid hands on me to do so. Afterwards, a number of friends came up wanting me to pray and prophesy over them as they also wanted as much impartation as they could get.

When I began prophesying over them, I found myself sounding remarkably similar to the way that Larry sounds when he prophesies. I'm not saying that my voice suddenly changed pitch, but the way in which I was speaking and describing things and was expressing myself sounded much more like Larry than like I usually do when I prophesy. Essentially, in addition to the impartation, I received a Prophecy buff. Numbers 11:17 provides a scriptural explanation for this buff: "I will come down and speak with you there, and I will take some of the power of the Spirit that is on you and put it on them. They will share the burden of the people with you so that you will not have to carry it alone." While teachers usually emphasize the part about the power of the Holy Spirit being taken from Moses and being placed on others, and while I mentioned about its relevance to impartation in a previous chapter there is another way to read the verse. The original Hebrew does not specify *whose* spirit is being taken from Moses although most teachers I have ever heard assumed it was Holy Spirit who was being taken. However, it could reasonably be read: "I will come and speak with you and take some of the power of *your* spirit and place it on them . . . (emphasis mine)" This version of that verse more closely explains what I experienced--that I received some portion of Larry Randolph's spirit, or more probably, a portion of the Holy Spirit as filtered and *influenced* by Larry Randolph's spirit. It is much like passing a light through a faintly-colored piece of glass. The light is just as bright, but there are slight tones of color that had not been there before.

Pastor Peter Tan, in his book *The Spiritual World*, explains it this way:

> There is an interesting phenomenon in the Spiritual World whereby angels and spirits in the highest spheres closest to God receive the life and light of God and pass it downwards through each sphere. There are no human words to describe it. It is like a 'refraction' of light and life through the beings in the highest spheres downwards. But this life energy that goes through each of these beings is somehow enhanced and changed according to the characteristics of each being. Thus, although it is the same light and energy, it now has an added 'flavour' as it is transmitted to the spirits in the next sphere. (65-66)

The very fact that an impartation came *through* Larry Randolph is congruent with Tan's revelation in the above passage—which somehow took on a Randolph-esque tone to it as I received it.

As stated earlier, buffs only last for a limited period of time in-game and if the buff is not renewed the effects will gradually fade or abruptly end. One way in which the Kingdom differs from RPGs is that while in-game buffs end, in Real Life the qualities of the buff may be permanently passed on and the effects continue whether the buffer ever returns to re-buff or not. While the effects of the permanent-buff are usually at a much lower level than the original buff, the fact remains that buffs in the Kingdom can become permanent, becoming more like a skill than a temporary buff. This is another example of impartation at work as discussed in the "Level Up" chapter, and this continues to be a very useful and valuable quality of Kingdom life. This is, in my opinion, an ultimate form of Power-leveling where no effort is put out whatsoever by the person receiving the impartation, but they continually reap the benefits of it nonetheless.

Buffs are not the only type of character-influencing ability in a game. Debuffs are abilities that work similarly but opposite to buffs, weakening skills and abilities instead of strengthening. They are commonly found in-game by darkness/evil-oriented characters, whether players or mobs. Player examples of darkness-oriented characters would be the Warlock, Necromancer, Death Knight, Vampire, or Werewolf. In-game, all of these characters exist as a purposeful choice of a player to serve Darkness and these players are the enemy of all players who serve the Light.

Debuffs are also referred to as "curses," and some examples are as follows:

> *Darkness* – a curse that makes the character temporarily unable to see and thus unable to attack for ten seconds.

Cripple – a curse that decreases the Strength stat by 20% for 5 minutes.

Bleeding – where an injury is prevented from healing for a period of time, causing continual damage over time much as if someone had continual blood loss from an injury.

Poison – similar to bleeding in that the poison status causes continual damage over time.

Note here that in-game both Bleeding and Poison can be either limited in duration if the buff is for a set length of time or it can last indefinitely until the wound is bandaged or an antidote is taken. This varies based on the rules of the individual game and the skill level.

It is unfortunate, but in the same way that buffs exist in Real Life, so do debuffs. We live in a world where forces of darkness are at work, and where there are people who willingly choose to serve the Kingdom of Darkness, whether by active choice to turn from the light or because they were raised by their family to believe that darkness is somehow right. The Real-Life debuffs cast by practitioners of dark arts (warlocks, witches, etc.) onto other people do have actual effects.

I know of a man whose family background comes from a certain tribe in Africa, and this man and his family, now in the USA, have a belief system which involves a ceremony that made this man the "scapegoat" for all of the sins of his entire clan—cousins, uncles, grandparents, everyone. This man lives a cursed existence. Everything he puts his hand to fails. His child was taken away by the courts due to a mistaken identity. His parents tried to protect him from this fate, going to some lengths after he was born to protect him, but the curse has still followed him. Not only that, but because he is not fulfilling his "duty" as the scapegoat, some of the compounded sins of his family are falling back heavily upon their own heads as well, and a unusual proportion of his family members have had tragic deaths and some have died at younger ages than normal.

While the above example is more extreme than some, the fact is that curses do exist and must be addressed in Real Life similarly to how they are fixed in-game. Ignoring a debuff in-game may not be enough to make it go away, and oftentimes a player will need to drink a potion or have it dispelled by a priest or healer for the effect to be reversed. As mentioned in a previous chapter, the best way to address a curse is to go through deliverance to remove the demon forces that are empowering that curse. Many good books have been written about demons and deliverance from demonic oppression, as well as addressing generational curses (things passed down from other family members, like in the example of the man from Africa), self-inflicted curses, and curses placed by others, but demons and exorcism will be addressed in more detail in a later chapter.

Ephesians 5:18-19 is a passage that compares a debuff with a buff. The passage states, "And do not get drunk with wine, for that is debauchery, but be filled with the Spirit, addressing one another in psalms and hymns and spiritual songs, singing and making melody to the Lord with all your heart." The effects of consuming quantities of alcohol are well-known, and like any other drug-altered state, can be placed in the debuff-category. While alcohol consumption and overconsumption can make one merry temporarily, it also causes dehydration, and a decrease of inhibitions which can lead to poor choices. It affects the central nervous system (CNS), decreasing balance, physical reaction time, and impairs vision. The morning-after effects usually include headache, light and sound sensitivity, irritability, and delayed thought processing. On the other hand, the effects of being filled with the Spirit include merriment and joy, but any resulting loss in balance (which can occur when drunk in the Spirit) rarely results in injury, and is the effect of the body being overcome by the power and glory of God, not by a detrimental physiological effects of a toxin to the CNS. While the long-term effects of alcohol consumption are liver cirrhosis, chronic nutrient deficiency, digestive and heart problems and sexual dysfunction (such as dysmenorrhea and erectile dysfunction), the long-term effects of being filled with the Spirit include but are not limited to love, joy, peace, patience, kindness, goodness, faithfulness, gentleness, and self-control. Being Spirit-filled causes zero headaches, no visual impairment, and no irritability. There is no sexual dysfunction, and decision-making is not impaired as a result of Holy Spirit filling us with His goodness.

ENHANCEMENTS

This chapter is title "Buffs and Enhancements" but so far all we have covered are buffs and debuffs. What I refer to as "other miscellaneous enhancements" are ways of boosting powers that don't fall into a specific category, but do have in-game correlations. As with all buffs, the purpose of these augmentations is to accelerate the growth process, whether in a game or in Real Life.

In-game the purpose of this acceleration is to help the individual reach a new level at a faster pace. On a very real level, acceleration is necessary in this time in history as the world as a whole appears to be living on the edge of crumbling economically, politically, and socially. The way the economies and economic policies, military actions, and fiscal and social policies are being poorly managed and purposefully mismanaged by various governments worldwide are pushing us as a World-community to a precipice, over which we will either fall horribly or fly gloriously. Which way it goes is going to be in part based on whether or not we accelerate and engage the supernatural workings of God in and through our lives to bring the necessary changes into this world--changes that will radically shift the dynamics of darkness that are increasing in the earth.

With this truth in mind it's important to discuss, as we did with buffs and debuffs, not just enhancements but their opposite reality-- penalties. Some games are even set up where there are multiple factions in game, usually the Light and the Dark, and at certain points in time, based on seasons, actions of players, etc. there are increases or penalties applied to everyone of that faction.

Penalties are a damaging part of the gaming-process, and any penalties incurred in a game slow down the growth and advancement of the character. In addition to the faction-based penalties, some boss-mobs exist in an area where there is an invisible force-field in place that has negative effects. Examples include an inability to teleport out of that area to safety, an inability to dispel negative status effects (debuffs), or inability to use magic skills inside that field. Real Life is no different. One example, noted by many who live in the USA, is that they have observed we live under what I call a "Dampening Field."

For whatever reason, a noticeable depressive effect on spiritual activity seems to happen for those living in the USA, and this is not just my personal observation. A great many believers have observed that doing missions work and traveling to other countries brings about a noticeable shift and massive increase in the level of spiritual activity, miracles, healings, etc. they experience. What is most notable is that the only thing the believers did to make this happen was alter their physical locale.

I have heard more than a handful of preachers give explanations for this effect, one being that the nation as a whole is under a self-inflicted curse due to the rampant abortion, akin to what the ancients did when sacrificing their infants to the god Molech. Others cite the heavy focus on science and intellectual pursuits bringing about unbelief in the people as the reason why the power of God appears to be dampened. A third possibility is that the level of opulence overall in this nation allows us to turn to our own physical abilities instead of as in poorer countries where if God doesn't do it they are doomed, whether with growing crops, medical care, or disaster relief and prevention. Still a fourth possibility is the idea that some sort of secret government technology has been employed in this nation to decrease the ability to engage the spiritual realm, bringing the effects we experience. Whatever the reason, this field has not always been in place, as evidenced by historical revivals and the works and miracles of such men and women as John G. Lake, Aimee Semple MacPherson, and others. During the Voice of Healing movement in the 1950s, people such as Jack Coe, A.A. Allen, William Branham, Oral Roberts, and Rex Humbard traveled all over the United States, seeing many healings and miracles in their meetings. In many ways far more than we currently experience today. If the Dampening Field were always in place, this could not have been so. Whatever the reason, it is important to be aware of its influence and to do things that mitigate its effects, but this requires a basic understanding of how it seems to work.

I describe the change in our spiritual effectiveness and liken it to a man driving a car at 50 mph with a 20 mph wind blasting directly against him. This causes a net reduction in speed, slowing his actual travel speed to 30 mph (assuming that for simplicity we are ignoring other aspects of physics such as aerodynamics). Using this same example, it is akin to that same man driving across the Mexico-USA border, and suddenly the wind is no longer pressing against his car. Now he is actually traveling *at* 50 mph when going 50 mph. While in reality there is no actual increase, it will feel like an increase to that man due to the lack of resistance as the true level his car's abilities are being realized. Because Americans are so used to living at a dampened level, it feels like a massive increase in level has taken place when in reality it's just a removal of significant national hindrances.

Any hindrance, in fact, can be considered a kind of dampener, which is why deliverance and inner healing are so important. When one is no longer being held back by demons and inner hurts, his function level rises significantly. There is a reason Hebrews 12:1-2a says, "Therefore, since we are surrounded by such a great cloud of witnesses, let us throw off everything that hinders and the sin that so easily entangles. And let us run with perseverance the race marked out for us, fixing our eyes on Jesus, the pioneer and perfecter of faith." Throwing off hindrances has a marked effect on a person's ability to operate in life. The good news is that dampeners and enhancements are both just different sides of the same coin. Where demonic activity causes a hindering, dampening effect, angelic activity creates an enhancing effect. There are many people who have found themselves in an increased angelic presence, under what is sometimes called a "portal" or "open heaven," or in other spiritual circumstances where they are being lifted up to a higher place simply as a result of the work of angels in their midst.

Much like dampeners, enhancements can be geographical. When one enters a location where an open heaven (an area where there are no spiritual hindrances, but an area buff instead) exists over the geography, the individual will experience the enhancing effects that result. Another way this can happen is if one enters the zone of influence of someone else who is operating in an open heaven. This is basically just a type of buff as touched upon earlier, but I differentiate it due to the nature of how the buff functions. If a man goes to a church meeting or spends time with someone who is having an open heaven over himself, he will typically be able to engage that open heaven at that time as well and benefit from its effects.

Below is an excerpt from the article "How Satan Stops our Prayers" by writer/prophet John Mulinde, who was speaking with a man formerly deep in witchcraft who had then become a follower of Jesus. This man shared some spiritual dynamics to John that explained at least part of why open-heaven experiences appear so limited in scope. The article explains some of what happens in the spirit realm that bypass our awareness, and how open heavens can manifest in response to our prayers. (Author's note: English does not appear to be Mr. Mulinde's first language--please read with this in mind). He writes:

> Some prayers appear like smoke that drifts along and vanishes in the air. These prayers come from people who have sin in their lives that they are not willing to deal with. Their prayers are very weak; they are blown away and disappear in the air. Another type of prayer is also like smoke. It rises upward until it reaches the rock; it cannot break through the rock. These prayers usually come from people who try to purify themselves, but who lack faith as they pray. They usually ignore the other important aspects that are needed when someone prays. The third type of prayer is like smoke that is filled with fire.

> As it rises upward, it is so hot that when it reaches the rock, the rock begins to melt like wax. It pierces the rock and goes through. Many times, as people begin to pray, their prayers look like the first type. But as they continue praying, their prayers change and become like the second type of prayer. And as they continue praying, suddenly their prayers ignite into flames. Their prayers become so powerful that they pierce through the rock. If the people persist in this kind of prayer and allow themselves to be inspired in the spirit and to keep going, something happens in the spirit. The fire

touches that rock, and it melts. The man said that when the melting begins, it is so hot that no demon spirit can stand it. No human spirit can stand it. They all flee. They all run away. . .

Then he said that after the person finishes praying, the hole remains open. He said that when people rise from their place of prayer, and move on, the open hole moves along with them. They are no longer operating under the blanket. They are operating under an open heaven. He said that in that state, the devil cannot do what he wants against them. The presence of the Lord is like a pillar from heaven resting on their lives. They are protected, and there is so much power inside the pillar that as they move around, the presence touches other people as well. It discerns what the enemy has done in other people. And as they talk to people who are standing with them, they too come inside the pillar. As long as they stay inside the pillar, all the bondages placed on them by the enemy weaken. (www.divinerevelations.info)

For those in the U.S it is especially important that we actively seek out and make practical use of geographical and situational enhancements. I'm not talking about spending all our time in some sort of spiritual search-mode. We are capable of operating in the spirit realm even if the tide isn't full, barometric pressure is below sixteen, the moon is in its fourth lunar cycle, and it's a Tuesday afternoon with a southeasterly wind, but it certainly makes some spiritual activities flow more easily with greater effect when we have an awareness and make use of these spiritual enhancements available to us. For example, while writing this section of this book, I was sitting in a coffee shop with my wife. My friend Hope called my cell phone, so I answered and we talked for a while. Shortly after answering the phone, I went outside where it was quieter with fewer people around. As I walked outside, I decided to pay attention to the spiritual atmosphere, partly because I had just been writing about it. In doing so I *looked* in the spirit, which is as simple as desiring to know and then expecting God will show me. I had a vision that highlighted this large circular area of the parking lot. I walked over to it and continued talking with Hope, and as I did so, I started pacing, which is something I often do when praying.

As the man that Mr. Mulinde spoke with had explained, sometimes when praying it takes time to break into a flow of spiritual energy or anointing, but as I prayed inside this area, it took me no time at all and I was immediately in that flow. Hope and I both could tell God was active at work, and that my prayers were being effective even at that moment. This is one noticeable benefit of being in and engaging geographical spiritual enhancements. I had the distinct impression the time we spent praying together in that parking lot helped open up the heavens over each of us personally and that the benefits we received from praying were further-reaching than just that particular prayer session. While I don't plan to drive to a coffee shop parking lot whenever I need to pray, my awareness of the spiritual geography around me illustrates the value of this truth. As to why that parking lot carried that spiritual dynamic that evening I cannot say, but I do believe God was further illustrating the importance of living under an open heavens in our lives, and what it can accomplish.

Once, when praying, I could tell that I needed to break back through into that realm of openness in the spirit, and I started worshiping and playing my guitar. I did this for a bit and felt myself not really getting anywhere fast, so I stood up to pace and pray. I prayed as I felt led for a few minutes then perceived the Lord calling me to sit with him on the throne for a while. As I did this, visualizing sitting on a throne with God, He instructed me to open up the heavens from the top-side as one seated *in* heavenly places, not from the bottom side as one trying to break through it upwards. In the spirit I took a staff and struck it on what I saw as rocky ground, splitting it open and creating a hole through which light was able to flow freely up and down between heaven and earth.

I began to worship again, which became easier as I had now opened up an increased spiritual "flow" into the atmosphere of the room. In a vision I observed an angel walk toward me; Jesus instructed me to observe, and I stopped worshipping. I watched a second spirit enter the room, but this one was a very dark, winged being who was evil. The first word I thought of when I was him was "basilisk," but if I were to describe him more accurately, he looked more like a cockatrice, a winged snake-like being with a body resembling a bird in some ways. Interestingly enough, the basilisk and the cockatrice are both serpent-beings, and both are found in various older translations of the Bible where newer translations use the words "viper" or "adder." This spirit was taunting Jesus into sending angels to engage in combat with him and his demons.

After this spirit left, Jesus reminded me of something I believe is important as this chapter comes to a close: "Enhancements will only remain effective if you are connected to Me—if you cut yourself off, the power and virtue will fade—apart from Me you can do nothing." John 15 speaks to the fact that He is the vine and we are the branches, and these spiritual enhancements are only sustainable if we remain in Him. Engaging these concepts outside of relationship with Jesus will bring minimal value to our lives, as there is no lasting foundation if it is not secured first in relationship with Jesus. The reciprocal of that message--that apart from Him we can do nothing, is encouraging, as *with* Him we are able to do *all* things, receiving spiritual buffs that stack (can be in place at the same time), accelerating the expansion of the Kingdom of God within us and around us.

Chapter 7

Maps and Portals

It is impossible to create an RPG without building locations for the RPG to take place; these are known as Maps--regions of the game that can also be shown on a physical maps. Some maps are dungeons full of mobs, while other maps may be cities, towns, forests, or deserts where players and computer-generated people called Non-Player Characters (NPCs) can interact. Most maps, however, are a combination of the two, combining areas inhabited by humans, elves, and other beings of a "good" alignment with mobs of "evil" alignment bordering them. To reduce the risk for confusion, the term "map" in this chapter will be referring not to the physical map one can look at, but the game-region, much like a county or city limits.

Maps tend to be level-based. By this, I mean that some maps are designed for players of low level. The mobs in various places throughout the map, the items they drop, and even the products in stores in the towns are designed for low-level players. Other maps are geared toward higher-level players. These maps are likely to have more secret quests, hidden dungeons, and higher-level mobs, ones that could one-hit-kill a low-level player. Still other maps are designated only for those players of the highest levels, oftentimes players who fight in parties. These boss-mobs are extremely difficult to kill, but the loot they drop is fantastic. As a result, the player's level dictates in part which maps they will spend time on as it is fruitless for high-level players to fight on low level maps and suicidal for low-level players to travel on high-level maps. Even if a player is on a map that matches his level, however, traveling at random through the map is not wise. This is because a player who doesn't know their way around could stumble into an enemy encampment and quickly be surrounded by mobs, all of whose attention and aggression are fixed on that player. Traveling aimlessly through maps is unwise, but it is possible to travel through even the most difficult of maps with little danger as long as one knows where he is going and how to avoid trouble.

The spiritual world is somewhat similar in the way its maps mirror those of RPG games. Heaven and Hell could be considered the Real-Life equivalent to in-game maps. While a good basic comparison, Heaven can't be relegated to a single map, and I have a hard time imagining Hell is either. The Bible is not extremely descriptive of spiritual locations, but it does shed some light on the vastness of the Heavens and is suggestive that Hell has at least a few regions to it. This means that Heaven and Hell would each include a series of maps.

The Old Testament speaks of Sheol and by definition it is the place of the grave--where one goes after he dies. Based on the scriptures that reference it, Sheol does not necessarily appear to be a place of judgment, but rather just the place where one exists after death. Comparatively, Matthew 5:22 references Gehenna, which is a place of fire, akin to Tartarus, a place referenced in 2 Peter 2:4 where angels that rebelled against God were cast into and bound with chains in the darkness. Based on the different definitions of each, Sheol and Gehenna clearly reference different spiritual locations or planes. Luke 8:31 is a passage where Jesus has a short conversation with a legion of demon spirits who beg Jesus not to send them to the Abyss. Since this is the first time this place is mentioned in the Bible, little is known about it, but, in the book of Revelation, a few more details can be uncovered. In that book the word *abyss* is often translated as *bottomless pit*, but more is revealed when seeing the meaning in the Greek. In Luke, there is only one word used to describe the Abyss--the word *abyssos*. In Revelation there are two words used--*abyssos* and *phrear*. While *abyssos* essentially means abyss, chasm, or place of immeasurable depth, the word *phrear* means a well or a narrower opening that opens up into a wider space below, suggestive of a cistern. The way I read this, it means that the abyss isn't just a single place, but rather a passageway *to* someplace (or possibly multiple places) and also describes or refers to the vast space at the end of that passageway.

Heaven, likewise, is made up of more than one location. Paradise is the abode of God that is designed for our pleasure. It is a specific area of the Heavens as the whole of the Heavens is described by a different Greek word, the word "ouranos." Psalm 115:16 states, "The Heavens are the Lord's, even the Heavens, but the earth He has given to man." This verse is suggestive that Heaven itself has different "heavens," or said another way that the realm we know of as Heaven is actually made up of a great many areas and levels, only one of which is Paradise. In 2 Corinthians 12:2 Paul states that he was caught up to the "third heaven" or "third ouranos." What this specifically refers to is unclear, but common logic suggests that there are likely a first and second heaven, and that Paul was given a larger body of revelation on this subject that he simply didn't verbalize. Taking it a step further, recognizing that seven is the number of days of creation of the earth and that heaven and earth were originally formed at the same time, there are likely at least seven different levels or areas of heaven if not many thousands more.

In the book *The Spiritual World*, author Peter Tan describes the spiritual world as a series of spheres--both light and dark, with the earth sphere in the middle. In one direction, the spheres continue to get darker and darker, while in the other direction they grow brighter and brighter. As a person grows and matures, he progresses from one sphere of light into another, but is able to interact with the "lower" spheres and shine light into spheres with less glory and light than the sphere where he resides, including even shining light into the dark spheres (25-31). This imagery closely matches the way RPG maps tend to run, with higher-level players in the high-level maps and lower-level players in the lower maps.

In my own travels in the spiritual realms, I have observed that there are places where only God, angels, and other beings of Light exist, and there are other realms of utter darkness. While I don't spend any time in places of darkness, it is possible to find in-between realms--places where angels and demons and other spirits all interact, much like on game-maps. While there are places in the Heavens that demons won't go, simply because of the brightness of the Glory of God that repels them, there are other places that they travel, even to the point of hindering and arresting the activity of the angels as they come to minister to us here on earth.

To explain a bit more in depth about spiritual travel for the unfamiliar, it is where one's body remains in place on the earth and the spirit or soul travels in the spiritual realms. There are two main ways this can be experienced, and the terms for them are in-body and out-of-body experiences. Out-of-body experiences (OOBs) are the ones everyone has heard about--someone goes under general anesthesia for a major surgery and at some point during the surgery, he finds himself sitting on the side of the room watching the medical team operate on his body, to the point where he may recall conversations the nurses and doctors had *during* his surgery while he was unconscious under anesthesia. OOBs are commonly reported during near-death experiences, but to be honest, near-death is a misnomer. Except in the case of surgery, where the drugs have created an extremely tenuous connection between body and spirit, usually the person has actually physically died with their heart, lungs, and brain no longer working, and shortly thereafter are brought back to life whether through prayer to raise the dead or through a series of jolts of electricity to the heart. Regardless of the method, the person dies, has an experience in the spirit realm, and their consciousness returns to their body to tell about it. While there is much debate about whether it is the spirit or the soul that does the traveling, I wish to avoid that debate here. What *is* clear is that during OOBs the *consciousness* leaves the body, a differentiation I emphasize because it most clearly delineates the various types of spirit-travel experiences.

When I say the consciousness leaves the body I mean that the man's awareness of his surroundings is based on where he perceives himself to be at that moment, not where his body is physically located. For example, assume this man lives in Olympia, Washington, is in a time of deep prayer, and his consciousness leaves and goes to Brazil. Even though his body is physically sitting in a chair inside a house in Olympia, his consciousness is unable to perceive that. Rather, what he is observes through his senses is the Feirinha do Largo da Ordeman, an outdoor Sunday marketplace in Curitiba, where he experiences the sights, sounds, and smells he would have if he were physically there. Even though he may be aware his body is supposed to be in Olympia, he is not able to connect any of his bodily senses with his physical location, to the point that he will likely say what Paul said in 2 Corinthians 12:3, "Whether in the body or out of the body I do not know; God knows." All of the senses that man would normally use to provide information about physical experiences are in that moment linked with the consciousness instead of the body, and therefore he is unable to tell for sure if he is in Curitiba or Olympia. In these situations the only way to tell is by an outside observer, someone who is able to attest to the fact that his body is in fact present in Olympia where it would be expected to be during that time.

The converse of this is where the consciousness remains with the body, which could be titled an "In-Body Experience (IBE)." When having an IBE the man is conscious of where his physical body is. In fact, he is usually able to function physically even while having the experience, such that if he wanted he could get up from his chair, walk across the room, even make a sandwich and eat it if he so chose. The caveat here is that once he does these things, eyes open and paying attention to the world around him, it will be far more difficult to maintain focus on the shift in consciousness, and therefore the experience may end.

I am convinced that the vast majority of spiritual experiences people have, especially those where they describe "being in heaven" or "being in the spirit" are actually IBEs, and every experience of mine in this book is an IBE, but I have learned years ago that an experience being in-body does not alter how real it is, although my mind may tell me otherwise at times. Many have difficulty accepting the existence of OOBs, but I have observed far more people having trouble accepting IBEs, and I believe the reason for this is a lack of understanding about how we as humans have been created and about the anatomy of our soul and spirit.

The human being is a marvelous creation, equipped with a variety of different layers to the person. By this I mean that each person has at *least* a spirit, soul, and body although someone with a deeper revelation may be able to more clearly divide the being into more parts. As all humans have the ability to spirit-travel, this is a basic ability that is inherent to the human form, much like how humans are born with lungs and the innate ability to breathe. It is impossible, therefore, for a man to *not* possess the ability to spirit-travel, rather he may simply lack the knowledge or experience to engage that reality. The ability to spirit-travel has been given a number of names throughout history, including translation, astral travel, and spirit-travel, but as the innate ability used is the same regardless of the name attached. It could be called "movement of the quoriaes eltavra through the framellated tanglenode" and it wouldn't change a thing about the actual practice itself. I have seen people get up in arms about terminology many times before, but the underlying point is that they are all the same, and as such I have settled on the neutral term "spirit travel" to describe it. There are many books and teachings out there from a variety of spiritual paths that instruct on this capacity, but the simplest explanation I can give is that the ability to spirit-travel is based in the intention of the human will. To spirit-travel we must first believe it is possible, then we have to engage our will to make a conscious choice to experience this travel. As we do this we will begin to experience IBEs although our first inclination will be to disregard them as being imagination only. These IBEs can eventually lead to OOBs as well.

The risk here is in believing that things imagined are not real when the truth is that most spiritual experiences take place in the imagination yet are very real. Imagination is the place where we experience visions and dreams, but it is much more than that. Imagination is the vehicle which allows our conscious mind to drive and experience the activity of our soul and spirit. Something taking place in the imagination doesn't necessarily mean it is completely made-up, but rather it can be the backdrop the mind uses to experience a nonphysical reality. Not only that, but imagination can actually influence physical reality. Visualization is a technique used by athletes, surgeons, and others in high-performance occupations that uses the imagination to allow them to experience a skill or event, and as a result to train the mind and body to respond accordingly in similar Real-Life situations. Even if something is imagined, it may actually be happening.

Imagination isn't simply mental-training, but has an added benefit--the ability to alter reality. Did you know it is actually possible to build muscle mass through visualization without ever doing any weight-training? A study performed in 2004 by Ranganathan et al titled "From Mental Power to Muscle Power--Gaining Strength By Using The Mind" demonstrated the visualization group (who did a mental "workout" with no physical training) were able to increase the muscle strength of the little finger by 2/3 that of the exercise group who actually performed physical exercises for strengthening (Abstract). Another study, published in the *North American Journal of Psychology* in 2007 performed by Erin M. Shackell and Lionel G. Standing demonstrated even more shocking results. The visualization group increased the strength in their hip flexors by 24%, whereas the exercise group increased it by 28%--only 4% more than those who only exercised in their minds (194-196). The underlying point is that the imagination is more than ideas that take place in a far-off fairytale-land where pixies, rainbows, and unicorns play; our imaginations directly affect our outer physical reality. It is no wonder, then, that we are able to have spiritual experiences simply by directing our will toward travel to other spiritual dimensions.

It is not, however, wisdom to travel at-will through the various spiritual spheres without any guidance whatsoever, guidance that I remind the reader God is more than willing to provide. One example-story of the possible hazards of spiritual travel is found in the book of Daniel, Chapter 10 where it speaks of an encounter Daniel had with a spiritual being. The being does not make clear whether it was a person or an angel, but the text states he, "looks like a man." This man tells Daniel that he came from God to Daniel and left to come to him on the first day that Daniel had set his heart toward humility and gaining understanding of a vision he had had. The man notes that he was opposed by the prince of the Persian kingdom *and* was detained by the king there. The only way he got free to come to Daniel was by the help of Michael, an angelic Prince. In order for this type of interaction to be possible, a few things must be true. There have to be a myriad of spiritual realms, some of which one must travel through to get to other realms. Some of these realms are clearly occupied by dark spiritual forces, and at least some of those forces oppose those who are attempting to come to earth. If we, too, want to travel in the spirit from map to map than we are likely to encounter mobs of our own to deal with, and at times we will need the help of others, whether humans, angels, or other Godly spiritual beings to address the obstacles and enemies in our way.

This does not mean that all spiritual map-traveling is dangerous, as we have the hosts of heaven assigned to us to watch over and protect us. However, it suggests that in the same way that meandering through an RPG map is not without risk, neither is traveling in the spirit. For every problem-story I have heard from others about risky spiritual experiences, I have probably heard five more stories of experiences that were beneficial, enlightening, and life-giving. The key is being wise about it. In the same way that a Game-Guide is usually written for a new RPG as an instruction manual, and anyone can read that guide in advance, it is wise to seek out counsel on spiritual travel before consciously engaging in it, whether by talking to someone or reading books on the subject.

While no one is an expert in every aspect of spiritual life, some have more experience in this area than others, and any information and wisdom that can be gleaned from veteran travelers is likely to be beneficial.

I was recently talking to a friend, Praying Medic, and as we discussed spiritual experiences and spirit travel he pointed out an observation given him by another friend--namely that the condition of an individual's heart has a lot of influence on his experiences when traveling through the spiritual maps. As like attracts like, one's heart condition works like a spiritual beacon, attracting positive or negative forces based on the kind of energy emitted. If I am predominantly fearful, angry, malicious, or wicked, I will gravitate toward the maps in the lower spheres where darkness reigns and will attract spirits with similar disposition. Even if I am not located in the lower maps, I would likely end up in the maps of the intermediate spheres where light and dark collide, and where I will at times find myself in the midst of a battle. If I am primarily loving, kind, faithful, and righteous, I will gravitate toward the maps of the higher spheres and will find myself in the presence of angels, saints, and God.

Heart condition is not the only determining factor, but is one of two major factors that dictate spiritual experiences when traveling through the various spiritual maps; the second one is belief. In the same way that my heart condition attracts and repels, so do my beliefs, and most especially my beliefs about God. If I believe in a God who is primarily angry and judgmental, I am more likely to experience the spiritual world from a lens of judgment and wrath. I may have experiences that are intended to help shift me off of that path and to bring new understanding of God's love and grace, but I am likely to experience a lot of suffering and pain even in my spiritual experiences. If I believe that God is primarily loving and supportive of my growth, then I will gravitate towards experiences, maps, and beings that not only support my beliefs but help me expand and deepen in them so that I am able to shine even brighter as a spiritual light in the earth and in the heavens.

Spirit-traveling through the various maps is made possible, in part, through the existence of portals. Portals themselves are simply doors--gateways between places. In a game-setting, portals are gateways between maps and realms, and in some cases even planes of existence, at times even transporting mortals to the realms of Gods or demons. Portals in Real Life are essentially gateways between spiritual realms--both light and dark, by which we can traverse the spiritual terrain of the celestial spheres. While an open heaven could be considered a type of portal, a gateway for divine light and glory to shine on the person, portals as a whole are a bit different, although the overall basic function of transport remains the same. In this instance, portals are gateways for spirit-travel, although some can be used to physically translocate throughout the earth. The most commonly known physical reality that correlates with this would be a worm-hole.

The most well-known example of spiritual portal-travel in the Bible is found in Revelation 4:1 where John, one of Jesus' apostles, was invited to come through a spiritual portal and to enter into the heavenly realms: "After this I looked, and there before me was a door standing open in heaven. And the voice I had first heard speaking to me like a trumpet said, 'Come up here, and I will show you what must take place after this.'" While that verse shows one way this experience can happen, it is not required that one be invited through a portal to visit spiritual realms. We often travel in the spirit in our dreams, and at times even see and experience "what must take place after this"--namely future events. I attribute déjà vu experiences to this reality--that I am remembering a current event because I somehow already experienced it in the past. Think about it--in order to feel like I have been somewhere or done something before, there has to be a reason I am having that experience--and the most logical reason is that in my sleep, while traveling in the spiritual maps, I experienced an event in the spirit realm that at the time of the experience had not come to pass yet in the physical realm. While I did not consciously remember that experience, my spirit was aware of it at the time that my body and mind were asleep and sends me a sort of spiritual notification when I am in the event coming to pass--a sort of "you're on the right track" reminder.

A variety of people speak and teach on this subject, and many more are starting to appear. In the past the only people who knew much about spiritual travel were non-Christians, and the terminology they use for it is "astral projection." Whether one agrees with this term or not isn't the point as all people have within them the same God-created mechanism by which they can travel through the spiritual realms. The term applied to that mechanism may differ from group to group, but the ability remains the same. The framework of understanding may also differ from group to group and person to person, which is why I recommend that anyone who wants to learn this, start with someone of Christian background and belief-system. Ian Clayton is a businessman as well as speaker who has had a good many spiritual experiences with travel in the heavenly realms. His teaching materials, while both dense at times and somewhat strange, are a good starting place for those who are interested in learning about spiritual travel or encountering God in the spiritual realms. Another man, Mike Parsons, has similar expertise in this area but tends to have, in my opinion, slightly more practical application that helps others step into these experiences for themselves. Justin Abraham, leader of the Company of Burning Hearts in Wales is a third person who teaches on this and related subjects in some detail.

While spiritual travel and use of portals is a common in-game theme that is similar to Real Life, it is also possible to *physically* travel across the Earth from place to place. What is often referred to as teleportation or translocation can easily be compared to the in-game function of using a scroll or spell with a "return to town" function. In-game this allows the player to teleport out of danger into a safety zone. In Real Life, translocation allows a person to physically move from one place to another without needing a specific pre-determined portal, spell, or other ability. It has the same general function as an in-game spell scroll but there are no limitations where one can teleport to. There are times, however, when a physical portal can appear and take someone to another location on the earth that is pre-set by God.

I had a visionary experience the night before writing this while praying with some friends and I sensed in the spirit a portal opening in front of me. I physically stepped through the location where I sensed it, and I started having a vision where I was in a vast space in the cosmos. All around me I could see stars far in the distance. The appearance of the universe around me could be compared to how a planetarium appears when all the lights are off. No single light is very close, but the feelings of being absolutely surrounded by space and an absence of limits are present. Just behind me were a series of doorways, all of which were open and glowing brightly. In this vision I didn't turn around, but rather leaned forward, as I saw that there was another doorway beneath me, in what would essentially be considered my floor, but as space lacks the same up/down functions as being on a planet, I simply leaned forward in my vision and started going through that doorway to the next place the vision took me.

I have heard others speak about a place that looks similar to where I was in that vision--a place of many portals that lead to different places. These are not just spiritual places, but actual physical places in the earth. Ian Clayton speaks of traveling through these portals and has literally traveled to other earthly locations using spiritual doorways. While I have not had the experience of physically walking through a portal myself, I have had other times where time or space was altered as I was traveling. My wife and I once skipped past 22 exits on a highway in the blink of an eye, and I know other people who have had similar experiences.

God is training his people to make use of these spiritual doorways, and the number of people who are stepping into these experiences is rapidly on the rise. The spirit-realm is becoming more readily accessed at this time in human history, and experiences that were once relegated to RPG games and fantasy books are now becoming part of the common human experience. Many even in churches have fought against this reality for decades, even centuries, attempting to push back that which they perceived as darkness infiltrating the Church. At times, however, this perception of darkness is not based on evil (although sometimes it is), but rather as a result of a new encounter that is outside the realm of past experiences. The first thing required to step through these spiritual portals and travel the spirit-maps is believe they exist, then believe it is possible. After that it is a matter of practice, practice, practice, as we train ourselves to adventure in the heavens much like we adventure in-game.

CHAPTER 8

GUILDS

Most RPG games boast a guild-system. In Real-Life history, guilds were usually profession-related. In-game, the activities of a guild vary based on the members, but guilds as a whole serve a few main function--they provide a social hub, a resource pool, a place of guidance, and help accelerate individual growth. In some games there may be skill enhancement and additional other perks for membership too. Let's consider each of these functions.

As a social hub, guilds can be a meeting-place for like-minded people. Regardless of the banner they gather under, guild members tend to have something in common, whether it be friendship with other guild members, enhanced gameplay, or other common interests. This social connection adds an additional element of depth to the game as humans are by nature social individuals. While a few prefer to play alone, gameplay can often be more enjoyable when people form parties, accomplish goals as a team, and develop new friendships. While it is possible to form parties without guild assistance, being part of a guild provides a player with instant acceptance to parties from other guild members, even if the player seeking the party and the party-leader have never met before. Guild members also provide each other free information. This can be in regards to good places and ways to grind and level, where to find specific items that they need to move forward on their quests, tips on how to improve their character, and more. Being part of a guild allows the player to take advantage of the collected knowledge, wisdom, and experience of all members, and in this regard churches are no different.

While being a social hub is not the main function of a church or para-church ministry, both are often a gathering place for their members to socialize in addition to the mission the church or organization promotes. Those who are deeply committed to prayer, worship, and intercession may find themselves gravitating to places such as the International House of Prayer (IHOP) in Kansas City where there is a mixture of all of the above centered around music, while others may seek out a regular intercessory group at their church or nearby ministry. Those who are highly evangelistic will most likely get involved in a ministry with a vision of sharing the good news of Jesus' death and resurrection. Others may have a passion for demonstrating the love of Christ through social justice and acts of service and may be found feeding the hungry or tending to the needs of the homeless, shut-ins, or other socially-challenged people-groups. All of these are outlets, and all of them provide social interaction with like-minded people, while giving the satisfaction of working toward a common goal. Like guilds, knowledge, wisdom, and mentorship are often available as a result of these regular interactions, and some churches have mentorship and leadership programs to train others and help them "grow up" into greater maturity as followers of the faith.

As mentioned earlier, guilds also provide a resource pool for the members. Often times, guilds have a "monthly upkeep" much like a church might have a mortgage, and there are usually guild-quests that members can do to help maintain these costs. This could be compared to volunteering one's time or services at a church, helping to landscape, clean, or even repair or remodel part of the building based on one's skill set. In exchange for the ability to keep running, guilds have a pool of resources available to the members. Somewhat like a thrift shop or trading post, the guild members donate items they don't need or that they feel other members may benefit from in the future. These can be crafting materials, weaponry, armor, or other miscellaneous in-game items. As the players have probably received similar benefit themselves from the guild, there is a sort of pay-it-forward attitude among members, and items get passed back and forth between players regularly based on need.

This act of donating to the guild for the good of other guild members is comparable to Real Life where one church member who just lost his job is given a large order of groceries from a food-donation to the church by another member, or another member loaning his truck to another family who is moving. These sorts of interactions happen regularly in-game and in Real Life, but there is a spiritual component to this interaction as well. Not everyone is in need of a physical item. Sometimes it is a word of wisdom or encouragement, a healing touch, or even deliverance from a demonic spirit or stronghold. It is times like these when being connected to a "guild" of other followers of Jesus can provide the strength that is needed to continue forward. Please keep in mind here that a church-guild does not necessarily have to be an organized church as many are familiar with, but is made up of any gathering of believers whether they have official 501(c)3 status or not--Jesus wasn't an official sect leader and neither were the apostles, but that didn't stop any of them from living the lives God designed for them. Living as a Real-Life guild doesn't require any of the common trappings of organized religion, but if it has them that's okay too.

In-game growth acceleration can occur as a result of the existence of the guild itself and is not just an additional benefit that comes from partying with the individual members. While this is a difficult phenomenon to explain, it is a result of the natural attributes of a guild. In the same way that Real-Life corporations are considered an individual entity, in-game guilds function a bit like their own characters because as with character and skill leveling, benefits accompany each new guild level. For example, a guild at Level 1 may provide a 3% increase to each player's attack and defense as well as a 5% increase in health, whereas a Level 6 guild may provide a 9% increase to attack and defense and a 12% increase in health. Oftentimes being part of a guild will also provide decreased cost at merchants, decrease downtimes between usage of certain limited skills/spells, and usually provide some basic stat increases to improve the character's overall health, spiritual power, etc. In addition to those benefits, guild membership often increases experience gain and stat proficiency increase by a small percentage. All of this contributes to the speed of the character's leveling and skill development. As a result, guilds of higher level are typically more well-known than low-level guilds, and there are usually a great many low-level guilds and only a scant few high-level guilds.

Ministries have levels much in the way that guilds do. Many are completely unknown to most people. Like a low-level guild, if one weren't at their physical location, one wouldn't even know they exist. On the other hand, much like high-level guilds are well-known in-game, high-level ministries are often well-known, but usually at their level of effectiveness. To explore some examples of high-level guilds, we will look at three, one in the USA and two in other countries. Iris Ministries, based in Mozambique, Africa, is headed by

Rolland and Heidi Baker. Freedom Ministries, headed by David Hogan, is based out of Mexico. Both operate very strongly in signs, wonders, and miracles. The functional significance of this correlation between guilds and ministries is that just like guilds, ministries can and do level up in Real Life, partially evidenced by the fact that both Iris and Freedom Ministries did not begin from day one with a heavy operation in the miraculous, either by their founders or members.

Iris Ministries' first significant level-shift took place after a dramatic series of encounters at the Toronto Airport Christian Fellowship, a church in Toronto, Canada in 1994 during the beginnings of a series of nightly meetings that lasted for years, an event now known as the Toronto Blessing. God had visited this church in a powerful way, and people were being touched and transformed on a daily, even hourly basis. Heidi and Rolland were burned-out missionaries and this church and these meetings were their last-ditch effort to find some sort of help. After their visit and this outpouring from Heaven, during which Heidi had a dramatic series of spiritual encounters, their ministry started to climb to new levels both in the natural and the spiritual. Miracles broke out, but also more things in the physical realm lined up to bring expansion and increase in their ministry and as a result of that, in the past ten or more years they have significantly contributed to transformation in Mozambique and surrounding nations.

Freedom Ministries has undergone many similar-yet-different transformations as God has visited them deep in the jungles of Mexico and nearby countries. While it might sound like the God-visits alone have caused all of the leveling up (and certainly that has been a significant part of it), many other factors are involved in a ministry reaching new levels. In the same way that destroying mobs can help level up a character, Freedom Ministries had dealt with any number of high-level demon spirits controlling various regions of their work, and fighting against black-magic witches and warlocks under demonic control. As they battled through evil spiritual encounters and attacks, and as they overcame, their ministry would hit new levels. Additionally, at times during these encounters they would obtain nontangible spiritual plunder, of sorts, from the demons they overcame, much like in-game drops which will be discussed in a later chapter.

In the USA, Bethel Church in Redding, CA is known for being a high-level church as well. People travel from all over the world to attend this church for healing and life transformation. They have even had a unique manifestation where a literal cloud of sparkling gold-colored dust floated high above the heads of the people during the church service. In and of itself, the purpose of this cloud is not well-known, but it serves as an obvious sign that demonstrates this ministry is operating at a higher level than the unknown church down the street who rarely has anyone get healed when prayed for, much less golden sparkling clouds of heavenly glory appearing in midair. It is not specifically important whether a ministry has glory clouds appearing, but what is important is that all churches and ministries operate in miracles, healing, signs, and wonders as these are the things that mark followers of Jesus different than the rest of the world. Any church or ministry that does not have any healing or miracles must question what they are doing. This begins with the leadership.

Leadership is an important quality in the function of a guild, and one of the unique things about in-game guilds that are different than most other aspects of gameplay is that they are run by players, not the GM. This means the guild leaders and members dictate the way it runs as each person influences guild interactions. There are times when people have disagreements, and even at times leading to the break-off and formation of new guilds. It is not uncommon for an individual player to get kicked out of a guild for his behavior or perceived behavior as well. Fortunately or unfortunately, Christian ministries are the same as guilds in these ways, up to and including church-splits and excommunication. Awareness of this fact can be important when navigating church-life.

For those who are or have been in-game guild leaders or officers, almost all ministries, and actually almost all organizations and businesses in general operate under similar principles. Leaders are able to give out ranks and privileges to their members, and they retain all forms of administrative control. This can be a good thing or a bad thing depending on how well the ministry is run and how skilled the leaders are, but this is another important aspect to consider when navigating one's spiritual walk in any ministry-type environment. Groups are made up of individual humans, and humans make mistakes, thus no organization will ever be perfect. If we know to expect something less than perfection out of imperfect people, it becomes easier to give them grace when things go wrong.

One of the major benefits of knowing that ministries operate like guilds is that if we are intent on personal leveling, we can seek out high-level churches to join. This is one aspect of the Kingdom which I personally find important, and here is why: I realize that especially if a church is high-level, I would easily gain as much if not more than I could add through my participation. When I have been in a place to church-shop, I have kept my eye out for high-level churches because I value spiritual acceleration and want to level up faster as well as help others do the same. All in all, due to the perks of being part of a high-level ministry, it can be desirable to be part of one, as the effects carry over to influence daily life, causing demonic and emotional hindrances to be removed faster, enhancing character growth, and bringing about an increased level of operation in the supernatural in less time. And what's not to like about that?

CHAPTER 9

NPCs, Items, Drops, and Personal Storage

While at first glance NPC's, Items, Drops, and Personal storage may not appear to be definitively related, there are close enough relationships between them in-game, as well as how they function in Real Life, that it seemed appropriate to cover them all in-depth in the same chapter. I have broken the chapter into multiple sub-headings for clarity's sake, but the interrelationships should become clear as you go.

NPCs

Non-Player Characters (NPCs) are a staple in any RPG. These are characters that are generated by the game to provide quests and other services to the players. No RPG could function without them and for good reason. First, having a portion of the characters in a game being computer-generated creates significant stability. Humans are only able to log in and playing for a portion of the day whereas

NPCs are there all the time. If a character needs his armor fixed but the blacksmith is another player instead of computer-generated, if that player is taking three days off from the game it will be very difficult to get the armor fixed. Certainly, there may be other blacksmiths, but the same issue applies to any situation like this--computer-generated characters solve these problems and create stability.

In addition to stability, NPCs can provide additional combat support. Many RPGs have mercenary NPCs who can be hired by players and who level up alongside the players. This means that a mercenary who is with a player for a long period of time will be a similar level to the player and have developed its own skills and fighting ability as well.

NPCs can be compared to Angels and other servants of God. Like NPCs, all of God's servants in Heaven are eternal--unlike humans they do not die and they are able to assist humans as we forge ahead spiritually and battle forces of darkness. Angels in the Bible are commonly referred to as messengers, and the word *angelos* means exactly that. From the beginning of the Bible to the end, angels carry out God's purposes in the earth and obey His commands--just like NPCs following the will of the GM.

We know that angels are involved in heavenly ministry--flying around God's throne and carrying His glory as God travels through the heavens, but their tasks don't end there. The Bible speaks of angels delivering messages from God to humans and instances where they bring healing virtue. Hebrews 1:14 says, "Are not all angels ministering spirits sent to serve those who will inherit salvation?" Angels minister to all humans, and are also involved in the judgments of God such as the angels in the book of Revelation that pour out the bowls and open the seals. They protected Lot and his family in Sodom and ushered them to safety from the city's destruction.

Angels struck down Israel's enemies in multiple battles spanning generations. They set both Peter and Paul free from multiple imprisonments. Michael the Archangel and those under his command participated in heavenly battles on at least two documented occasions, and those are only the references found in scripture. Since then, many other men and women have reported angelic visitations and encounters, and major spiritual events has been ushered in partly through the work of angels, as have various revivals throughout history. They supported healing and prophetic ministries such as those of John G. Lake and William Branham. In fact, angels are far busier than we realize, and there are far many more of them at work daily in our lives than we are aware of.

One function angels play that does not appear to be delegated to other servants of Heaven is that of spiritual warfare. Like NPC soldiers from a Kingdom Army, they engage in spiritual battles on our behalf, fighting against the demonic hordes that mass against us in the invisible realms. They work behind-the-scenes of the Cosmic Gameplay to bring about the positive "game content" we currently experience in our own lives. Certainly, angels are not able to prevent every calamity, but even that fact is like a dark cloud with a silver lining, explained below.

Judges 3 starts out with these two verses: "These are the nations the LORD left to test all those Israelites who had not experienced any of the wars in Canaan (he did this only to teach warfare to the descendants of the Israelites who had not had previous battle experience)." For as God brought the children of Israel out of Egypt and led them through battle into the Promised Land, there were those who were not yet old enough to fight, and those who had not yet been born. They would not have learned about how to war against darkness if God had not provided a way for them to be trained. Likewise, God does not send out all of the angel armies at once from heaven to put His enemies under his feet in order that we, the Descendants of Adam, might learn to make war and take dominion over the Earth and all of Creation once again as He commissioned us to do in the very beginning.

Angels are not the only kind of NPC who help us. There are countless men and women of God who have gone on before us into heaven--either through death or like Enoch, through not-dying yet still phasing from the earth plane to reside in Heaven. Hebrews 12:1-2a states, "Therefore, since we are surrounded by such a great cloud of witnesses, let us throw off everything that hinders and the sin that so easily entangles. And let us run with perseverance the race marked out for us, [2] fixing our eyes on Jesus, the pioneer and perfecter of faith."

The Bible seems to suggest that those who have gone on before us are not actually in some far-off realm called "heaven" playing harps on puffy clouds, but rather are integrally involved in our lives, going so far as to call us "surrounded" by them. And why else would we be surrounded by them except to both continue to participate in and cheer us on in the finishing of our race? It is the very goal of reaching the "the end of the game" that causes these saints, also known as Witnesses to cheer us on. While there are those who say this is too far-fetched and is an impossible reality, are not all things possible with God? For those who say this understanding of the saints who are alive in God interacting with us is some sort of idolatry (as some have been known to say), I ask what part of now-departed saints cheering us on to fix our eyes on Jesus even more firmly could be idolatrous? No, the Witnesses are certainly others like us–people who seek to know and understand Jesus and the depths of his great love that drove him to the greatest sacrifice, yet from the Heaven-side of things. We are only now beginning to gain more insight into the interaction of the Witnesses with us humans here on earth, but these interactions are designed to enrich our lives and to prepare us for things to come–offering us wisdom gleaned through their own experiences, bringing messages from the Father in Heaven and even bringing us supernatural gifts and even physical ones to ready us for the quests God has laid out for us to embark upon in this life.

The Bible goes on to mention other NPCs--the Four Living Creatures, Principalities, Powers, Thrones, Authorities, Rulers, Dominions, and the 24 Elders. Their various functions are mostly unclear, and it remains quite possible that in the end all of these beings are simply different classifications of angels. What I have come to understand thus far is that Powers are somewhat like the "Elemental Spirits" of myth and legend. After all, Satan himself is referred to as the "Prince of the Powers of the Air."

From other anecdotal sources such as *The Magic of Findhorn* by Paul Hawken and retellings of personal experiences such as those by R. Ogilvie Crombie in his audio recording set titled *Encounters with Pan and the Elemental Kingdom,* it is possible to accept the existence of entire categories of spirits whose functions are entirely related to plants and plant growth and governance of the stars and other celestial bodies. While the Bible says very little about many of the above-named entities, or at least says little about them in any clear fashion, one thing is certain–the universe is full of a mass of NPCs who help maintain the game-play environment on our behalf. (Please note that not everyone will have a grid for the material in this paragraph, but I have gleaned much heavenly truth from the above named sources using study, wisdom, and discernment, and have gotten similar revelation of my own that corroborates it.)

Mind you, these spirits maintaining the game-play on our behalf does not directly translate into "they will always ensure all things work out in our favor." Even though God *has* made a commitment to make all things in our lives into something good, my point is that while angels don't work against us, Jesus in John 16:33 told the disciples that "In this world you will have trials." In Hebrews 12:2 (*Phillips*) says, "For he himself endured a cross and thought nothing of its same because of the joy he knew would follow his suffering." Jesus knew that even though He purchased a far better reward for us that as a result of bringing His will into the earth we too would share in his sufferings. We are not alone in this, however, as God has given us many promises in regards to what we receive as we share in His sufferings--we will be comforted, we will attain the resurrection of the dead, and we will also share in his joy and his glory, to name a few. This is not an easy path we walk, but there is no other path like it--either in this life or in the life to come.

ITEMS

Remember that we are not here all alone on the earth. In addition to Heavenly NPCs we are also given items, much like those we receive when playing an RPG game, to help us on our Real-Life quests. Personally I have had numerous times where angels have given me spiritual items, much like NPCs provide rewards for completing quests. While these spiritual items may not seem important, being invisible and intangible to most (although I have friends to whom spiritual objects are both visible and tangible), they are a part of a greater reality that we are only beginning to glimpse–the realms of Eternity. To believe something is insignificant and unimportant because we do not taste, touch, or feel it would only demonstrate our ignorance. Ultraviolet rays from the sun can't be tasted, felt, or seen, yet these rays can have significant influence on us, causing great, even painful damage to the skin. Likewise, spiritual items from heaven are very important, and they can be quite beneficial even if we don't always understand the benefits in the here and now.

Take Ephesians 6:13-17, for example:

> Therefore put on the full armor of God, so that when the day of evil comes, you may be able to stand your ground, and after you have done everything, to stand. Stand firm then, with the belt of truth buckled around your waist, with the breastplate of righteousness in place, and with your feet fitted with the readiness that comes from the gospel of peace. In addition to all this, take up the shield of faith, with which you can extinguish all the flaming arrows of the evil one. Take the helmet of salvation and the sword of the Spirit, which is the word of God.

There are a number of items discussed here—the passage mentions a belt, breastplate, shoes, and shield --all important pieces of armor, and all of which are integral for the player to use in his spiritual journey. Next is "flaming arrows of the evil one." This is part of what all the armor is to protect against, but this passage is clear that these items exist—the former to protect against the latter. Finally there is the helmet of salvation and the sword of the Spirit— two offensive weapons to counter the arrows and other enemy attacks.

If we look back to the beginning of the Ephesians passage, however, we observe that it mentions a complete set—the Full Armor of God. It's possible to wear only parts, but like any Set of Armor in-game, there is a synergistic effect that takes place when wearing the whole thing. From a gaming perspective, the armor of God is comparable to wearing a complete set of Epic-level Armor of Divine Blessing, one that is imbued with the nature and attributes of God.

One key to note here is that the believer in the Ephesians passage—referring to all believers as a general whole, is given melee-class armor and weaponry like shields and swords and not ranged weapons like a sling or bow and arrows. This is because the Kingdom is always advancing and there really is no place for defeat, retreat, or hiding and trying to snipe enemies from afar. That isn't to say that spiritual arrows don't exist, nor that followers of Jesus can't use them, but the primary armor given is that of a close-range battle-class, not a supporting attack-class. Everyone is meant to take part in the fight and there are no sidelines.

Recently, as I was taking stock of my own spiritual standing, I decided to take a look in the spirit at the condition of my armor, and the results were less flattering than I would prefer. As I looked at my sandals, they were the old kind that one might see in Ancient Greece or Rome–the kind that strap up the leg. However, mine were worn and parts of the leather straps were broken. Looking at my belt, it was on but unbuckled. My breastplate was tarnished and my shield could use some buffing although it was in much better shape than my breastplate. Fortunately, my helmet was just fine, but my sword needed sharpening and polishing—it was certainly dull in a spot or two. In order to fix this I had to pray and do some spiritual "repair" to my armor to return its durability, sharpness, and luster.

The Bible is full of other clothing and accessories--both good and bad. Isaiah 61 speaks of a robe of righteousness, garment of praise, a crown of beauty, and garments of salvation. Ezekiel 13:20 speaks of magic charms--items that the enemy used to ensnare God's people. These items, and the accompanying experiences, are not limited to scripture alone. No, this is a lived-out, Real-Life game we play.

When addressing the topic of spiritual items, it is near impossible to ignore the fact that this escapes rational thinking--that intangible and invisible objects and beings can play a real role in our daily lives. If we are having difficulty grasping this concept, we might consider Hebrews 11:3 which says, "By faith we understand that the universe was formed at God's command, so that what is seen was not made out of what was visible." If God formed all of the visible universe out of invisible substances (not *small* objects like atoms, but *invisible* ones), then invisible substances play an important role in the activity of this universe, including the planet we now occupy.

To give some examples, two friends of mine from a number of years back, Jen and Ben, both operated in a unique manifestation of the gift of discernment, which manifested through physical touch. By this I mean that they were able to *feel* spiritual objects and beings that are normally intangible. The downside is that they were unable to *see* the items they felt, but both learned through practice to use their gifts more effectively. Hebrews 5:14 addresses the operation of this gift, stating, "But solid food is for the mature, who by constant use have trained themselves to distinguish good from evil." In the Old Testament Hebrew, the word that describes this ability to perceive, discern, intuit, and have heightened consciousness is the word *yada*, first mentioned in Genesis 3:5 as the result of eating of the Tree of the Knowledge of Good and Evil. This word *yada* is best characterized by the senses, which means that by eating of that tree all mankind gained the ability to gain discernment and perception through the senses. In Hebrews 5 Paul explains how this ability can be put to righteous use through regular training. In short, the scriptures suggest that when we operate in this gift we do it specifically through the five senses, and my friends are living examples of that fact. On more than one occasion Jen, who lived in my town, had found herself minding her own business and going through her day when she would walk into something firm but invisible. While we usually think of spiritual substances as intangible, to Jen, objects in the spirit had both physical dimension *and* weight. I recall one time she called me on the phone and asked me what spiritual item she was holding. As I usually operate in a sight-based discernment, I looked in the spirit at what she was holding (on the other side of the phone), and began to describe it to her. I saw an object with a rounded base that tapered slightly toward the top, was open on the inside and which appeared to have considerable weight—in other words, a heavy ceramic pitcher. Everything I described was exactly what she felt with her hands even though she couldn't see the pitcher itself.

Ben lived in another state, and he would take time to practice his gift of discernment with another seer friend of his. From the stories Ben told me, they would get together, start praying, and Ben would practice discerning what the seer saw in the room. Keep in mind this wasn't limited to good things either. Ben had been suffering from a number of symptoms of a malady that sounded a lot like Lyme's disease and had this problem for a while. One day when he, the seer, and their wives got together and prayed, they began discerning a bunch of black things stuck all over Ben, which they proceeded to pull off of him. Shortly after they did this, his symptoms evaporated! These are just two examples of discerning spiritual realities, and an important key to remember is that things we see in the spirit directly influence the natural world, and changes we make in the spirit can alter physical reality.

If we can discern some spiritual things, it stands to reason that we can discern others like them. In the same way spiritual armor can be equipped, spiritual accessories can be too. While some computer games limit the number of accessories a player can wear, possibly only two bracelets, a necklace, and two rings, Heaven does not limit the number of items it will give us--all of which are designed by God to enhance our spiritual walk. Some of my most memorable spiritual experiences were angels handing me spiritual accessories–rings specifically. One of the first experiences I had with spiritual items was while I was in my apartment back when I was single and in college. I was in the living room praying when I discerned in the spirit a box sitting on the floor in front of me. I didn't see it with my physical eyes, but in my mind's eye I could see this box and exactly where it was on the floor as well as what it looked like—one of those white gift-boxes from a department store to put clothing in.

Not quite sure what to do and not having had something like this happen before, I decided to open the box, hoping that by doing so I might be able to "see" what was inside. In faith, believing I would be able to see the contents, I physically moved my arms, pantomiming lifting off the box lid. In acting this out, I found that the box was now open but I still couldn't see inside. I reached in and pulled out whatever was inside, believing and hoping I would then be able to see it clearly. As I picked it up, I saw a big shaggy white robe. Continuing to act this out physically, I "put on" the robe.

The *very moment* I did this, I suddenly discerned that there were sandals on my feet and a ring on my right index finger. The ring itself was gold, set with a large, bright green gem about the size of a nickel. As there is only one verse in the Bible that mentions a robe, a ring, *and* sandals together, I knew immediately that this was a reference to Luke 15:22, "But the father said to his servants, 'Quick! Bring the best robe and put it on him. Put a ring on his finger and sandals on his feet." While I didn't completely understand the significance of the experience at the time, I have since been given multiple other rings, each with a different colored stone. The next ring I received had a red stone and the third one was blue.

The unique thing about the blue stone is that it went on my left ring finger—signifying marriage. What I didn't know, which God did at the time, is that my future wife (whom I married about two years after I received the blue ring from heaven) was expecting a sign from God about her husband-to-be involving blue sapphires, due to it being an older tradition than diamonds for marriage. When I showed up in her life, I came wearing a ring with a blue stone in the spirit on my wedding ring finger—her blue sapphire!

Just recently, I was over at a friend's house and discerned in the spirit a long red rod in my back going up and down my spine. It was about an inch thick, but positioned as if it was in some way fusing my spine or similar. I asked my friend to remove it, and she had to work at it for a minute or so before she was successful. When she finally *did* remove it, I looked at her and noticed her physical face was a bright red color—which it had not been before. She could feel physical heat on her face while she was taking it out as well, almost as if what was in my back was a red hot poker just out of the forge fire. She later explained what took so long was that it felt as though it had been there a long time and as a result had become attached to other things within me. This is yet another example of spiritual objects that have physical effects, demonstrating that spiritual items have far greater significance than we previously imagined.

To further illustrate, while writing this chapter I was tagged in a Facebook post by a woman whose pen name is Faith Living. She had written a blog post "My Awesome Broadsword" about a battle she had in a dream, and in it a man/angel threw her a broadsword. Even as this was happening, she knew this sword was a Word from God--not meaning that the sword was the Bible, but a specific prophetic word that God had spoken to her through a prophet years prior. She wasn't quite sure what to do, but she knew God was wanting her to remember and apply that word in this circumstance to win this battle. As soon as she remembered what that prophecy was in the dream, she was able to wield this broadsword mightily. All fear left. She and the angel routed the attackers and won.

Hebrews 4:12 says, "For the *word* of God is alive and active. Sharper than any *double-edged sword*, it penetrates even to dividing soul and spirit, joints and marrow; it judges the thoughts and attitudes of the heart" (emphasis mine). In the dream, the sword itself was an object in the spirit realm--specifically a prophetic word. Interestingly enough broadswords are double-edged whereas rapiers may have no edges on the blade at all, and katana and other oriental swords often have only a single edge to the blade. This is yet another example of how spiritual items are useful in daily life, as this spiritual object, both a prophetic word and a sword, was used for defeating enemies in a spiritual battle. And for those who are willing to accept it, I suggest that Faith Living didn't simply dream, but her spirit fought an actual spiritual battle in the night while her body was asleep.

There is a risk of being misunderstood when talking about spiritual items and objects. Because many RPG games use a lot of magic, amulets, potions, spells, etc., there is a risk of mixing concepts in our minds--namely God's power versus witchcraft, sorcery, and other dark arts. To avoid that confusion, let me be clear about one thing here--when referring to "items," this is not the same as taking literal physical objects, praying over them, chanting, blessing, sprinkling with water or otherwise, and attempting to somehow create a "relic of power." The only place in the Bible where someone did this sort of thing on purpose is Acts 19:11-12 when it states, "God did extraordinary miracles through Paul, so that even handkerchiefs and aprons that had touched him were taken to the sick, and their illnesses were cured and the evil spirits left them." And even then, the objects themselves were mundane and did not become permanent powerful relics, but rather were temporary carrying mechanisms to relay the power of God from one place to another. No, I am speaking here of objects that exist in the spirit realm that have no physical counterpart. In spite of that fact, the apostle Paul using these mundane objects is of note and could look similar to some occult practices, and as such no discussion about items would be complete without addressing it.

In this instance, Paul was not using some sort of spiritual Alchemy or Enchantment skill to transmute substances into spiritual objects although it might be considered a type of Miracle skill. The closest approximation to a game-description I can give is that he was infusing objects with divine energy, but it was not his intent to create a lasting power object like an amulet that one would wear constantly. Rather, Paul was using the fact that divine power is transferable and he used an intermediary device to take divine power from him and release it onto those who were not physically present at the time. The items themselves were unimportant and he could have used anything at all to make this happen. I have watched videos online of a man doing the same thing with a plastic spoon. What *is* significant is the fact that we too have been equipped with this Power-Transfer Skill and can release the Kingdom on the world around us, even to the unsuspecting.

To take the idea further, imagine this: You are sitting on the bus after a long day and are ready to go home. Home is a 30-minute bus ride away, so you will be on the bus for a while. The seats on the bus are filling up rapidly, but the aisle seat next to you is still empty. Before anyone sits down, you place your hand on it and say a quick prayer, releasing the power of God onto the bus seat. An elderly woman hobbling with a cane slumps into the seat next to you and sighs. You get into a short conversation with her where she tells you that she's been feeling quite exhausted and has had a very long day. As she sits there, you observe her slowly perking up, and she informs you by the time you get off at your stop that not only is she feeling invigorated, but her hip that has been bothering her all day isn't hurting anymore.

God allows us to use normal, everyday items such as the chair in the above example and allows us to release his power through us into them and from them into the world around them. Moses had a staff he used in everyday life, and God used it through Moses to work miracles. Elisha died and years later his skeleton raised a dead man's body back to life. The Catholic Church has passed around bits of saints' bodies as relics for centuries, and on occasion, people actually did get healed when touching or being in proximity to the relic. While these are some examples from history, the key to keep in mind is that it's not about a focus on creating items of power, but about knowing the Person of Power. With that said, we are wise to take every advantage of the items that He brings us through his NPC-servants. What God gifts us with is meant for us to use, both for our benefit and those of others.

DROPS

One of the more enjoyable aspects of any RPG game, beyond skills and guild interaction, is that of the Drops System. A drop is basically anything left behind by a mob after its death. Drops in-game are typically graded based on the level and type of mob. A low level mob such as a fox, wolf, or boar will drop a small amount of money (usually coppers), low level ingredients for crafting, and possibly a low-level weapon or armor. Usually animal mobs will give off drops that are consistent with their type, such as pelts, tusks, claws, etc., much of which are items used for crafting. Low-level humanoid mobs such as goblins or kobolds will drop basic weapons, small amounts of money, and occasionally low-level clothing. A higher-level mob such as a Mountain Troll or Undead Ogre will offer different drops, providing a range of weapons, gems, crafting materials, or other enchantable items. The higher level mobs will drop more money, and all other items they drop will be higher-level and have more stat requirements and options, as the higher the level, typically the better the drop.

While drops are not the only way of obtaining in-game rewards, they are representative of a spiritual principle that is much like in-game drops, which I will term here as Heaven's Reward System. The

Bible is clear that there are heavenly rewards for our earthly actions and as such these rewards can be likened to in-game drops. From simple things like smiling at someone or performing a simple act of kindness to quitting one's job to spread the Kingdom in a far-off country, there is an outcome for each. In-game drops are somewhat random inside a set of parameters set up by the GM, but drops are calculated a bit differently in Real Life. In Real Life, we can receive not only Heavenly drops but Earthly ones. Earthly drops would be akin to the natural outcomes and rewards for our actions, whereas the Heavenly drops are the rewards we receive that may or may not materialize in this Earthly realm. The good news is that in the same way that spiritual items can have influence on the material realm, Heavenly drops can be accessed here and now, not just some far-off day in Heaven.

Matthew 6:16-18 speaks to this difference in the system, looking a little at how heavenly drops can be obtained:

> When you fast, do not look somber as the hypocrites do, for they disfigure their faces to show others they are fasting. Truly I tell you, they have received their reward in full. But when you fast, put oil on your head and wash your face, so that it will not be obvious to others that you are fasting, but only to your Father, who is unseen; and your Father, who sees what is done in secret, will reward you.

Rewards vary based on whether other people give accolades for the accomplishment or not. This doesn't mean every single act must be done in secret, but that actions that are done without seeking earthly reward will be given rewards in heaven, whereas actions done with earthly rewards sought after will have no rewards in heaven.

There are other actions and internal states that the Bible says cause one to receive Heavenly Drops. These are in no particular order: Righteousness, faithfulness, showing mercy and kindness to an enemy, caring for widows and orphans, repentance and returning one's heart to God, following God's commands obediently, according to one's actions, deeds, conduct, and heart, using wisdom, kindness to the poor, loving those who are unloving, doing acts of good in secret, welcoming God's messengers and honoring them *as* God's messengers, being hated, excluded, insulted, and rejected as evil for God's sake, according to one's labor in the Gospel, laying a solid foundation as a Christian leader, preaching voluntarily as opposed to involuntarily, confidence and faith in God, seeking God in faith, continuing in the teachings of God, being a servant of God.

Jesus himself instructed his disciples in Matthew 6:19-21, "Do not store up for yourselves treasures on earth, where moth and rust destroy, and where thieves break in and steal. But store up for yourselves treasures in heaven, where moths and rush do not destroy, and where thieves do not break in and steal. For where your treasure is, there your heart will be also." There are treasures in heaven *and* on the earth, and Jesus was simply instructing his disciples to focus on obtaining drops that have heavenly rewards as opposed to those with earthly benefits. Earthly benefits aren't bad, but they're not eternal.

Our overall actions are not the only way in which we can receive Heavenly drops. Like in-game, where defeating mobs deliver many kinds of drops, Real Life is no different, although the items dropped are again, usually spiritual in nature. Remember as mentioned earlier, spiritual items have the ability to impact the material world, so obtaining spiritual drops does not mean they have no value—only that their use is a bit different than that of physical items.

Apostle John Mulinde writes about spiritual items in his essay "How Satan Stops our Prayers – Combat in the Heavenly Realms." In it he relates an explanation of various aspects of satanic warfare as explained to him by a former Satanist:

When they overpower an angel of God, the first thing they go after is the answer he is carrying, and they get it from him. They then give it to people who are involved in cults or witchcraft, so people might say, 'I got this because of witchcraft.' Remember what the Bible says in the book of James? All good things come from God. So where does the devil get the things he gives to his people? Some people who cannot have children go to witch doctors and Satanists and become pregnant! Who gave them the baby? Is Satan a creator? No! He steals from those who don't pray through to the end. (www.divinerevelations.info)

Drops that come from demons and other mobs are originally derived from heaven and come in response to our prayers. When evil spirits fight with angels and win, they are able to take the items that the angels were carrying to bring to us in response to our prayers. In fact, when our prayers go unanswered this can be a reason why--it was stolen! Not only can demons give these things to human followers of darkness, but at times they will store up these items for their own use. Ian Clayton once gave an example in an audio message (found on his website sonofthunder.org) where he had defeated a demon principality in the spirit, and he then went to plunder that spirit's lair. One of the things he took while he was there was something that he identified as being another person's property– someone that he knew and recognized and whose spiritual possession had been taken by this particular demon. The message did not relate how he returned that item to its owner, but it demonstrated that not only can spiritual items be stolen, but that they later become drops when that spirit is defeated.

Personal Storage

In-game a player typically has a Personal Storage Locker where they store all of the drops they have collected during their adventuring. These storage facilities go by a variety of names: Warehouse, Personal Storage, Storage Chest, etc. Regardless of the name, this storage system allows the player to take the drops he has collected, quest rewards, crafted items, and any other objects or money and store them. This frees up the limited space that a player has in his backpack and allows him to collect and store new items. While some games require a player to travel to certain pre-designated locations (such as certain in-game towns) to be able to access this storage, other games allow the player storage-access anywhere he is located. Even if he can access this storage anywhere, there are limitations to this, in that he cannot make immediate use of or equip an item in his storage if it is not first placed in his backpack, also known as an inventory.

Additionally, in the same way that a backpack has space limits, so does Personal Storage. What this means is that at times the player will have to do something with all the items he has collected to free up space for new ones. In other words, the game prevents hoarding. What usually happens is that a player will trade in or sell lower-level items after he has upgraded his equipment and made any necessary adjustments. With the resulting equipment upgrade, an older model can be sold for money or traded for another item with another player. In some cases, he might just give it away!

We too have been given a Personal Storage although since it's in heaven, we can know that it is of far higher quality than a dusty warehouse or cold metal shipping container. John 14:2 says, "In My Father's house are many dwellings; if it were not so, I would have told you; for I go to prepare a place for you." Jesus has already gone before us and prepared a place for each of us—a place where the elements cannot destroy what we store, and where there are no thieves trying to pick the lock and steal what is kept there.

When we have overcome a mob and received Heavenly drops, our settings automatically place them in our Personal Storage unless they are automatically equipped, as may occur with equipment that is of higher grade than we were using prior. We can access this storage at any time and from any location. Ephesians 1:3 says, "Blessed be the God and Father of our Lord Jesus Christ, who hath blessed us with all spiritual blessings in heavenly places in Christ." The Scripture tells us that we have been blessed with all of these spiritual blessings, but that we have to travel to heavenly places to our storage to access them. As discussed in an earlier chapter, we have the ability to travel through spiritual portals into heavenly maps to visit our Personal Storage at any time, even if we are physically on earth.

Personally, I envision my Storage as a mountain in Heaven that is filled with treasure troves of items. This imagery may not work for some, but I have found it useful when engaging spiritual realities. From time to time I may go in the spirit and put things in that storage or take them out, but either way this visualization is a method I have used to some effect, both with myself and others in times of prayer

.

CHAPTER 10

QUESTS

I cannot think of a single role-play game that does not include quests. Quests are the in-game equivalent of life's responsibilities--things that make us do things. For example, if a player were Level 1 in a brand new fantasy world full of swords, magic, mythical beasts, and exploration, what would make him go out and explore instead of staying in town where it is safe? Quests add a sense of depth to a game, giving the player excuses to have adventures, solve puzzles, and just have fun. At the same time, quests often have elements of danger or difficulty, and starting a quest does not provide any guarantee that he will be able to complete it successfully.

There are a number of types of quests, all of which correlate to Real-Life actions that we can take as followers of Jesus: Individual Quests, Party Quests, Guild Quests, Repeating Quests, Level-based Quests, and Chain Quests. While these are the main quest-types, they can overlap with one another, such as a Level-based Individual Quest or an Individual Repeating Quest. We will look at the individual types of quests in-game and look at their correlation with events seen in the Bible, then discuss their relevance to our lives today.

Individual Quests are ones that can be completed by any player without additional assistance from other players. Party Quests are obviously quests that require a party to complete, as the difficulty level is usually too great for an individual player, or there are elements of them that require more than one player to complete it. Guild Quests are only available through guilds. Repeating Quests can be completed regularly--even daily at times. Level-based Quests have certain level requirements--either a minimum level to be completed or a maximum level at which they can be completed. Chain Quests are the most difficult to complete as each element is dependent on successfully completing the prior one, and each quest is as difficult or more-so than the last. Quests come with rewards, with the rewards typically increasing with the difficulty of the quest. Quest rewards are already covered in the previous chapter on Items and Drops, so will not be discussed in depth here.

In addition to in-game, all of these types of quests can be found in the Bible. Individual Quests are those that are performed alone. One Biblical example of this would be when David's father sent him out to the battlefield to deliver food for his brothers. In addition to being a simple quest, almost impossible to fail, it was one he carried out alone, thus an Individual Quest. Keep in mind that all Individual Quests are not necessarily simple. Shortly after David completed the above quest, he was given another Individual one but this time by King Saul and at a much higher difficulty level--to defeat the as-yet undefeated Philistine champion Goliath, who was part-giant.

Party Quests are obviously those that are carried out in a group. Paul was offered a Party Quest in Acts that brought him to Macedonia. As explained in Acts 16: 6-10, "A vision appeared to Paul in the night: a man of Macedonia was standing and appealing to him, and saying, 'Come over to Macedonia and help us.' When he had seen the vision, immediately we sought to go into Macedonia, concluding that God had called us to preach the gospel to them." In the surrounding passage, Paul is traveling with Timothy and at least one other person on this quest--the writer. The vision was the Quest Invitation, and the response was the party immediately set out to complete it.

Repeating Quests are less common but that doesn't mean they can't be found. One example of a Repeating Quest is in Matthew 10 when Jesus called the twelve apostles together and sent them out to the cities of Israel in twos. He instructed them not to take provisions for the journey, but to receive provisions from others as they traveled, and to heal the sick, cleanse those with leprosy, resurrect the dead, and cast out demons on their journey. Later on in Luke 10 he called together seventy-two disciples, presumably of which twelve were the twelve apostles who went on the first journey, whom he sent out on the same mission all over again. One of the benefits of a Repeating Quest is the players gain experience and rewards each time they complete the quest. In the disciples' case, they gained Real-Life experience performing miracles, healing others, and casting demons out of the afflicted, but they also learned how to deal with people in unfamiliar and at times scary situations. They learned how to lead and teach groups of people as they traveled from town to town and how to actively put their faith to work for them to see their needs met. Those who did it the first time had an easier time the second time through, and because they had the basics of the quest down they should have been able to delve deeper into the experience the second time. Not only that, but I suspect Jesus did not allow the first twelve to remain in pairs, and split them up with some of the more timid disciples and/or those he thought would need the most in-person assistance. After all, Jesus was training his disciples to be effective, and what better way to do that than with teaching assistants?

Guild Quests are akin to ministry-related mission trips and other assignments that an organization might give to their members. These are often related to something that will benefit the ministry organization, but not always. As seen in 2 Kings, Elisha the prophet was found both handing out and performing guild quests. The following is one specific example in 2 Kings 9:1-3, found as Elisha spoke to what was essentially a school of prophet students:

> Now Elisha the prophet called one of the sons of the prophets and said to him, 'Gird up your loins, and take this flask of oil in your hand and go to Ramoth-gilead. When you arrive there, search out Jehu the son of Jehoshaphat the son of Nimshi, and go in and bid him arise from among his brothers, and bring him to an inner room. Then take the flask of oil and pour it on his head and say, 'Thus says the Lord, 'I have anointed you king over Israel.'' Then open the door and flee and do not wait.'

Chain Quests can be found in various places in the Bible, and Moses sets a perfect example. His first quest in the chain was to follow the instructions at the burning bush--an easy place to start. The quest level jumped up significantly when he had to convince Pharaoh to let the Israelites leave Egypt. He had some difficulty with this quest, having to go back time after time to use and level up his Miracle skill, demonstrating new miracles to Pharaoh. As a result, he was positioned very well for the next quest in the chain--escaping from the Egyptian army. With his Miracle skill at a high level from its constant use, he parted the Red Sea waters, led the Hebrews to safety, and destroyed the Egyptian army. He went through a number of other side-quests along the way, including a crafting-type quest to construct the Tent of Meeting, but the final result of his quests were success--the Hebrews entered the Promised Land. At times there were penalties he and the Israelites received due to poor choices made along the way, one of which resulted in him not being able to enter, but the overall quest to lead the Israelites to the Promised Land was a success, even if it was 40 years behind schedule.

There are some quests that are class-specific as well as others that are related to a specific region or specific timing based on natural events. One good Real-Life example of this is my friend Hope, a prophetess, and on multiple occasions she has been given assignments from Heaven. One particular trip Hope was sent to Montana to pray over, among other things, a series of bridges and waterways. As she did this she could feel the demonic resistance and witchcraft that were opposing her. Unbeknownst to her, her visit to the region coincided with a particular gathering of high-level witches and God gave her this quest to halt and disarm the spiritual powers of darkness at work in that region.

To simplify all quests down to the common denominator, think of them as missions of some kind. What are the missions God has given *all* people? Love the Lord your God. Steward and take dominion over all the earth. Make disciples of all nations. Preach "The Kingdom is at hand." Heal the sick, cleanse those with leprosy, raise the dead, and cast out demons. These same quests are available to every believer regardless of what point in the timeline we are born. It is not so much important that we make sure to complete these quests daily, but that we understand these are real Kingdom missions--quests of importance that can be completed as long as we make them an integral part of our daily lives. There are times when we might engage these quests while at work, at the store, or at random other points in the day, all of which have nothing to do with "intentional ministry" at some officially-sanctioned church gathering. I remember hearing an audio CD of Bill Johnson, Pastor of Bethel

Church in Redding, CA where he told a story about a man who visited his church and wanted to be a part of the "Mall Ministry." Bill told him "We don't have a mall ministry." The guest was persistent about wanting to join all of the people who went to the malls and healed the sick and injured that he heard on the stories Bill told in his sermons. Bill then realized what this guest was referring to. Explaining further he told the man, "No, we really don't have a Mall Ministry. We have parishioners who shop." There is no need for a super-special moment where a shaft of light shines from heaven with an angelic choir in the background and a glowing orb of blue light settling overtop of the person in need of a touch from heaven. In our daily lives if we feel the desire to reach out with God's life-giving power and bring positive change, then we can do so in love and watch God meet the person in need with demonstrations of the Spirit's power.

The one thing we can count on about quests is that there are no such things as impossible quests. Some are highly difficult, but God does not hand out quests that cannot be completed. With that said, however, there are a number of reasons why quests may fail. In-game quests tend to fail when the player either misses out on timing, is ill-equipped for the quest, whether due to a lack of skills and training or due to inadequate supplies, or is overwhelmed by the enemy forces, possibly leading to the player's death. Real-Life quests can fail for the same reasons, including enemy attacks, misunderstanding God or the nature of the quest, not following through with timing or having a lack of personal character.

There is a real enemy out there that we fight against, and enemy attacks are a reality. The goal of our spiritual enemies is to cause death and destruction wherever they go, so if we are in the middle of a quest it should be no surprise if death and destruction attempt to push their way into our endeavor. When we misunderstand what the quest is about, it can also lead to failure because our energy is spent on things that don't move the quest forward. In-game this quest could look like one with a quest-goal to fight through a labyrinth and obtain a treasure, with a time restriction to complete it. In that instance, the quest is more about speed to reach the treasure than it is about kill-count of the mobs inside the labyrinth. Even if the player evades some mobs entirely and still reaches the treasure, the quest has still been completed, as it's partly about the method, not just the results. Likewise, Real-Life quests are often more about the process and what it builds in us than it is just about the end result. Character issues are a significant factor in quest completion. The fact is that if the quest participant grows during the quest-process, he is far more likely to complete the quest than someone who is so intent on completing it that the quest doesn't change him at all.

If we recall the lessons from the chapter on "Stats and Skill Trees" we will remember that anyone with enough use and practice can grow and enhance skills. Given enough time theoretically we could complete any quest on this planet if it just came down to skill proficiencies. However, there is more to questing than brawn or expertise. After all, 1 Corinthians 13:1-8 says:

> If I speak in the tongues of men or of angels, but do not have love, I am only a resounding gong or a clanging cymbal. If I have the gift of prophecy and can fathom all mysteries and all knowledge, and if I have a faith that can move mountains, but do not have love, I am nothing. If I give all I possess to the poor and give over my body to hardship that I may boast, but do not have love, I gain nothing?
>
> Love is patient, love is kind. It does not envy, it does not boast, it is not proud. It does not dishonor others, it is not self-seeking, it is not easily angered, it keeps no record of

wrongs. Love does not delight in evil but rejoices with the truth. It always protects, always trusts, always hopes, always perseveres. Love never fails. But where there are prophecies, they will cease; where there are tongues, they will be stilled; where there is knowledge, it will pass away.

These verses clearly express that we can operate in any skill to the God-level, but at the same time if we don't have love and the other fruit of the Spirit (joy, peace, patience, kindness, gentleness, faithfulness and self-control) our quests and other acts mean nothing. Basically, to fall grossly short in the realm of character is a surefire way to fail quests left and right, even if it appears at first glance like we followed all of the quest requirements.

There is good news, however, which is found in John 15:1-8:

I am the true vine, and my Father is the gardener. He cuts off every branch in me that bears no fruit, while every branch that does bear fruit he prunes so that it will be even more fruitful. You are already clean because of the word I have spoken to you. Remain in me, as I also remain in you. No branch can bear fruit by itself; it must remain in the vine. Neither can you bear fruit unless you remain in me.

I am the vine; you are the branches. If you remain in me and I in you, you will bear much fruit; apart from me you can do nothing. If you do not remain in me, you are like a branch that is thrown away and withers; such branches are picked up, thrown into the fire and burned. If you remain in me and my words remain in you, ask whatever you wish, and it will be done for you. This is to my Father's glory, that you bear much fruit, showing yourselves to be my disciples.

This section of verses promises that if we remain in Him and He remains in us (which has to do partially with ongoing relationship with Him) then there is nothing that we cannot do. The metaphor of the vine is actually quite encouraging as well. Normally these verses are interpreted to say that Jesus is the vine stalk and we are the branches attached to it and if we don't stay attached, then we can't get the life-giving sap from the vine, but that's not how it works. You see, Jesus is the *whole* vine and we are the branches *in* him. As long as we remain in Him, fruit happens. The branches don't work really hard at growing fruit, but rather the whole vine simply grows fruit over time. It is really as simple as that. Even those of us who are afraid that we lack the character we need to be successful in carrying out even the smallest of Kingdom quests need not fear. We simply make our first goal to draw near to God knowing that as we do this He will draw near to us. Fruit will automatically grow within us, and as we remain in Him and his words remain in us all the benefits that come from knowing him will be ours--that if we ask anything we desire it will be done for us.

So then, what is the value of understanding and learning about quests? First off we build momentum when questing and leveling, and purposeful action produces better results than unintentional action. I feel I must caution the reader here that there is a difference between developing and training what we have been given out of a desire to display more of God's love and power versus working hard in order to earn that love and power. Jesus already paid the price, so we must understand and believe that God is actively giving it to us instead of working hard to try to please God enough to earn it. What I mean by this is that it is possible to get so doing-focused that we actually lose out on the being-part of life and spirituality. We are not designed to be automatons who simply do-do-do, but instead we are meant to experience life together with God. When we understand and carry out quests from that internal position, we are far more effective.

Ultimately questing is about bringing Heaven to Earth, just0 as Jesus prayed in The Lord's Prayer. For a long time it has been believed that the point of life is to get others "saved" so they go to Heaven when they die. And while if a man is going to die then heaven is a good place to end up, the plan has never been to bring those on Earth to Heaven, but to bring Heaven to Earth. This is accomplished through questing.

CHAPTER 11

EVENTS AND SERVER RESET TIME

In-game Events are typically regional or global in nature, and something that a large number of people can join in on. In-game, these often coincide with Real World holidays, providing a celebratory outlet for Real-Life happenings or at times during a large patch or upgrade to the game itself. Any Event is a pre-determined set of actions or happenings that are set into motion by a trigger-action or catalyst of some kind. As mentioned, sometimes a date on the calendar is the "Event trigger," but other triggers exist, such as the completion of a high-level quest that opens up an Event with in-game regional impact.

The Bible is chock-full of Events and the life of Jesus alone is full of them. The first Event in the gospels is a Census, during which Mary and Joseph travel to Bethlehem where an Angelic Choir visits the shepherds in the fields at night heralding the birth of the new King. The next major Event-trigger is that of the Star in the East which signals the Wise Men to its occurrence, whereby they too travel to homage to the new King. Another major event is that of the

Crucifixion although that one appears at first to end on a low note--
until the resurrection three days later with world-changing results!
Even in the book of *Acts* after Jesus ascends to heaven, it is quickly
followed up by an Event: the Baptism of the Holy Spirit; the ripples
of that Event continue onward even to this day.

While it can be easy to label something an "Event" simply
because it is important or significant, two Greek words actually
describe this type of happening, both of which are found in the Bible.
The word *chronos* has to do with cycles of time, is a root of the word
chronological, and covers things in time-order. The second word,
kairos, deals with appointed moments of fixed time which are
ordained by God, not cyclical and seasonal events like Chronos time.
The in-game comparison to this would be that Chronos events are
holidays like Christmas and Easter and Kairos events would be those
special events decided by the programmers or GMs due to game-
significant markers or event-triggers that only they know of.

CHRONOS EVENTS AND SERVER RESET TIME

In every RPG I have ever played or seen, there is some sort of
night/day server reset, which provides some semblance of realism to
the game inasmuch as Real Life has both night and day. When the
server hits the 24th hour and starts over at 0001 minutes (or however
the server counts), invariably some items reset along with it. One
specific item that comes to mind is time or phase-sensitive quests.
Some quests must be completed within a specific allotment of time,
and some quests are DAILY quests--ones that must be completed
that day. Effects of that quest cannot be put off for another day, nor
can they be banked in advance to cover a player on a day when he
doesn't get to it.

The idea of a server reset applies to Real Life as well. God gave
the Israelites manna from heaven every day (with the exception of

the sixth day where they had to collect enough for two days), and the manna would not last longer than a single day. If someone failed to collect manna that day he could not go back later and get it--the food had spoiled by the next morning. Jesus knew the importance of completing daily quests, and I believe this underlies part of why he prayed "Give us *this day* our daily bread. (emphasis mine)" Jesus knew that there are some things in Real Life which cannot be stored up to be brought out on a rainy day, but rather must be engaged in on a daily basis. As such, he instructed his disciples, and subsequently all believers, to seek out their blessings for each day.

Psalm 68:19 says, "Blessed be the Lord, who daily loads us with benefits, even the God of our salvation." In looking at that verse a little more closely, it is even vague in the original Hebrew. The word "daily" is the word *yowm* which according to *Strong's Concordance* denotes not just a single day, but a period of time. This can and does include a day, but it could also be synonymous with era, period, or even lifetime. The phrase "loads us with benefits" doesn't actually say that straight-out either, and multiple translations translate it differently. Some say that God loads us with benefits, while others say that He carries our burdens. The reason for this is that the phrase itself is actually just a single word *amac* which means "to load, carry, or carry a load." Regardless of the minutiae of meaning, whether God is loading us up with good things or we're loading Him up with our bad things, or both, the fact is that there is a significance to times and seasons and we have to work with those times and seasons as they cycle. Whether in-game or out of game, this is a form of Chronos time.

When one period of time has completed, we cannot go back and do something inside that time that we haven't already done. Things that go unfinished simply remain unfinished because it is a new day and time for new things. There is a warning in that, to be diligent with our days and times, but there is an encouragement and admonition here as well--do not miss out today on what God has for us because God has things specifically portioned to us for today—things that we couldn't have received yesterday and may not receive tomorrow. These things are specifically for today.

Understanding the cyclical nature of Chronos events provides a context for repeating patterns, both great and small. Gregg Braden in his book *Fractal Time* explains this concept:

> . . . it's clear that cycles are involved and that each has a beginning. In every instance, that beginning –the seed event – sets the conditions that will repeat at various future dates. From our understanding of natural rhythms and cycles, we can calculate when similar conditions and events will repeat throughout the cycles of time.' So here's the question: Is it possible that everything from the war and peace between nations to the love and heartbreaks of life began with a seed event somewhere in our distant past? In other words, are we living out a pattern that was initiated with the beginning of time?" (Braden *Fractal Time* 121).

A perfect example of repeating cycles, as related in *Fractal Time*, surrounds the keywords "Surprise Attack." Just after the September 11, 2001 destruction of the Two Towers, Gregg Braden had a realization about the cyclic nature of events and decided to look at whether it would have been possible to predict the attack based on events and conditions in history. Using *surprise* and *attack* as keywords, he reviewed events in history fitting that description, and aptly settled on Pearl Harbor as a previous event fitting that descriptor. He eventually set up a computer program that, using the Golden Ratio (also known as the Fibonacci Sequence or 1.618), calculated the next point in time when the seeds for another event involving *surprise* and *attack* would have been likely to occur.

Interestingly enough the program spit out August of 1984 as the next period when the seed for those events would exist (in the USA). While no actual attack occurred, this was during the Cold War. The Soviet Union had anticipated a nuclear attack from the US and had planned a preemptive strike. While it is impossible to know just how close the US was from nuclear disaster, it is confirmed that this calculation was indeed able to predict and/or identify seed-periods for repeating events (Braden *Fractal Time* 29-32).

On an individual level this also plays out. Most people know someone who gets depressed around a certain time of year, and oftentimes that can be traced back to a tragedy in their life--death of a loved one or some other severe trauma or loss. I know a number of people who claim that a particular time of year for them is particularly fraught with problems. For one woman it is the November/December holiday season, and after serious marital problems ending in divorce, it has always carried a cloud of doom-and-gloom for her. For another man the last few weeks in September carry this weight of darkness. In the case of the former it is possible that through inner healing and a choice to create new and happy memories during that time of year she could overcome and rewrite that cycle. For the latter individual, he does not seem to recognize how his poor choices renew the cycle, and that were he to seek as a whole to make better life choices, come out from under a curse in prayer, and stop sowing into the darkness-cycle, he could learn to embrace the growth that season has to offer him instead of fearing it. The power of that curse-cycle could be broken and he, too, could overcome its effects.

While Chronos Events are cyclical in nature, they are not guaranteed to occur. As Gregg Braden demonstrated in his book, these "seed events" are just that—seeds. As each cycle comes around, it is possible that the event will "bear fruit" and produce the results of that cycle, and it is possible it will not realize itself and remain dormant until the next cycle comes around. As was seen with the Soviet Union, the surprise nuclear attack did not materialize, but the conditions were present for it to occur. While it is impossible to know what thoughts, actions, or events might tip the scale in one direction or the other for any cycle, it is valuable to know that events can be avoided. The good news is that it is possible to avert disasters, catastrophes, and war, but the bad news is that if great evil can be averted through actions, so can great good. The ability to recognize repeating patterns and cycles in life gives one additional ammunition as they work towards releasing the Kingdom of Heaven into the earth–both in partnering with Godly cycles and working toward unraveling demonic ones.

In my own life, I have had a habit for the last eight or nine years of staying up late on Christmas Eve to listen to what God wants to tell me about His plans for the coming year. This involves things on a global level, in my nation and region, as well as things for myself personally, my family, and other friends and acquaintances who God wants to send a message to. This is an event that both I and my wife can anticipate each year as it happens at the same time and same date every year. While I have my own personal yearly-event, there are other holy days and feast day that the Bible lists as significant: Yom Kippur, The Feast of Trumpets, The Feast of Tabernacles, Passover, Purim, and Rosh Hashanah. While there are certainly other holidays that have developed over time that could fit this pattern, the above-mentioned are the most clearly seen in scripture.

KAIROS EVENTS

There are times in everyone's life when God hijacks us in his timing. One example is known as a divine appointment, where we meet someone seemingly at random during our day and it turns out that we have connected with the right person at the right moment. Regardless of the outcome--whether it's that we land a job interview, learn something new, or even simply exchange encouraging words with each other, God is doing something. That interaction can be complex or exceedingly simple, but either way it will contribute to our overall level-grinding process and life-growth.

Divine appointments are by no means the only type of Kairos moment. While other Kairos moments don't have a specific name, they all involve God doing something without any known or obvious intervention on our behalf to make sure they happen. On the day of Pentecost, when the Holy Spirit fell on everyone in the Upper Room in power, it was a Kairos Event where he lambasted them with his goodness. And while Jesus had hinted to them about a week prior that something was going to happen, he didn't tell them what or exactly when that was going to take place. This was a Kairos-moment where God ordained that the time had arrived and He showed up.

Kairos Events happen in the present-day as well, and the more notable ones have long-lasting effects. We usually call them Revival in the Church-world, but the most marked Events are ones where the Holy Spirit showed up in power with unique and often not-seen-before manifestations. The most recent ones in the US are what is known as the Brownsville Revival and the Toronto Blessing. Both took place at churches, but the former was known more for its fire of purity that God was bringing in, and the latter for a restoration of joy and freedom. Both were very significant, and like with all Events, have had a lasting impact on the world.

All Events have significance of some kind, but the level of importance can vary. The events noted above are all God-related, but it is also possible for Satan to create Events. The 9/11 bombing in September 2001 could be considered a Demonic Event. These events are always a form of Kairos although there is no fullness of time involved. Rather, the demonic realms delight in causing mayhem, chaos, and death whenever possible and will take any opportunity whether great or small to bring more darkness into the earth. Oftentimes these opportunities are of human-origin, in that we through our own actions, thoughts, and deeds allow demons to enhance the effects of already-brewing darkness within us.

Peter Tan in *The Spiritual World* expresses it this way:

> At times in societies where an entire community, city or country is taken by a deep set of dark emotional outbursts, feelings of hate or anger that dominate them, it is like the gates of hell are let loose and all manner of evil looking spirits are attracted out from the deep darkness underneath the earth and dominate the entire community or society; causing humans under their power to do their bidding like possessed zombies destroying everything in their path. This sometimes happens when a society has experienced deep seated oppression and injustice for a long time. The undercurrent of pent-up indignation and anger burst like a volcanic eruption and attracts the worst kind of evil spirits to the earth plane. Anarchy takes place and all manner of evil and wickedness are committed by men irrationally. (21-22)

This passage denotes the type of demonic influence behind the "mob mentality" that can happen when large groups of people get together and experience a shared heightened emotional state, often resulting in riots when some of those same people might normally be quite mild-mannered or downright docile (This can happen with any emotion, the most notable being anger and rage).

While at first this topic may seem to have limited usefulness, the value of understanding Events is significant. First, the nature of the Event itself will usually reveal the source of the event--God or the enemy. Once the source is discerned, the appropriate response can follow, including the right kind of prayer and action, and this gives the individual guidance on whether to join the Event by helping it or to actively oppose it. Second, knowing it is possible to calculate the possibility for cyclical events to reoccur allows the individual to target their response in relation to world-events to help prevent them from occurring in regards to the negative, or to promote their realization in regards to the positive.

CHAPTER 12

REPUTATION AND TITLES

Competition and comparison can be some of the most fruitless aspects of life, but there are two sides to any coin. While it is possible to form bad habits of comparison, there is a measure to which we are able to reasonably gauge our own life experiences relative to the experiences of others. To some extent this isn't an unhealthy pattern but simply another way of understanding how the world works. What can be irritating, however, is when this comparison doesn't seem to match with what we would normally expect to see in a world that we perceive as being relatively fair. The laws that make up the natural world are actually much more impartial than we like to believe, but there are invisible governing forces that influence our life experiences in some unexpected ways. Some of these forces are represented through the RPG lens of Reputation and Titles, which we will look at in depth this chapter.

REPUTATION

Reputation in any RPG is important. Depending on how high a reputation (known as Fame) or even how low it is, it can influence the price of items in a market, the quests one receives (including certain special quests being withheld if fame is not high enough), and more. Some items or professions could even be restricted if the proper level of fame is not reached. Fame is usually obtained through special pre-defined actions. Some examples: new discoveries, unlocking pre-set achievements, obtaining new levels, or even as rewards for completing certain quests.

Unlocking pre-set achievements could include things such as: 5 player-kills, 20 player kills, etc.; level 50 reached, level 100 reached; etc. In Real Life some achievements might be: salvation, water baptism, baptism of the Holy Spirit, casting out 50 demons, casting out 100 demons, healing 5 sick or injured people, healing 30 sick or injured people, etc. While it is impossible to prove that achievement rankings exist in the real world, as mentioned in a previous chapter it is a known fact that there *are* rewards in heaven, so the concept is quite plausible. As no human has access to know what actions do and don't carry additional achievement bonuses with them, they are acquired naturally as a result of living life.

The counterpart of fame is infamy, and infamy can be obtained through special actions as well although these actions are far less-positive. Player killing, NPC killing, stealing, and completion of certain evil-aligned quests can result in increased infamy and is usually only useful if one is evil-aligned, as there are few benefits to be had from increased infamy. People are typically less trusting of someone with high infamy, and if infamy is high enough, it is possible that merchants may refuse that player service entirely. The player may be locked out of certain quests due to the negative alignment their high-infamy status brings them. The only people who may give increased trust and/or relationship with those with high infamy are evil-aligned characters, including warlocks and necromancers as well as evil-aligned NPCs such as bandits, vampires, werewolves, etc. Unlike in-game Real Life has no long-term benefits to being evil and cultivating darkness, and any of the spiritual benefits are short-lived; there is no value to infamy whereas there is great value in high levels of fame.

While there are not always clear Real-Life correlations to reputation and infamy from a point-based perspective, the principles still come very much into play. Luke 2:52 explains, "And Jesus advanced in wisdom and stature, and in favor with God and men." If we understand that RPG-fame is synonymous with Real-Life favor, we can see that this verse clearly divides Fame into two separate categories--God-Fame and Human-fame. In the [currently nonexistent—see Appendix 1] *Gamer's Standard Bible* (GSB), this verse would say, "And Jesus increased his Wisdom stat and leveled up and increased his Fame with God and men." Jesus, the Perfect Man himself had to increase in Fame with both God and other humans. If Jesus needed to increase his Fame, how much more do we need to do the same, following his example?

A good example of Fame with man is the following: everyone has met that person who had no skill in a job whatsoever and waltzed into an interview and got hired when we might have applied for a similar position and actually *had* experience and *still* couldn't get our foot in the door. If we are spiritually inclined, we may have met that person who has always been highly spiritually sensitive or easily engages miracles, healings, or the supernatural because it's just always been that way, when we feel like we have to actively hunt down those experiences just to get the drips from a leak in the fountain of Heavenly Glory. I used to feel like that person for a long time, and sometimes still do.

How about that car salesman who is a horrible person but always gets big sales, or the waiter who is an absolute lazy jerk and womanizer but somehow makes far better tips than you do. Or the underperformer who somehow gets great reviews, jokes with the boss, and can get away with anything short of murder as compared to the unlucky fellow who only ever gets called into the boss's office are to get reprimanded for doing something incorrectly when he wasn't trained properly to begin with. These are the most obnoxious versions of fame-in-action where it seems like the Law of Sowing and Reaping has been completely suspended in favor of the horrible-person-who-possesses-high-fame. And while it feels that way, Sowing and Reaping is actually hard at work. Fame is a force that when released causes the world to work toward the benefit of the one who has released it. Thus, the jerk-face who gets great tips or the well-liked underperformer has somehow tapped into a level of fame that causes people to overlook his shortcomings. This does not mean that these people can forever live as miserable examples of humanity without repercussion, but it could delay it for some time in certain areas of life where the fame is applied.

Increased Fame with God basically decides how favorably God looks upon any of us in any situation. This subject is somewhat controversial, and it is a bit difficult to explain for a few reasons. What Jesus accomplished on the cross wasn't just removal of sin. It was a complete eradication of the nature of sin inside us that forces us into downward spiraling behaviors, thought patterns and decisions, freeing us to make life-giving choices instead. The work didn't stop there. Jesus set himself as the standard and example in Heaven before the Father, effectively making him the lens that the Father looks through when judging our lives. It's not that God is somehow struck unintelligent when Jesus walks in the room; it's that Jesus purchased the right for the Father to only view us from the perspective of what Jesus finished on the cross and nothing else. Thus, when the Father looks upon us, he has chosen to always view us in a favorable light.

There's more. It is imperative that the nature of the Father's personality and disposition be calculated here. James 1:17-18 says, "Every good gift and every perfect gift is from above, coming down from the Father of lights, with whom can be no variation, neither shadow that is cast by turning. Of his own will he brought us forth by the word of truth, that we should be a kind of first fruits of his creatures." The Father is the Giver of perfect gifts who doesn't hide in shadows and who doesn't change his mind and flit from mood to mood. He is the most stable, kind, considerate, steadfast Person of Love that one can ever meet. There is NO darkness in him whatsoever. He is *always* favorably disposed toward us and bears us no ill will.

The most oft-referenced Bible passage that describes love is 1 Corinthians 13:4-7. It is commonly read at weddings for this very reason. The Bible also tells us that God is love, and if we want a clear picture of what God's love is like, we have only to switch out the word love for God in this passage. With the change it reads as follows: "God is patient; God is kind; God is not envious or boastful or arrogant or rude. He does not insist on his own way; He is not irritable or resentful; He does not rejoice in wrongdoing, but rejoices in the truth. God bears all things, believes all things, hopes all things, endures all things." If we know that God is as this passage says, then it is hard to believe that with God that the odds are not ever in our favor, and that he is somehow NOT favorably disposed towards us.

Nonetheless, there is still some sort of game-style modifier placed on our lives that influences when, what, and how God answers our prayers, speaks to us, and the degree to which supernatural experiences grace our lives regardless of God's nature of favor toward us. This doesn't make God a liar, but it does mean that the situation is far more complex than we might understand, and definitely more complex than we might prefer. Everyone is loved by God and looked upon with unconditional positive regard, but some people simply get better results than others, and the best way to understand this difference is that some people have more Fame than others. We may not always understand how it works, but it does both exist and work. Functionally, Fame with God influences our effectiveness on the earth inasmuch as we are more able to manifest Heaven's power in the here-and-now.

If quantity of Fame is important, then it is important to increase that Fame, both with God and man. So how does one do that? Hebrews 11:6 says, "And without faith it is impossible to please God, for whoever would approach him must believe that he exists and that he rewards those who seek him." Faith itself is a prerequisite to pleasing God, and God's good pleasure means that we will have increased Fame with Him. We have each been given a measure of faith *by* God so no one is without the faith needed to please Him. However, it is a fact that some will invariably nurture that faith more than others. Developing faith is done first and foremost by hearing, and hearing comes by way of the word of God. Faith can also be cultivated through practice, meditation on Godly principles, and experiencing the supernatural. A second means by which fame can be increased is through prayer. It is not that prayer forces God to like us, but it brings our hearts and minds more in alignment with His, and as we reflect Him more and more his favor becomes more able to manifest in our lives.

On the other hand, some players have a very high infamy, to the point where it seems they have purposefully developed it. It is much easier for evil-aligned characters to gain infamy, but anyone can raise theirs provided they do all the wrong things. Stealing, deception, and vandalism are ways one can earn infamy, but none of these are the fastest. The worst players tend to sport something known as a Murderer's Mark, which the system places on them when they kill other players. The term for this is a Player Killer, abbreviated as PK. PKers are to be avoided as they value the lives of others only for the experience they gain by killing them. They do not care how they mess up the other players' gameplay. While some in-game maps are specifically designed for those who enjoy PK-ing, normal gameplay does not involve rampant murdering of other players. As mentioned before, Real Life has no value for infamy, and the best recommendation is to get rid of it in two ways: first by getting rid of it, applying the power of the blood of Jesus to our lives in prayer, and second by not obtaining more of it, making good choices that simply don't accrue infamy.

TITLES

A Title is a system label that a player receives for his actions and any resulting reputation. Titles act as an additional buff over and above any other items, spells, and party buffs he may have. While designed to affect the stats and skills of the player who holds the title, they can at times have broader effects such as increased Leadership over a party, debuffs to certain mobs, and other area-effects such as increased health regeneration for those in a ten-meter radius. Titles are helpful because they provide an extra edge over any competition, including mobs.

Titles are usually obtained through certain actions. For example, if a player is grinding in an area full of goblins, after killing 100 of them, they might acquire the title "Apprentice Goblin-Hunter" that provides an additional 5% attack against Goblins when the title is equipped, as well as an extra 5% of gold and drops from all mobs. If a player continues to hunt Goblins, he may eventually be granted a new title: "Journeyman Goblin-Hunter" that does everything the Apprentice title did but adds an additional +5 to Strength and Dexterity stats and increases the % attack to 10% against Goblins.

There are also Rare titles--ones that come in limited quantity, such as the first to discover a dungeon or explore a new area, winning a tournament, or being the first to perform a certain action. "Firsts" titles are usually obtained by players who begin a game early on, but that does not mean that there aren't other hidden Rare titles that can be discovered as the game progresses.

Some titles can be obtained by defeating certain Bosses, reaching certain pre-set character levels, participating in events or performing certain actions repeatedly. One example of this could be someone who jumps nonstop for an hour might receive the title "Spring-foot Bouncer" which reduces stamina usage when jumping and adds an additional 10% to jump-height. While a fairly useless title, it is the result of a repeated action.

Titles in Real Life can be obtained in similar ways. For example, a number of years ago I saw a short video online of a man who, by faith, was sticking bobby pins to a wall. After watching this I immediately grabbed a nickel off the desk in front of me and stuck it to the wall; it stayed there for about five minutes!! I ran and showed my wife and then called friends who tried it with the same results. Over the subsequent years I have introduced this particular miracle skill to a good many people, and my grandkids and I sometimes grab handful of coins and stick them to the wall just for fun. Mind you, this is not limited to coins, and can be done with anything. I have seen plates, silverware, small household tools, a USB drive, and even playing cards stuck to walls, doors, filing cabinets, the ceiling, and even glass.

The point here isn't so much about the skill, (although if you haven't by now you should try it) but about the title that accompanies this action and others like it. "Sticky-Wall Apprentice" is the title one might imagine receiving after they too begin sticking things to walls (without glue or other physical alteration of the substances). "Imparter of Miracles" is the title one receives for sharing miracle skills with others. "Apprentice Bearer of Persecution" is the title one receives after having people rant him out, accuse him of being a liar, fraud, deceiver, or similar as a result of sharing the miracle and skill with others. . . not that this has *ever* happened to me. . . While all of the above mentioned titles are made up, they personify the types of in-game titles that Real Life could give. However, there are real titles with real functions, which I explain below.

Functionally, titles release a certain measure of authority into a situation or area and create noticeable spiritual recognition of the person's achievements. While humans typically cannot see titles, other spirit beings can. This is demonstrated through an encounter some Jewish exorcists had with a demon they were trying to cast out of someone. Acts 19:13-16 says:

> Then some of the itinerant Jewish exorcists took it upon themselves to call the name of the Lord Jesus over those who had evil spirits, saying, 'we exorcise you by the Jesus whom Paul preaches.' Also there were seven sons of Sceva, a Jewish chief priest, who did so. And the evil spirit answered and said, 'Jesus I know, and Paul I know; but who are you?' Then the man in whom the evil spirit was leaped on them, overpowered them, and prevailed against them, so that they fled out of the house naked and wounded.

While impossible to know exactly what the demons knew about Jesus and Paul, it is certain they knew *something*, and more specifically that Jesus and Paul possessed something the seven other men didn't have. I suggest that what both Jesus and Paul had obtained were spiritual titles that clearly displayed that the power and authority they operated in that were far above that demon's pay grade. What is equally clear is that the seven sons of Sceva most certainly did *not* possess the necessary titles to address the demon, and were trying to cast it out based off of borrowed merits. Whether in-game or Real Life, the system cannot be cheated.

There are actual titles found in and based off the Bible that carry spiritual boosts with them. These are bestowed upon believers who have engaged the Kingdom of God in a variety of ways: One who is Faithful and True, Overcomer, Man of God, Child of God, Friend of God, and Bride of Christ are just some of the titles found in the scriptures. These titles carry privileges although unlike RPG Titles, Kingdom titles carry responsibilities or restrictions in addition to the customary benefits. One who is known for being a Friend of God cannot engage in the same behavior as someone with the title "Pagan," "Witch, "Unbeliever", or the like, and there are penalties if they do. The information section on the title might read like this:

Title: Mouthpiece of God

Options: +100 Fame
+3 to all stats
3% exp bonus when title is equipped
Effects will stack with other titles

Restrictions: Available to Prophet Class only
Repeated acts of mediumship, necromancy, witchcraft, or other dark arts will cause automatic title change to "False Prophet." Negative title change includes automatic loss of 5 levels, 3% decrease in all attributes and stats, +200 Infamy and 8% more exp. needed per level. "False Prophet" title cannot be unequipped. Can be restored to "Mouthpiece" status. Restoration of title status will not return lost levels.

At the end of the day, there are underlying lessons to take from the existence of titles. It could be argued that the demons' response to the sons of Sceva was the result of their low Fame instead of lacking a title, but whether the response was a result of a lack of title or low Fame matters little. The forces at work in this world are much the same as the forces at work in RPGs, and subtle, invisible forces such as Fame and titles do have a sizeable impact on aspects of daily life. As we become more aware of how our actions alter our Reputation and bring us titles we will be able to enhance our effectiveness in the spiritual realms as well as on this Earth.

Ding! A system message appears.

By performing a certain action you have gained the Title: Deliverer
+10 Affinity with Angels
+20 Authority over Demons

CHAPTER 13

CLASSES AND CRAFTING

In RPGs, certain skills and actions are available to all players--skills such as running, riding, and basic combat skills such as empty-handed fighting. These simple skills ensure that players have the basic abilities that one would have in the real world, but to deeply influence the magnitude to which a player can grow and develop, it requires a *class*. As such, the importance of classes cannot be overstated, as they are crucial for a player's in-game development.

A class typically involves a player selecting a main "type" of character. Most classes fall into a series of categories: Support, Magic, Melee, and Crafting are a few of the major class categories. Classes are also known as Professions, and the in-game ramifications of choosing a class extend to all aspects of character development similarly to how having a profession in Real Life does, including the level of financial prosperity, location, and extra-curricular activities that are required. For example, if a player chooses to be a Blacksmith, he will probably craft weapons and sell them to make money as opposed to spending all his time hunting mobs as a Warrior might.

He might also settle down and remain mostly at a single location, having set up or joined a smithy to do his work. A perfect scenario for a blacksmith is to find a steady supply of raw materials and customers as both together will almost ensure prosperity.

A Mage, Enchanter, or other magic-using character will typically spend more time with arcane learning. They don't tend to care much for physical weaponry, nor do they wear metal armor, and as such are rarely found in a blacksmith's shop. Mages can often be found in or near libraries seeking new spells and abilities, and some may gravitate towards larger cities with bigger libraries. While mages are not bound to these stereotypes in any way, often venturing forth to discover new dungeons and uncover hidden and ancient secrets, the lifestyle of a magic-user will be very different than that of a crafter. These are just two examples of how class influences gameplay, but usually a great variety of classes can be chosen and tailored to fit the player's desires.

Magic classes include the Mage/Wizard/Sorcerer, which typically involves magic-working on the surrounding environment. Magic users tend to wear cloth or leather, and usually cannot equip metal gear as the iron negatively influences their magical work. An enchanter is a magic-class that deal with materials and the making of magical items instead of working with their surroundings, adding magical options to clothing, weapons, and other gear. An enchanter might have a secondary class involving jewelry, tin-smithing, tailoring, or other production-based abilities, but any heavy armor he has in his possession will only be temporary--long enough for him to enchant it and give it back to its owner.

Summoners form magical contracts with animals and magical creatures, transporting them magically to the Summoner's location to do their bidding. Necromancers are a type of summoner but only work with dark magic and the undead. Shamans are a bit of a

CLASSES AND CRAFTING

crossover class that combines a bit of the magic class, including some summoning and magework, with the support-class based healing abilities. Due to their high mana use, all magic-users tend to stock up on mana potions and items that enhance magical abilities and add resistances instead of using health potions like a close-combat fighting class might. Raw materials are only useful if they are spell ingredients, and magic-users often purchase pre-refined materials instead of starting from scratch like the crafting classes, with the Enchanter as the occasional exception.

Support classes work best in a party setting because they tend to have low attack power but are vital when dealing with high level mobs, large mobs, and when one is a long distance away from a respawn point. Priests/Clerics are the mainstay of this class, providing instant healing, healing-over-time, and even resurrection. It is unwise to attempt any quest that carries significant risk with it without at least one priest, and that priest's life must be protected at all costs as the priest can always heal and resurrect the rest of the party, but once the priest is dead the level of risk rises dramatically, and a quest can become significantly more difficult and take much more time. Priests also buff the party with divine blessings that provide temporary stat increases and increased health and mana, as well as removing negative status effects such as poison, decay, and plague. Priests are especially helpful when fighting the undead and evil-aligned characters such as vampires as the priests' holy spells, including healing spells, can often be used to harm the undead. Some types of priests will also carry curses that debuff mobs, but these are more common with priests aligned with evil.

Bards are another kind of support class that use the power of music. They have the ability to raise the attack power of their party members, provide temporary stat increases, and at times, their music can speed the rate of health and mana regeneration. Their music can

185

also cause confusion among enemy mobs and can be used to apply negative statuses on the enemy, decreasing their speed, regeneration, and causing confusion, etc. Bards are very useful during raids as their music carries over a large distance and can at times be used to affect tens or even hundreds of players.

The Shaman, as a magic/support crossover class, have healing magic that provide basic healing and at a high enough level can resurrect other players. Paladins and Monks are crossover classes and while both have support magic available to them they focus on melee. The main advantage of a melee/support crossover class is that they can usually fight solo, but this comes with a disadvantage in that their healing skills are limited and those skills usually reduce the number of combat skills they possess.

Melee classes focus on attack and defense, typically fighting with metal weaponry. The Defender is a party-based player who attracts all of the enemy attention while other players such as the Archer, Mage, and Warrior continue to deal damage unhindered by enemy attacks. Defenders are also known as tanks. They have high defense and health and thus are able to sustain higher damage than other Melee players. A Warrior/Fighter trades some of his health and defense for attack power, but still has significantly higher health than a Mage. This class is excellent for solo-play and players of this class easily fit into any party. An Archer/Ranger focuses on ranged attacks and their goal is to kill the enemy before it reaches them. Archers can use skills that allow them to fire off multiple shots rapidly; they often have other skills that can be used for reconnaissance such as far-sight and night-vision. The Rogue/Thief/Assassin class is the least savory of the Melee classes by far. They excel at misdirection, stealth, and their main goal is to avoid direct confrontation wherever possible. They will use poison to weaken enemies prior to combat, and where possible will sneak up from behind to go for one-strike kills. While it can be fun to play as a Rogue or Thief, these players are often the target of negative attention due to their insistence on walking on the shady side of life.

Crafting classes are those that deal with production, using raw materials which they refine and develop in their work. Crafting classes are often behind-the-scenes in that they tend to have low prestige and are therefore not as commonly chosen by players, but Crafters provide all of the materials that all of the other classes use for daily life and work. The most common of these are the Blacksmith, Tailor, Alchemist, Jeweler, and Cook. As their skills are turned toward the functional and artistic rather than the military or arcane, none of them are built for fighting. Most people don't realize this but without crafters, whether NPC or player, none of the other classes would be able to function properly. Food would go to waste instead of being turned into delectable dishes, clothes and materials would decay instead of being mended and sewn, and broken armor and weaponry would simply rust instead of being repaired and repurposed. In other words, even classes that are not on the front lines are important, and in some ways equally so as those who go out dungeon-hunting and mob-fighting. It is as important to have the right equipment for a task as it is to complete the task itself.

Finally, some games allow another category of classes that is actually an amalgam of the others, aptly named Multiclassing. If done well, this class can enhance a character using complementary skills and abilities between the multiple classes that allow for optimal gameplay. For example, someone who is an Enchanter with a secondary Crafting class of Jeweler will be able to both produce accessories for sale and enchant them. A dual-class Warrior-Archer will sacrifice some strength in battle, but will make up for it through increased agility and thus reduced likelihood of being hit during battle as well as giving the option of ranged attacks, allowing the player to attack from both distance and at close range.

Multiclassing has its own risks as one can create a very poorly multi-classed character. I have always enjoyed the idea of a Warrior-Mage dual class that allows me to use both physical and magical attacks, and if it could be done well, that would be fun, but that is rarely the case. The problem is that this type of dual class has one inherent weakness--being spread too thin. A Warrior-Mage has to split stats between the physical and magical, putting stat points into Intelligence and Wisdom for the Mage class and also into Strength, Vitality, and Dexterity for the Warrior class. Basically, instead of focusing on one or the other, the player has to enhance every single stat instead of having primary and secondary stats. The end result is usually that it makes for an all-around weaker character, a Jack-of-all-Trades who will never come close to mastery in anything.

So how does this correlate into Real Life? As we each learn and grow in life, we exhibit certain tendencies, whether through our chosen profession or our hobbies or other interests and passions. I'll use myself as an example to explain what this might look like and how it could translate into a class.

I am conscious that my strong desire to heal people began to manifest at age 13 and I began pursuing learning in pressure points, herbal therapy, energy medicine, etc. I also looked up poisonous local plants for two reasons--I was curious, and as a Boy Scout I thought it might be a good idea to know what was harmful versus helpful. I have always loved plants and enjoyed gardening and the outdoors, and all of this predispose me towards an alchemist or healer class.

I am currently a nurse by profession and have plans to become a doctor at some point although I'm not sure what type--Osteopath, Naturopath, Chiropractor, Doctor of Oriental Medicine, or Medical

Doctor, but it will probably be one of the five. I am also a very spiritual person and God is a central part of my life pursuits. Healing-and-spirit related functions predispose me toward a priest-type class. When we combine both the spiritual and healing functions I could easily dual-class as a Priest-Alchemist or Priest-Healer support class.

Why is this important? If I understand what makes me tick, so to speak, having awareness of the things that interest and excite me and get me going, then I will be able to better figure out my "place" in the midst of the many options in life. For example, I have a friend who is a very informative and inspirational writer. This man has a range of influence that seems to be ever-increasing, and he has had a good number of invitations to speak at churches and other gatherings. However, to date he has turned down almost every single one of them. Why? Because he has already found his place--at this point he doesn't see himself has a public speaker nor does he have the interest, even though there is nothing physically hindering him from speaking publicly. He knows that his "place" and his passion are as a writer, one who influences people through the words written on the page rather than a stage presence. He has gone to some length to protect a level of anonymity even in the midst of being a published author so that he *can* be a writer instead of a visible celebrity.

If I understand that I am a Priest-Healer than I will gravitate toward the following pursuits as my primary foci: spiritual battle against forces of darkness, divine healing for those in any kind of sickness or pain, providing practical physical solutions for healing in addition to the mystical, and manifesting and releasing the Divine Nature of God in demonstrations of power. Even this book you are reading falls under the category of my Priest class inasmuch as it is the imparting of spiritual wisdom to others, although it could be the work of a Scribe as well.

Multiclassing is not without its own Real-Life difficulties. As someone who enjoys physical activity but also enjoys reading, writing, and engaging the spiritual, I have to find a way to make time for all of it. While there is some clear-headed thinking and meditation that can be accomplished while running, it is difficult to make adequate time to train both the physical *and* the spiritual, and at any given point, one will take pre-eminence over the other. In some ways I actually end up being a bit more of a Generalist with no specific in-depth mastery as a result, but at the same time I am versatile in many situations that require broad-based skills or a variety of spiritual abilities.

Knowing that there is Real-Life significance to having a Class, I have broken down some of the more well-known in-game classes and given them some Real-Life spiritual correlation, as well as included some others that may be less-familiar or are Real-Life specific. This is by no means exhaustive, but focuses specifically on the spiritual aspects of RPG classes and their correlation with Real Life. I have broken this list into three headings: Performing Classes, Crafting Classes, and Equipping Classes. The former involve the performing arts where the *performance* is the product, the second craft *tangible objects* as their product, and in the case of the third they *are* the product. While the last one sounds a bit confusing, I will explain each in depth.

PERFORMING CLASSES

As mentioned above, these classes involve performing arts. Bards and Dancers are the only classes mentioned here, but as you read on it will be apparent that there are a variety of specializations and sub-classes. While actors are not mentioned below, they are a mix between the Dancer and Bard classes and their effects will mirror that combination.

Bard: The Bard-class is a sound-based class, which includes storytelling, inspirational speaking, and musicians, both vocalists and instrumentalists. There are two different sub-classes available: Music specialization and Voice Specialization. Music specialization is correlated with musical ability, whether instrumental or vocal. This specialization will involve Worship Teams, Worship Leaders, and others who create music that brings the essence of Heaven into the Earth realm. Someone who is a preacher, inspirational speaker, or storyteller (oftentimes a teacher or similar) falls under the Voice Specialization. These people value the spoken word over music and use their words to alter mindsets, plant new ideas, and to share wisdom and revelation with their hearers. It is possible to level up both specialties, but there is no specific benefit to leveling both over one or the other.

The benefits of the Bard: Oftentimes this class will help temporarily increase faith and divine affinity. Their actions open people up to divine encounters and at times precede people receiving healing or having other needs met by God.

Dancer: This class provides buffs to the viewers as well as debuffs to the enemy spirits at work in the room. Dancers can have a myriad of styles, including but not limited to Ballet, Hip-Hop, or Liturgical dance. There are other sub-classes of the Dancer class, of which the main subclass is Flagging. The history of flagging dates back thousands of years and was originally used in actual warfare situation for communication, but over time the uses evolved and now they are used in both spiritual and nonspiritual celebrations. A visit to a local dance club rave will demonstrate high-level talent in this class although with the talents possibly not used for the highest benefit possible.

Benefits of the Dancer: Flagging oftentimes will provide buffs and blessings, especially when the flag is being waved over you.

Dancing does the same, but usually involves the dancer dancing near the buff-recipient, whereas flagging gives buffs via waving an object over or at the recipient. In reality the dancing and flags are a means to an end since they provide a physical means of releasing spiritual virtue. It also provides good personal physical fitness as an added bonus!

CRAFTING CLASSES

Tailor: This class is responsible for making clothing and other church paraphernalia that is used for a variety of purposes. My father is an Episcopal priest, and growing up I witnessed a number of operations of this class. First, the priests in most highly liturgical settings wear some sort of gown or robe over their clothing. They also may wear some sort of shawl or drape that has decorative and/or spiritual significance. All of this is called one's vestments, and my father has some that have been crafted by those in his congregation and as gifts.

In liturgical churches parishioners alternate between standing, sitting, and kneeling, and no one likes to kneel on an unpadded floor. One church in particular that my father served at had a group of women who would make padded kneelers using counted-cross stitch, embroidery, and other sewing skills. While it might not seem like a big deal, the padding or lack thereof and the potential pain associated with it can actually make a difference as to how meditative and focused one's prayer-time is while on his knees, which translates ultimately to potential increase in faith and divine affinity, and that doesn't even take into account the love and devotion to the faith that went into the creation of the kneelers themselves. In-game these items would be highly valued by all religious classes due to the buffs they would provide.

The Tailor class typically also makes clothing for liturgical dance, as well as wall hangings and seasonal decorations that hang on pews, the altar, and throughout the rest of the sanctuary. It is, in fact, actually possible for one to craft physical items that contain a measure of spiritual blessing or benefit with them, and this depends not so much on the skill level of the tailor, but on his spiritual capacity. When something is crafted with love, care, and often even is prayed over while being made, there is a Divine essence which begins to saturate it. Over time it will carry an aura of blessing with it, permitting those who are wearing or using it to receive just a measure more of heavenly light and grace as they use it. This benefit applies not just to Tailors but all crafting skills involving physical materials.

Used by the Flagging support sub-class, flags are another notable item that Tailors are responsible for crafting. As mentioned before, there are entire groups of people who use flags in worship, a practice which also dates back to Biblical times. Flags can be used as items of celebration, can herald spiritual warfare, or almost any other creative use one can think for them. I have used them on many occasions during worship or intercession.

Blacksmith: This class doesn't sound at first glance as though it could have any relevance to spiritual life, but that's only if one is expecting the Blacksmith to work with physical materials. In Real Life the Blacksmith is a fairly unknown class although people use it much more often than they believe. It is actually possible to craft spiritual weapons, and there are two ways that I am aware of that this happens. The first is through our words and prayers. In praying for others for inner healing and deliverance, I have at times observed various weaponry sticking out of their soul-body (the body that I envision that represents their soul). Sometimes as I pull out these weapons--often arrows, daggers, darts, and swords, some of which are poisoned--I am able to recognize that these are the words, thoughts, or prayers of others. This means that as we think and speak and pray, we are creating spiritual/soul objects with our words, and they are sent out to accomplish that which we are intending them to do--which in some cases is to wound others. While it is possible that we don't intend to wound someone at all times with our words, those thoughts and words, such as gossip and slander and false accusation, can be damaging nonetheless. Thus, it is important to be aware that spiritual Blacksmithing is not only possible but a highly active class, in some ways a sort of Word-smithing, quite fitting as the Word of God is portrayed in the Bible as a sword.

The second means by which we can create spiritual weapons is to literally create them. I have on multiple occasions either made or duplicated weaponry for people in the spirit, and I know others who have done the same, including my wife. I was in a church service once where I was talking to a couple and telling them about making spiritual weapons (this is done essentially by willing it to be so). They said something along the lines of, "Oh, yeah, we do that too!" and proceeded at my request to make me a chakram, a circular weapon derived from India that is much like a Frisbee with no center, and which the outside edge is a sharp blade. Shortly thereafter I threw it at a woman. While this might not sound very nice, this particular weapon was made with the intention of being used for light, goodness, blessing, etc. and I surmised that if I was using it on another person and had that same intent in mind that it would cast blessings upon her, not injure her. Whether that assumption was true or not when I threw it at this woman, her body actually jerked in such a way as it would have if she had physically been hit by a flying object. She had her back to me at the time, so she wasn't responding to anything she saw happening in her surroundings--it just actually works because as mentioned before, spiritual objects are *real* objects. This is not the only time I have witnessed or directly caused something like this to happen, but it is one example that outlines the reality of spiritual weapon-crafting.

There is another aspect to Blacksmithing that is also nontangible but deals with relationships, not spiritual objects. Proverbs 27:17 states, "As iron sharpens iron, so one person sharpens another." In our interactions with one another, we each sharpen each other, a Blacksmithing-based skill. Over the past number of years, social media has been a significant place of sharpening for myself and many I know. It is a testing ground for ideas, both spiritual and mundane, and there are many writers who have discovered their voice first by writing blog-notes over social media and sharing other material there. Each of us has valuable wisdom and insight to share, as well as new revelation and ideas that help others on their journey. Sharpening is a vital aspect of our growth as human beings.

Alchemist: In Christian religious circles this class mostly crafts essential oils. While some other spiritual groups may have other uses for this class, there is not much alchemy to be done as health and mana potions don't exist in Real Life. Yes, there are drinks with herbs and caffeine in them that can give a physical or mental boost for a time, and I suppose those too could fall under the Alchemy domain, but I will focus on essential oils here.

The Bible mentions oils in a number of places with a variety of uses. Olive oil is the most common and although typically a carrier oil and not essential, it is both a health-food item and a staple of ancient Middle-Eastern life. Mary poured oil of spikenard on Jesus' feet and washed them with her tears and hair. Jesus' body was prepared with frankincense and myrrh, both fragrant oils with healing properties. There are other oils mentioned in scripture, including a number in Song of Songs/Song of Solomon, all of which have medicinal benefits, some of which fight cancer, pathogens including

MRSA, and even physical trauma. There is a directive found in James 5:13-15 which states:

> Is anyone among you in trouble? Let them pray. Is anyone happy? Let them sing songs of praise. Is anyone among you sick? Let them call the elders of the church to pray over them and anoint them with oil in the name of the Lord. And the prayer offered in faith will make the sick person well; the Lord will raise them up. If they have sinned, they will be forgiven.

While the verses above state that the prayer offered in faith is what makes the person well, there is still reason to believe the elders used essential oils to anoint the person. Essential oils have healing properties in and of themselves, and the energetic benefits of these oils combined with prayer can have powerful results. An Alchemist would be the one responsible for the production of these oils, and there are some ministries whose entire method of ministering center on the significance and use of essential oils both in scripture and in present-day.

Artist: The title of "Artist" is a broad designation as art can be broadly defined. For the purpose of this discussion "Artist" refers to those using paint, metal, cloth, or other more typical mediums of art. However, please keep in mind that any medium used for art can carry the benefits of this class. As a class, Artists are not really fit for anything other than crafting and support, but the support that can be provided is considerable. I have heard stories of people who have been healed or received revelation as a result of gazing on a particular painting. In the cases I have heard, it seems the painting in question addressed something for them on a soul level and may have also carried a certain air of heavenly revelation with it that set them free from invisible spiritual chains that were holding them back.

Art itself is highly expressive due to being completely based in the creativity of the mind of the maker, and as such is a fantastic medium to share ideas in a non-threatening manner. It offers inspiration and encouragement as well as hope and peace, depending on the scene that is depicted. Some art can have an interpretive meaning with one or more messages contained in the symbolism therein.

EQUIPPING CLASSES

Equipping classes are not product-based in the same way that Crafting classes are, nor are they like Production classes although the Equipping Classes may contain aspects of each of the others. Their purposes are listed in Ephesians 4:11-13: "So Christ himself gave the apostles, the prophets, the evangelists, the pastors and teachers, to equip his people for works of service, so that the body of Christ may be built up until we all reach unity in the faith and in the knowledge of the Son of God and become mature, attaining to the whole measure of the fullness of Christ." As explained, these classes are to *equip* believers to carry out the command of Jesus--to go into the world and make disciples of all people so that they too may bring the Kingdom of God to the earth.

Some Equipping classes can be hereditary or decided before the person was even born as was the case with Jeremiah the Prophet. In Jeremiah 1:5b God speaks to Jeremiah and says, "Before I formed you in the womb I knew you, before you were born I set you apart; I appointed you as a prophet to the nations." As mentioned in the first chapter, this class-setup is decided at least in part if not fully prior to being born, and in the same way that the Bible talks about blessings being visited on a thousand generations, those blessings sometimes come in the form of a spiritual class.

Apostle: This is a class of Builders. Their specialty is in gathering groups of people together and helping them sort out their strengths and weaknesses to function well as a whole. This class can often be found leading teams of people, regardless of group size, into new endeavors. They are explorers and while they push at the walls of the "established" church, they are also instrumental in engaging new understandings and beliefs within the currently existing church systems.

Prophet: This is a class of Revelators--those who hear God and pass the understanding forward. Prophets are able to help sort out the strengths and weaknesses of others and call out God's plan and destiny for their lives. Exploring the spirit realm and seeking out new revelation are common past times for this class, but sharing that revelation in a manner that others can understand is not a prerequisite, and some prophets live in obscurity due in part to their inability to communicate effectively the things they have seen and heard to others.

Evangelist: This is a class of Hunters or Fishermen, but not the kind that kill. Evangelists reach out to others in their sphere of influence to help bring them into belief in God; they also help prepare and train others to do the same in their own social circles. Evangelists have a broader reach than at first glance, as basic belief in God is not the only focus of an Evangelist. There are those who seek out others already within the realm of Believers and help take them to new heights by sharing with them new beliefs and revelation from God. While Prophets are responsible for obtaining that revelation, Evangelists are very adept at disseminating that information.

Pastor: This class is the Shepherd class, primarily involved in the growth and training of new converts to the faith (i.e. Noob players). Optimally, this class helps others grow into their own gifts and callings and to find their own class(es) that God has designed for them. While this can be done in a vast number of ways, the Pastor class is possibly the most supportive of the Equipping classes, having little function other than helping others to function at their highest. While that statement might make it sound like pastors are unimportant, that is not the case. I am simply stating that the function of a true Pastor is similar to a parent raising a small child. Once that child is full-grown the relationship changes--the child no longer needs help growing up, but can enter into an adult relationship of relative equals. This relationship-transition between parent and child is similar to what the Pastor class should experience if they are doing their job correctly.

Teacher: This class is somewhat self-explanatory, in that the primary function of a teacher is to teach. They take their own revelation and that gleaned from the Prophets and Apostles and come alongside the Pastors to help train others. While Teachers are especially effective with noobs, they can be of benefit to anyone at any age or maturity level if they have information to share that is new or unfamiliar to their audience.

There are useful correlations between in-game classes and Real Life, and when one is able to grasp the underlying functions of a class and the benefits and consequences of specialization, it becomes easier to apply the wisdom gained to Real-Life situations. I have found it helpful to pigeonhole other people to some extent based on their gifts and abilities. The goal in doing so is not so much to limit them to the mental categories I assign them (although there is a risk of that) but it helps me to remember their strengths and weaknesses, which is helpful when interacting with them. I trust the same will benefit the reader as well.

CHAPTER 14

KINGDOM ECONOMICS

Another practical aspect to this RPG model of mine that I hit on time and again in my own life which touches on another characteristic of RPG games is the economic system. In any game there is a mode of commerce by which all players and NPCs function. This commerce system allows the player to buy and sell items and make money as well as purchase new weapons, armor, and enhancements. The more a player uses these new items to help him level up and complete quests, the more money he can make. The more money he makes, the more high-level items he can buy to complete quests more easily. And the process continues. Some games have an entire Class, the Merchant Class, dedicated to this reality. As any good merchant knows, the money systems of these games function on the principle of Compound Interest, even if the game packaging doesn't directly come out and say so.

Compound interest is demonstrated by an upward curve on a graph, which basically shows that the more money that is gained, the faster more money will be gained. The larger the money grows, the faster it grows. Knowing this is useful for game-play in that using wisdom and cunning in-game to grow one's monetary supply early on will reduce hardship later. I used to play the game *Fable* and discovered that supply-and-demand was a significant part of selling to NPCs. If I bought all of any item from a merchant, then bought more of it from the next, and bought it again from a third, I could resell all of them back to the third merchant for a higher price, as they had none and the demand was high. I then turned around to buy them back from that merchant, but due to such a large supply (that I had just provided), the price fell below my original purchase price. With the profit I made on each transaction I started doing this with low-level items--carrots, cabbage, and simple cloth. As the game progressed and I continued this tactic, I was able to afford to do this with precious stones. As one can guess, I never had money problems again as each transaction made me notably richer; to be honest, I traded back and forth about fifteen times per transaction before continuing on my merry journey to total game domination.

I want to make several significant points of comparison between gaming and Real Life regarding commerce in general, but specifically in regards to compound interest. First, Jesus taught about compound interest both directly and indirectly. First he stated in Matthew 25:29, "For whoever has will be given more, and they will have an abundance. Whoever does not have, even what they have will be taken from them." Jesus told numerous parables and teachings throughout the gospels about sowing and reaping that indirectly demonstrate the building-on-effect that compound interest has on things in this universe. But whether direct or indirect, the Bible is very clear as to the power of compound interest. And we, not being unaware of spiritual things, should also be aware of how to apply them in our lives. Have you ever noticed that rich people seem to have a much easier time making money than poor people do? A main contributing factor is compound interest, a principle I explained back in Chapter 3 regarding leveling up.

As mentioned before, compounding, while powerful, is like other laws--highly impartial. If we have a garden and plant a seed that we desire to cultivate, then we profit greatly from its compounding action. If, however, that plant were a hardy weed, by the end of the summer our garden could be so overrun that we give up our garden for lost and try again the following year. Compound interest doesn't care whether we want that plant there or not--it will simply cause it to produce in such a fashion that it multiplies rapidly.

Compound interest isn't the only aspect of Kingdom Commerce that needs to be addressed. Commerce as a whole is a significant motivating factor in Real Life in the same way that it is in-game. For example, as a gamer it is a simple fact of life that in order to even *play* an RPG one must have the resources to play it, which requires two things: time and money. The time a man spends at work, at 40 hours per week, is 40+ hours that cannot be spent playing the RPG. One of the main reasons he is *at* that job is to earn money for life expenses. Essentially, while he needs time *and* money, he spends his time at a job in order to obtain money. So if enough money was obtained, the individual would have both the time *and* the money needed to play more. If all life expenses were paid for, the person could theoretically play the RPG for much longer periods of time each week and level up in much shorter periods of Real-Life time. The Kingdom is no different.

While yes, there is a measure to which we engage Kingdom realities everywhere we go and we are able to pray and to minister to others at work, it's not the same as what I'm referring to. If we have to work most days, we are unable to spend as much time with uninterrupted worship and prayer, to go to conferences and other meetings, or have unfettered time fellowshipping with other believers as we would if we were not as job-bound. Having more money at our disposal meets a *very* practical need--it allows us more time to purposefully self-enhance (as discussed in the Leveling chapter). For that matter, it would give us more time to volunteer, help out the single-parent family down the street with yard work, or any other needs that require time to fulfill. For those who say money isn't important to them, not only are their priorities seriously out of order, but also actions speak louder than words, as most who say this still get up each day and go to work. Money isn't important? Then why spend so much time working for it?

In my own life I am and have been seeking ways to increase my financial standing and increase the amount of money I have coming in each month to the point where one day I won't have to keep getting up and "going to work" each day. Certainly I will still have responsibilities to attend to and will still spend some time on business-related work, but much more of my time will be freed up for pursuits that I consider more significant--namely Kingdom ones. For me this looks like a lot of prayer and worship, but will include overseas ministry, volunteer work, and a serious amount of healing and miracles, along with an occasional vacation with my wife.

While increasing the stream of income each month is an effective way to address the issue of increasing available money, there is another way to solve the problem of not-enough-money and that is to alter the flow of time. What if we were able to work for 8 hours and get paid as normal, then come home and spend eight hours-*worth* of prayer yet only about five minutes of *actual* time had passed? Or if we own our own business or are self-employed and were able to get six hours of work accomplished in two hours, it really wouldn't require "extra" time at all. After all, everyone has five minutes to give to God a day, right? It's just that some of us count a little differently than others. While I recognize some may find this to be a pipedream, I cannot help the fact that what I share here is actually quite possible.

My wife and I have had a few different experiences of being physically transported while driving together, but one in particular highlights my point about altering time. We had been at a gathering at some friends' house two hours north of us. It was snowing heavily and the roads were getting rough. A number of cars on the highway had already escorted themselves into the ditch, so we were taking it at half speed. We spent one hour of the trip at half speed and one faster, but still not normal speed, and arrived home in the regular two hours. Our two-hour trip *should* have taken three to four hours, but instead we arrived in the same amount of time as if we had traveled the whole distance at full speed, which we did not. This is not the first time that sort of miracle has happened to us either, but possibly the most easily verified by simple math.

Ian Clayton, in a message titled *Transrelocation*, spoke about how he always manages to finish mowing the lawn faster than his son, and he used to never understand how. As he shared in his message, his son is young, physically fit, and has no difficulty mowing the lawn, so it is unreasonable that he completes it in one third of the time it takes his son to perform the task. He has also, as a business owner, had his employees remark about how much work he gets done and that they didn't know how he managed to fit so much work into one day. He eventually realized that this was all possible, both the lawn-mowing speed and the work tasks, as a result of time not treating him the same as it treats other people. Whatever the reason he has stepped into a place of heightened experience in this area where time simply doesn't bind itself to him in the same way that it does for others. We know that Heaven exists in Eternity, but Ian seems to tap into that Eternal realm frequently, and when he does this time ceases to pass in the same way for him. It could be he has altered his mindset and belief systems to embrace this time-alteration skill or it may be a skill he was gifted with, but regardless of the why-and-how Ian has hit on a useful method to increase our own Kingdom Economy and God is offering us this same ability as well.

While this is certainly an important skill that can and should be made use of regularly, I will confess a single limitation I have hit with it--I do not have this ability within the realm of my control at this juncture, having yet to have done this at will. And in reality, in order to learn to engage it more, it will likely take more time--the very thing that I am trying to free up via this method. Ironic, I know, but in spite of this, the truth of Kingdom Economics remains: that to be able to increase in Kingdom pursuits, we must be able to free up time, and this can be done by freeing up money directly or by freeing up time instead. Regardless of which method or combination of methods is put into practice, the ultimate goal is this: To spend our lives making the Earth the same as it is in Heaven. God-willing (and He is), we will do just that.

CHAPTER 15

RESPAWNING AND RESURRECTION

In most RPGs the player is pseudo-immortal. Much like a phoenix, while the player can be killed he will invariably rise again by way of a function known as "respawning." Respawning, by definition, describes a process when an entity, whether player or monster, is reborn or recreated after it dies. Monsters usually respawn quickly in-game to provide adequate gameplay experience, but when players die something similar occurs. As mentioned above, players rarely stay dead, and games where player-death is permanent are infrequent as no one likes to start over from the very beginning of the game. Death as a whole is very unforgiving, and the thought of putting all of that effort into the growth and development of a character only to have them die at level 34 would be extremely aggravating to the player, which is why it is so rare.

A respawn point is the location where a player reappears after he or she is auto-resurrected in-game. This happens in a designated "safe point," usually a nearby town or other place that protects the player from meeting another untimely death immediately after respawning. There are often penalties to dying which can include losing levels, experience, skill experience, and even gold or items, but since the player has come back to life he is able to continue moving forward in spite of setbacks.

Resurrection is an in-game skill which is usually only available to the priest-class, and is somewhat self-explanatory, although a little bit different than respawning. With a normal player death they will respawn in a safe-area as mentioned before, with any subsequent penalties incurred. On the other hand when the Resurrection skill is used the player will not incur any of the penalties of normal death, so no experience, gold, or items are lost. Additionally, his body remains in place instead of teleporting miles away to the nearest respawn point, which means he can continue to fight with his party as though nothing happened. Usually he is resurrected with only a portion of his health and mana intact, but that is a very small price to pay. In some instances this skill can decide between victory and defeat when fighting Boss mobs, as the instantly available manpower can turn the tide of battle.

Both Respawning and the Resurrection skill have a Real-Life corollary. As mentioned in an earlier chapter, Jesus, through the process of his death and resurrection, took control over the domain of death and regained mankind's right to not only reverse the effects of death and bring about resurrection, but He removed the right for death to harm us in any way. It is almost like before Jesus came we had a permanent status debuff called "Unto Death" which made us susceptible to physical death, and what Jesus did was give us permanent immunity to the "Unto Death" status. In other words, in reality Jesus died to solve the problem of death, not the problem of sin. Jesus addressed sin because death was sin's payment, and in order to stop people from dying he had to deal with sin fully once and for all.

Imagine this scenario in-game: You are the leader of a large town of people, all of whom are players and none are NPCs. You have fought and endured many hardships with these players but no matter what you do, all of them eventually die. Sure, new players come and take their places, but this particular game has no respawning and each player only gets one access to the game. When they die, that is it. You will never play with them again. Now let us pretend there is a high-level Assassin with a specialty in high-level poisons who is secretly going through the town and poisoning players. He calls himself "The Executioner" and believes it is his job to kill off anyone who has any infamy at all, and due to the fact that everyone makes mistakes, every single player has at least one point of infamy. No matter how many health potions or antidotes they consume or the number of healings and curse-dispellings they receive from the priests, nothing removes the poison and nothing changes their infamy. Slowly, one by one each and every player dies in front of you. Plus, the computer doesn't leave it off at simple death. No, the graphics are unspeakable, blood everywhere and screaming--horrendous screaming. No matter whether you turn your volume off or not, you still somehow hear their screams of agony as they take their dying breaths.

Now imagine that you have searched and searched for a solution and you finally stumble upon a dusty pamphlet in the corner of the library that had fallen behind other books some years ago. You pick up the pamphlet and read it. The contents are clear--there is a way to remove the poison and expunge the infamy from the town forever, but the price is that you have to be poisoned in their place. Because you love your townspeople and are a true leader at heart, not wanting to see their suffering, as it is the only way you decide to willingly lay your life down to save theirs. It's not the infamy itself you are concerned about, but rather the death that the infamy causes.

However, the infamy is what causes the Executioner to poison everyone to death. You would go to any length at all to stop the dying, but in reality the solution is simple: confront the Executioner, destroy the poison recipe, and drink his stores of the foul brew down to the last drop so they can harm no one ever again. Once this is done each member of the town simply has to touch you, transferring all of their infamy and the poison to you, and they will be saved.

This is what Jesus did. He knew that we each were dying slowly of a toxin, an insidious poison deeply entwined within our very being that ever so slowly rots even our very DNA--a toxin known as sin. This sin is the only thing that makes it possible for people to die, and once sin has been done away with, there is no longer any reason for people to perish. Jesus surgically removed the toxin and disentwined it from us so that we no longer have to die. You see, sin is the measurement of death. It is the thing that tells the enemy, agents of darkness, to send dark energies our way. Sin is the attractive force in our lives that brings on decay, disease, and ultimately death. Without sin, there is nothing to attract death-bringing forces to us, and therefore we should in theory live forever. Unlike the in-game scenarios where we can resurrect indefinitely, Jesus has given us the ability *both* to resurrect an indefinite number of times if we die, *and* the ability to never die.

Our problem is that by and large we don't really believe that Jesus conquered sin *and* death. We are so poison-focused that we really only acknowledge that Jesus died to set us free from the toxin of sin, allowing us to die poison-free. I heard a minister once say that "They can die, but they can't die sick. It's not the will of God for them to die sick." News flash! It's not the will of God for them to die *at all*, sick or not! We have completely missed out on the fact that the *real* goal was to prevent death, not just do away with sin! This truth is not something most have ever heard preached from a church pulpit, nor is it a popular view. For whatever reason, people get very angry when told they can live forever and don't have to die, but what is true is not always popular.

Let's think about this logically. Death is an overwhelmingly common experience, but something being super-common doesn't mean it is the *only* option. That's like going to a clothing store and buying dress pants because *everyone* wears dress pants, even though there is a sportswear section in the back corner of the store with really comfortable clothing that you would actually prefer to wear. It is not that there aren't other options, just that few people actually avail themselves of the other choices. Scripturally speaking, Hebrews 9:27 says that man is appointed once to die and then the judgment comes, but it goes on to state that Jesus died *as* me, *in place of me*, because he died once in place of *all mankind*. And if that is true, which it is, then my personal one-time death-quota has already been fulfilled and I may now keep on living. There is no double-jeopardy in the Kingdom of God. I cannot be re-punished for sins that were already paid for, unless of course I *choose* to accept the punishment, which I flatly refuse.

Based on what Jesus did, why on earth would death still be required? Jesus paid for our sins to remove death, and if we still had to die to get to heaven then Satan would be God's best friend. He would actually be *helping* God by killing us to get us back to heaven, but that's not how it works and the idea itself is absurd. In John 10:10 Jesus clearly outlines job descriptions for Satan and himself. He states, "The thief comes to steal and to kill and to destroy, but I have come that you might have life and have it more abundantly." Satan is responsible for death, Jesus for abundant life.

This holds true pretty much anywhere we turn in scripture, but two things have to be done before we will see it that way. First, we have to believe that Jesus was speaking literally when he spoke about eternal life. We have to stop interpreting verses that say "eternal life" as meaning "eternal life in heaven as a spirit being after we die" and take them at face value. Second, we have to look at things consistently. Why would God provide for literal physical resurrection from the dead if eventually people had to die anyway to get to heaven? That would be extremely self-defeating, would it not? Jesus himself said in Mark 3:25, "If a house is divided against itself, that house cannot stand," and Heaven is not a divided house. In John 6 Jesus spoke somewhat plainly on this topic to the Jews. He pointed out that Moses and their forefathers ate manna in the desert and died, but Jesus was providing bread from heaven that they could eat and not die. He gave a one-to-one comparison between eating heavenly manna and physical dying, and eating heavenly bread and living forever. The only way to read that passage with any sense of scriptural literacy is to be consistent and recognize that when Jesus compared the two he was talking about physical death and physical immortality.

The in-game Resurrection skill is almost an exact correlation for what happens in Real Life. When someone dies, his spirit and body become disconnected. The spirit makes its way to heaven or hell or wherever, and the body remains as a lifeless shell back on earth. The body is there for a certain length of time, and during that time period others can come and pray and command that spirit back into the body. If it is successful, the person will physically revive and continue living his life (no, this is not the precursor to the zombie apocalypse). If it is not successful, he will be buried and everyone else will have to grieve and move on. This is the part where Real Life diverges from in-game in that there is no special re-spawn point. There is no way for us to earn our way to a higher karmic level through reincarnation. Once my sins are forgiven I can't get a "better" karma rating since I am as holy as it gets. Thus, death without resurrection is permanent--well, mostly permanent.

There are a few places where the New Testament states that all who are believers and have died will be physically resurrected in new physical bodies at the "End." I personally like to emphasize the *new body* part of this. God is so interested in abundant life that even the dead will not stay dead and will eventually be resurrected anyway even if a resurrection attempt failed and they were buried. In-game it is akin to having beaten the last Boss and the end-credits are rolling. You watch your character and all of the other players who have died get new bodies and go flying into the sky. For those readers familiar with "Sword Art Online," an anime miniseries, it's like the end of the second part where Kirito and friends fly from Alfheim into the new SAO world that appears in the sky. The players don't cease to have bodies as they head toward the floating new world, but rather they just continue forward from where they are at that time.

A lot of people have a hard time with this concept. I suggest the difficulty is that it flies in the face of what they are *used to*. God is able to do exceedingly abundantly more than we can ask or *think*, and I promise you that someone *thought* of immortality a long time ago. The Chinese have stories of immortals dating back thousands of years, and even in the 1990s there was a six-season TV show about it, *Highlander*. If filmmakers can film about immortality for six seasons, I am pretty sure God can one-up them. After all, if *all things* are possible with God, why can't He just transform our bodies without us having to die? Is there a rule that says God is unable to transform our bodies into glorified ones unless we die first? Not that I have ever read.

As I said before, it's not a popular idea but it really should be. We spend billions of dollars each year on healthcare, supplements, surgeries, and this in the United States alone, all in an effort to have a higher quality of life. Deep down beneath it all, none of us want to be sick or die, and many people are actually afraid of death. The gospel of Jesus Christ is literally the "Good News of Jesus Christ" and what could be better news than discovering that we don't actually have to die? Paul wrote in 2 Timothy 1:9b-10 that, "This grace was given us in Christ Jesus before the beginning of time, but it has now been revealed through the appearing of our Savior, Christ Jesus, who has *destroyed death and has brought life and immortality to light through the gospel* (emphasis mine)." If there was ever something that sounded too good to be true but actually was true, this is it, and the scriptures state it plainly.

The fact that the vast majority of people die goes to show that somehow, even though Jesus already defeated death, that the rest of us are really slow to figure it out and appropriate that reality for ourselves. How is this so? It is common knowledge that science presupposes from the time we are born that we are slowly dying. There is a perceived scientific limitation on our cells based on the telomere, a piece of cell anatomy that essentially decides how many times that particular strand of DNA can be replicated. Each time a cell replicates, the telomeres shorten just a fraction. Eventually the telomeres reach a point where they are no longer able to shorten further, and replication ceases. The reason I say this is a perceived limitation is that our beliefs dictate our reality, so if we believe and have faith in the ever-slowly-dying process, that is the result we will get. Modern science, and more specifically the work of geneticist Richard Cawthon and his colleagues at the University of Utah, have found that the enzyme telomerase can alter the shortening process of the telomeres, but that is the best they can do at this time. It can be purchased on the market but is expensive, averaging around $600 for a 1-3 month supply, and that still doesn't create immortality but only slows the aging process by anywhere from 3-10 years.

So how does this not-dying thing work? To proceed we must first look at how health and healing work in-game, then review the Real-Life corollaries. In-game the player's Health level decides how much life he has and how close to death he is. Health regeneration is actually a relevant aspect of this process of immortality and can be defined as the process by which the in-game body heals itself over time. When a player has lost health, if nothing further happens to them to kill them, they will eventually regenerate their health back to 100%. What decides whether a player is living or dying is based ultimately on whether their health is draining or filling. When health is decreasing at a faster rate than it is regenerated, it is safe to say that the force of Death is manifesting. When health is regenerating faster than it is being removed, the force of Life is active. There are skills and items that can influence this in-game, with negative statuses such as poisoning slowly decreasing health over time and where some foods, potions, and skills increase health over time. In reality, both forces are active both in-game and in Real Life, but there is this constant interchange between the two.

If the forces of Death and Life both exist, then it is conceivably possible for more Life to infuse within us than Death at any given moment, and this does happen at times. Any time healing takes place in the body, there is a measure of Life that is at work greater than Death at that given moment. This is true even more so when divine healing takes place. I have personally witnessed people divinely healed of torn tendons, ligaments, broken bones, and a variety of minor sprains, pains, and injuries through prayer in under five minutes each. Without divine intervention some of these injuries take weeks or months to recover from and still others require surgical repair with the body part never returning to its original strength. When I have seen healings take place the Life of God powerfully worked in those injuries and restored them in moments. If that Life can work so powerfully at specific times and yield such dramatic results, why cannot that same Life energy regularly infuse our bodies to an extent that it overpowers the Death that attempts to work within us? The truth is it can, but to change our experience will first require us to change our beliefs.

If we truly want to experience the many things this vast world has for us, it will require many more lifetimes than we have typically been living, and immortality is the only real solution to that problem. If we look back into Genesis in Chapters 3 and 4 at the genealogy list and do the math, we see that Enoch and many others, while not completely immortal, lived a dozen of our lifetimes, and that was the common experience of their day.

We truly can change our experience, but to do that we have to start believing things that we previously believed impossible. We have to change the things we think and the things we say as well as the way we live our lives. The old saying that goes, "Whether you think you can't or think you can, you are probably right" applies here. The belief and acceptance of death is a pervasive worldwide reality. Try telling ten people you know that you plan to live forever and not die and listen to their responses. I would be shocked if more than one out of those ten people responded with anything remotely approaching agreement. What I have personally found is four typical responses.

1. "Yeah, whatever. That's impossible. You will die like the rest of us." These people are as skeptical as can be and aren't nice about it. This category is the group of people to avoid as they will actively hinder your pursuit of immortality. Identify the Category 1s and then never discuss this topic around or with them.

2. "Hahaha. Let me know how that works out for you." The Category 2's are also completely skeptical, but are just nicer than the

Category 1s. They don't really want to burst your happy little bubble, but they don't believe it for a moment.

3. "Let me know if you ever figure that one out." These people have an underlying wish that it might be possible, but they really don't believe it is because they've never heard of anyone doing it before. If you did ever figure it out though, there is a chance they would legitimately listen with open ears and open hearts because above all else, this group need *permission* to believe differently, but have never gotten it and as a result they perpetrate the myth like everyone else.

Those three options above are the "collective consciousness" of humanity as a whole--it is a culture that believes death is the final option and will allow for no other. These people propagate an erroneous belief about death because they live from the knowledge of their experiences, not from the realm of possibility. God's way is for us to experience what is possible, and in living from past experience these three categories of people limit themselves to only what has previously been tasted and seen by the common man. Even if there were a few men and women in history who did exactly what I am talking about (and there are), the collective consciousness is such that it won't allow these few outliers to alter the course of humanity slowly marching toward death, so such nails that stick up are usually the ones that get hammered down, and those who talk about such things as though they are both possible and real get drowned out by the naysayers.

You will notice I promised you four categories but listed only three.

4. "Really? Tell me how!!" I don't mention it with the rest of them because it has been so rare to find someone who actually fits into that category. Historically, most people who might be 4s are actually highly excitable 3s, but that is changing. Even the conversations I have had with people six to eight years ago on this

subject are different than those that I am having with a select few people today, as the consciousness is starting to shift.

We are entering a period of time where this truth of Immortality will be increasingly common as compared to the past. The wishes, hopes, and dreams of the many will actually be an experiential reality instead of just an in-game concept as has largely been the case up to now. My greatest encouragement is to surround ourselves with like-minded people who are relentless in going towards the goal to obtain the prize. Each day is a brand new opportunity to choose between Death and Life and to receive the power of Life within us in a greater measure. God is not only willing to pour out his Life upon us, but He is able and will do it if we ask--He's always had it for us, but His love demands that He has to wait for us to make the choice and ask Him. Matthew 7:7-8 says, "Ask and it will be given to you; seek and you will find; knock and the door will be opened to you. For everyone who asks receives; the one who seeks finds; and to the one who knocks, the door will be opened." Ask and keep on asking, and as the revelation grows within us, so will the abundant, everlasting life of Christ.

CHAPTER 16

COMBAT

Most computer games, and almost every game that involves a character leveling up in some fashion includes some aspect of fighting or warfare. The exact method of warfare differs from game to game, but the underlying presence of combat remains. In both reality and in a game setting, the combat will vary depending on the situation. For example, when a group of five is fighting a group of twenty with a similarity in strength, it is much better if the group of five can cause long-range damage by spells, archery, throwing weapons, bombs, etc. before the twenty fighters reach them. Each enemy they pick off from a distance increases their chance for victory, and for that matter, their chance of survival. When there is a single high-powered enemy, it is recommended to fight alongside powerful allies, and preferably as many of them as possible. Sometimes more fighters really is better, but in the end the method of combat is dictated by effective combat tactics.

Other things influence combat as well. For example, armor and weaponry play a big part in the way a battle goes. As mentioned above, arrows can come in handy especially when an enemy can be taken by surprise, but when they get close, it is important to be able to switch to a weapon that is appropriate for close combat. While there are movies, such as the *Lord of the Rings* series, that demonstrate highly illogical fighting methods such as where Legolas regularly shooting people with arrows at point-blank range, it doesn't really work like that outside of the movies. Armor plays a part in that its ability to protect the wearer will dictate part of the long-term outcome of the battle. If the armor is in disrepair, is not equipped, or is of low quality, the player is at a higher risk for death or loss of that fight than if his armor is high quality, in good repair and is worn properly.

Combat skills and the level of expertise in those skills also play a part, ultimately to the point that a skill that is more developed will deal a greater amount of damage over a shorter period of time. There is a calculation that can be used to decide how effective a character is at dealing damage over a short period of time, and this has the ability to affect gameplay. Known as Damage Per Second, or DPS, this tells the player how effective their character is in battle based on overall damage dealt. Keep in mind that this is a number that includes the player's weapon of choice and skill proficiencies, as well as any other buffs or enhancements from his armor. In other words, there is no single most-important part of a combat situation as each part plays its own role.

As has been seen throughout this book, the Kingdom of God resembles an RPG game, with a number of aspects of combat that match the spiritual realms, each one having its own place and importance. Before explaining further, however, it is important to understand what this "heavenly combat" actually looks like. For some this concept conjures up images of witches and warlocks casting curses and dark spells over a campfire in some remote province of Africa or South America. For others this involves a Catholic Priest wielding a flask of holy water, shouting, "The love of Christ compels you!" For yet another this might include visions of angels and demons hovering above the earth clashing in an otherworldly battle unnoticed by the people below. All of these are correct in their own way, yet none of them paint the whole picture.

To gain a better understanding of spiritual combat, we must start by knowing who the enemy is. Ephesians 6:12 says, "For our struggle is not against flesh and blood, but against the rulers, against the authorities, against the powers of this dark world and against the spiritual forces of evil in the heavenly realms." The battle first and foremost is not a fight against other people. It can be easy to fight back against others who are doing unkind things to us, (and there are times when we do need to take legal action) but as a whole, our focus needs to be on the spiritual battle we are in, and that battle must be waged accordingly. Verbally or physically attacking others will never solve spiritual problems, and it may well compound them. Unlike some games that make use of redemptive violence, such as murdering evildoers to reduce the overall ratio of good to evil in the world, this does not exist in the Kingdom of God. We do not fight fire with the same fire, but rather we operate the opposite as those in this world do battle--we operate out of love at all times. And we are not left without assistance, as both protection and weaponry are afforded us for this selfsame battle. Ephesians 6:13-18 goes on to explain further:

> Therefore put on the full armor of God, so that when the day of evil comes, you may be able to stand your ground, and after you have done everything, to stand. Stand firm then, with the belt of truth buckled around your waist, with the breastplate of righteousness in place, and with your feet fitted with the readiness that comes from the gospel of peace. In addition to all this, take up the shield of faith, with

which you can extinguish all the flaming arrows of the evil one. Take the helmet of salvation and the sword of the Spirit, which is the word of God. And pray in the Spirit on all occasions with all kinds of prayers and requests. With this in mind, be alert and always keep on praying for all the Lord's people.

The armor is not just a conceptual construct, but literal armor. In *How Satan Stops our Prayers: Combat in the Heavenly Realms* John Mulinde discusses a conversation he had with a former follower of Satan who often had made war against the followers of Jesus and what that man had explained to him about the Armor of God:

> The man said that when prayer breaks through like that, the answer will always come. He said he did not know of a single case in which prayer broke through and the answer did not come [from heaven]. He said that the answer always came, but that in most cases, it never reached the person who asked for it. Why? The battle in the heavenlies. He said that after they [the demons] succeeded in cutting off the open heaven and restoring the rock, they would watch the person and wait because they knew the answer would definitely come.

> Then the man said something that really shook my faith. It was because of what he shared next that I fasted for ten days asking, *'Lord, is this true? Can You prove it to me?'* The man said that every Christian has an angel who serves them. Now we know the Bible says that angels are ministering spirits who minister to us. He said that when people pray, the answer comes in the hands of their angel. The angel brings the answer, just like we read in the book of *Daniel.* Then he said something that was difficult to receive: If the one who prays knows of the spiritual armor

and is clothed with it, the answer comes by an angel who is also clothed in full armor.

However, if the one who prays doesn't care about being clothed in spiritual armor, their angel comes to them without spiritual armor. When Christians are careless about the kinds of thoughts that enter their minds and do not fight the battle for their minds, their angels come to them without helmets. Whatever spiritual weapon you ignore on earth, your angel does not have it when he serves you. In other words, our spiritual armor is not protecting our physical bodies; it is protecting our spiritual exploits.

The man said that as the angel was coming, they would watch him to find the areas that were uncovered and then attack those areas. If he didn't have a helmet, they would shoot at his head. If he didn't have a breastplate, they would shoot at his chest. If he didn't have shoes, they would make a fire, causing him to have to walk through fire. Now, I am just repeating what the man said. Actually, we asked him, '*Can angels feel fire?*' You know what his reply was? 'Remember this is the spiritual realm. They are spirits dealing with spirits. The battle is intense. When they overpower an angel of God, the first thing they go after is the answer he is carrying, and they get it from him. They then give it to people who are involved in cults or witchcraft, so people might say, 'I got this because of witchcraft." (divinerevelations.info)

As Mulinde and the man he spoke with explained, the Armor of God is real. It is a spiritual armor that has real form and substance and actually protects from spiritual attacks. This armor is important because it not only protects us but allows the angels God has assigned to us to use similar armor to ensure their and our protection, as well as to ensure that the answers to our prayers reach us.

The real question is: How is this armor engaged? Armor is only useful if it can be equipped, which it can. Personally I use the power of declaration. For instance, at times I have prayed and said, "Right now I put on the Belt of Truth, the Breastplate of Righteousness, the Shield of Faith, Helmet of Salvation, and Sword of the Spirit in Jesus' name." I have also envisioned myself donning armor to protect myself. According to Hebrews 11, faith is the *substance* of things not seen. If we choose by prayer or even physically acting out putting on invisible clothing to equip spiritual armor by faith, we can expect that the actual substance is being applied to us, and therefore to our angelic forces as well.

I believe we need to actively engage the attributes of that armor to wear it. As an example, Isaiah 59:17 says, "He put on righteousness as his breastplate, and the helmet of salvation on his head; he put on the garments of vengeance and wrapped himself in zeal as in a cloak." To explain what I mean by sharing the above verse, by my count there are twenty-two different places in the Bible where nonphysical objects are used as clothing, whether by God, people, or other forces of nature. The attributes they were clothed with were salvation, thick darkness, joy, shame, disgrace, gladness, splendor, majesty, cursing, righteousness, strength, dignity, zeal, vengeance, terror, despair, gloom, majesty, power, imperishability, heavenly dwelling, and even Christ.

While this is a lengthy list of intangible things that one can be clothed with, the point remains that wearing them looks like something. In other words, there is an experience to go along with the idea of wearing the above-named attributes. When clothed with terror there should either be something that makes us terrified or something about us that terrifies others and being clothed in gloom will likely bring a dark rainy cloud with us wherever we go. If putting on garments of strength, dignity, or righteousness, there should be something about us that causes us to stand with our shoulders just a bit higher and that causes others to stand up a bit straighter when we are around them as the shame, disgrace, and burdens fall off.

To engage the attributes of the armor of God, I believe we need to purpose to live according to those attributes. We ought to live lives that are truthful, righteous, peaceful, and full of faith. We must actively pursue and engage physical and emotional healing and deliverance from darkness in our thoughts and actions. In order to do this, to emulate the way Jesus lived, we simply follow Him. As we embody His attributes more and more, the armor becomes even more effective in our lives. Having it and using it, however, are two different things. The armor of God is spiritual in nature and is available to anyone, but as Paul mentioned in Ephesians 6, he exhorted them to actually put it on. This means that it is possible to have it but not wear it. It is important that we actively clothe ourselves with spiritual armor and "put on" the attributes of our King so that we, too, may be equipped for spiritual warfare.

After the armor is equipped, the scriptures exhort us to take up the Sword of the Spirit, which is the word of God. Some interpret "the word of God" to specifically mean the Bible, but I suggest that is not the only option as the text doesn't actually make that specification. God is alive and well today and still speaks to us. Any time God has spoken to us about something, it is a form of weaponry against works of darkness. One example of this is a friend of mine who we will call "Justin."

Justin has some serious health problems, including type II diabetes, which eventually led to kidney failure and he spent three days each week at dialysis to remove the toxins that his body was no longer capable of excreting. To make matters worse, he developed a pretty bad ulcer on his heel and the heel bone became infected. He was on antibiotics for months to kill the infection, but during that time Justin and I prayed somewhat regularly for his foot to be healed. However, instead of getting better the tissue in the wound started dying and the wound developed an odor that over a few weeks went from bad to really bad. One day as I looked at the foot and saw that large blisters had formed on the top of the foot, completely opposite the heel wound and where there had been healthy tissue just days prior. As a nurse, I was concerned that the wound needed further medical care, and long-term might eventually require amputation if it did not improve. True to form, two days later Justin had be admitted to the hospital. A few days into his stay a cluster of doctors gathered at his bedside for their daily rounds, one of whom remained behind to speak with him further. This surgeon informed him that he was going to lose his foot and that they would amputate in two days.

As one can imagine, Justin was having one of the worst moments of his life, but God had other plans. A pastor friend of Justin's was reading through Proverbs that morning when he read a verse that struck a resounding chord within him and which he knew was meant for Justin. Proverbs 3:26 says, "For the Lord will be your confidence, and your foot will not be taken." This pastor called Justin to give him this word, which elevated him significantly. Here, God was telling Justin to place his confidence in Him and that in spite of circumstances his foot would NOT be taken. Justin took this word to heart.

The next day another surgeon from a different surgical specialty walked into his room and said, "Your circulation in that leg is too good. We aren't going to take the foot." Months later, through some more ups and downs and with another threat of amputation, Justin and the rest of us continued to stand on that word, continuing to pray and decree that his foot would be healed and NOT taken, and even with the setbacks his foot was healed, not taken. A word from God, whether scripture or not, is a faith-weapon. It is something that we can remind ourselves of when we are experiencing difficulties and trials and use it to engage our faith to not only believe for the best outcome, but to see it manifest.

Scripture and activating faith are not the only ways to engage in spiritual warfare. Another method that Jesus used often to deal with demon problems was to cast them out. This is most commonly known as "exorcism" but is also known as "deliverance" and "spiritual warfare" depending on who one talks to. It is important to understand that any believer can do it and while tools can be used, there is no special ritual, school degree, or study program required, and exorcism can be performed even if no crucifix or holy water is present. After all, Jesus' disciples were ordinary men and women who simply followed and learned from him, and they even cast out demons *before* Jesus went to the cross. Think about that!

One of the most notable cases of demon exorcism Jesus dealt with was in Mark 5:1-15 (also found in Luke 8) where Mark shared:

> They went across the lake to the region of the Gerasenes. When Jesus got out of the boat, a man with an impure spirit came from the tombs to meet him. This man lived in the tombs, and no one could bind him anymore, not even with a chain. For he had often been chained hand and foot, but he tore the chains apart and broke the irons on his feet. No one was strong enough to subdue him. Night and day among the tombs and in the hills he would cry out and cut himself with stones.

> When he saw Jesus from a distance, he ran and fell on his knees in front of him. He shouted at the top of his voice, 'What do you want with me, Jesus, Son of the Most High God? In God's name don't torture me!' For Jesus had said to him, 'Come out of this man, you impure spirit!"

> Then Jesus asked him, 'What is your name?'

'My name is Legion,'' he replied, 'for we are many.' And he begged Jesus again and again not to send them out of the area.'

A large herd of pigs was feeding on the nearby hillside. The demons begged Jesus, 'Send us among the pigs; allow us to go into them.' He gave them permission, and the impure spirits came out and went into the pigs. The herd, about two thousand in number, rushed down the steep bank into the lake and were drowned.

Those tending the pigs ran off and reported this in the town and countryside, and the people went out to see what had happened. When they came to Jesus, they saw the man who had been possessed by the legion of demons, sitting there, dressed and in his right mind; and they were afraid.

The significance of this story is threefold. First, it is important to note that a person can have more than one demon as spirits do not occupy spiritual space in the same way we occupy physical space. Second, note the significant physical abilities granted this man by the demons and how he responded to their presence in him. While he was more than half-crazy, he was able to break metal like it was a small stick. When the demons saw Jesus coming, *they* ran to him with the man's body. The man was not in control. My father is an Episcopal priest who has done his fair share of deliverance, and I have learned a trick or two from him, one of which is to keep my eyes open during deliverance. The reason for this is that with my eyes open, I am able to pay attention to what is going on around me, for the person I am praying for (and the demons in them) very well might react physically while we are praying, much like the man Jesus dealt with in the passage above. Incidentally this also means that I have learned to hear from God and have visions even when my eyes are open, a valuable skill worth having for many reasons, this being only one.

The third important aspect of this story is this--regardless of how many times we have to pray, we are to keep praying until we get results. If we reread the passage above, we observe that Jesus had to command the Legion out of this man twice, and the second time was even after some unique bargaining. Bargaining with demons as a general whole isn't the best plan, but there are times when bargaining with a demon will make the deliverance easier. It's essentially like granting a plea bargain to a guilty suspect when you have bigger fish to catch. The demon is still going to leave, but there may be options as to where the demon goes. The reason I point this out is to negate the concept that Jesus did everything he did because he was God-in-man's-body. While Jesus was perfect, he was operating as a man filled with Holy Spirit, the same Spirit who fills us. If it took Jesus two times to command a legion of spirits out, it should be no surprise if we don't always get the results we are looking for on the first try.

In fact, this is a little like comparing the DPS of two players. While each player is able to cause damage, the actual DPS of each player will vary, and sometimes it will even differ based on the kind of mob they are fighting due to their strengths and weaknesses. In a fight, regardless of whether a player is able to one-hit kill or has to continually attack to defeat the mob, the player will continue attacking until he or the mob dies. In the same way, casting demons out can resemble this. If it comes out with a single command, great, but if it requires multiples of attempts to get the person free then we must keep attacking until we have defeated it.

Some tips from my own experience with deliverance ministry are as follows. First, to know if a demon actually left can be difficult. To be most effective it requires the gift of discernment of spirits, but it is possible to tell sometimes even without special spiritual knowledge.

The Bible says in Psalm 104:4, "He makes his servants winds, his spirits flames of fire." Demons are spirits, and oftentimes respond to being cast out as though they are a form of wind (In Hebrew the word "spirit" itself literally means "breath"). On many occasions when casting demons out I have seen people burp, cough, pass gas, yawn, or even sneeze. This tells me that demons are leaving even without using some sort of spiritual sixth-sense. When I observe physical changes happening in their body, I know movement is happening, and if things are moving, I can build on that momentum to get the person free (Vomiting is another option which I have had happen to myself on multiple occasions although it looks like normal vomiting most of the time, nothing like movies might have us believe).

One other thing to keep in mind is whether the passage of air actually completed itself or not. For example, sometimes when doing deliverance on myself I will start to yawn but never "finish" the yawn. It's like the yawn started and stopped halfway. The same could happen with gas or a burp. I might feel it rumbling around but then it stops before actually coming out. Both of these are examples of spirits fighting to stay. If they can get us to think that they came out with a half-yawn, or if we just don't know what is going on, then they will stay and we will be none the wiser. Only when that burp or yawn resolves fully I can know it has left. Either way, I pay attention to these details. I usually tell this fact to people I am praying for, even though I think it might seem silly to them. I used to make a disclaimer about it being strange, but I have stopped because if I make it sound like I think it is weird, they will think it is weird too. I find it normal, so I might as well come across that way and model my expectation, and as a result the person I am helping will usually be fine with it too. If I have to explain further, I do my best to give a short explanation then keep going. The reason is that I refuse to give the demon spirits the ability and room through that person to question my every move, as it would just block me from actually getting the spirits out. Give a simple explanation, and if they disagree, that doesn't matter, as I will still use the passage of air as an indicator whether they believe me or not. I must point out here that yawning or other forms of air passage in and of themselves cannot be the only indicators one uses in this process, and it is important that supernatural discernment is used constantly during the deliverance process. While I have described what *often* happens it's by no means a guaranteed formula.

I have been involved in more discussions than I care to count about whether someone who is a believer can be possessed by demons or not, and it's a discussion I basically refuse to entertain any longer as it is usually indicative of an armchair-believer, interested in mentally understanding the concept from the comfort and safety of his couch, not actually ever casting demons out of anyone and not trying to learn for practical use. I will say this: Yes, Christians can have demons. I don't care if you call it possessed, depressed, or oppressed, and I don't care if you think they are in you, on you, over you, under you, or around you. They're devils. Get rid of them. Don't worry so much about the deep theology behind their location. If you find devils, make them leave, and leave discussion on pinpointing their exact position to someone else who has a goal of total ineffectiveness in deliverance ministry. While there is a measure to which understanding what we are dealing with is wise, I have yet to find a single time when knowing whether the demon was in someone, over them, under them, or next to them made a load of difference in whether I was able to cast them out or not. Regardless of where they are located, when we finish praying they should be long gone. Period.

Knowing that deliverance ministry makes use of the gift of discernment of spirits without an explanation of how the gift works is useless, so I have included a basic explanation. This gift defies easy description because it manifests in a variety of ways and can differ *so* immensely from person to person that it cannot be fit into easy boxes. However, I will explain some general guiding principles of ways one might experience this gift which leaves room for the reader experiment from there with his own gift (Keep in mind the gift is free for *everyone* who asks. Ask and it *will* be given to you).

First, this gift has a couple of uses. The most common definition I've heard is "To be able to tell if someone is speaking something from a Godly or demonic source or from their own soul." That's true, but it's a rather pathetic and limited definition that covers only a small part of the whole subject. There is *so* much more to it than figuring out the source of what someone is saying. However, this aspect of discernment is useful for testing prophecy, when combining it with a knowledge of the scriptures to compare against the word given. But again, there are other applications, such as when dealing with demons directly.

It is possible to train this gift for maximum benefit, allowing us to perceive the spiritual world around us through the gift. This has been touched on in previous chapters, but I elaborate in more depth here on what an actual experience with this gift might look like. Hebrews 5:14 says, "But solid food is for the mature, who by constant use have trained themselves to distinguish good from evil." This gift, as holds true with all spiritual skills, is learned and developed through *constant use.* All throughout the scripture where it talks about spiritual understanding, it refers to the five senses. In other words, when one discerns, he does it through sight, sound, taste, smell, and touch. There is a sixth that accompanies the other five at times which is an internal perception, explained later in this chapter. While some of the examples below might sound a bit outlandish, sometimes it *has* happened to people and they just didn't realize that's what it was. I have had a number of these happen to me personally.

Hearing: I have heard sounds before of things that most certainly were *not* there in the physical, such as barking (with no dogs present), a loud buzzing/whirring sound in my ear, and ringing of various pitches in one ear or the other. I have observed a telltale sign right before the ringing sound comes too, as I can feel the atmosphere shift right next to my ear before the sounds come. This is helpful because the sound can at times be quite loud and would otherwise catch me off guard, as has happened once or twice when that did not occur. A number of years ago I talked with a Nursing School classmate who wasn't even a believer and she's had it happen too. While to some it might seem like tinnitus (ringing in the ears), there is actually something spiritual going on, and is *not* the same as the medical condition, even though the symptoms may appear to be the same. Other sounds are possible too, including hearing entire conversations. I am not always sure what it means, but sometimes I suspect my angels are trying to talk to me, and when I focus in on listening, I often do hear divine direction at those times.

Taste: I've never had it happen but my wife and other friends have. It involves tasting things that are *not* physically there, and which are *not* being eaten at that time. For those it happens to frequently, they may develop a "language" of sorts, where certain tastes mean certain things and which convey certain information. For instance, a sour taste might indicate a demon is present and a taste of apples represent angels, whereas honey might indicates the presence of favor and God's love might taste like fresh cherries. These tastes and their meaning are highly personal and will vary for each individual.

Smell: This is similar to taste, although I *have* experienced it on a few occasions. Smell is a bit harder to discern than taste is, because it is easy to tell if something is actually in our mouth or not, but harder to tell if the fragrance we are smelling is from a natural or supernatural source. My wife went in the spirit into heaven once and afterwards smelled cool mountain air in her house, even though her house was in the middle of a town nowhere close to mountains. One of my own favorite memories was on New Year's Eve of 2005. It was a Friday night and the Watch was cancelled for the night, so my Watch partner Jen and I went to her brother's apartment where he and a number of other believers were hanging out. Somehow we got onto the topic of Old Testament sacrifices and one guy, Matt, remarked that God loves hamburgers, citing all of the cows which were burned on the altar. It was about 2:00 AM at this point and the delicious smell of hamburgers began to permeate the room. As no one was flipping burgers at that time, it was clearly a spiritual reality we all were smelling; about nine of us were present in the room who shared that experience.

Sight: This involves seeing things. Generally, we can assume that it means *literally* seeing something with open eyes, but it can also refer to visions in the mind's eye. Whether in the mind's eye or seen visually, it is important to understand that those things which are seen are actually taking place around us even if our natural eye isn't catching it. Historically it has been rare for me to see spirits physically, so I tend to rely on my mind's eye, but I once saw a shadow move across a wall when nothing was moving, and on occasion I will see flashes of light appear in my peripheral vision. I have seen many gemstones appear on the floor supernaturally, but on rare occasion when I went to pick them up the image disappeared because that stone wasn't physically there like the rest of them. Once I threw a spiritual fireball across the front of a church, and my stepdaughter literally watched the ball of light fly through the air. One night at bedtime a number of years ago my eldest granddaughter asked my wife if she could get the angel next to the bed to "turn the light down" because the light the angel was giving off was keeping her awake.

Touch: This involves the feeling of objects or persons in the spirit. As mentioned in the chapter on Items, I have friends who operate strongly in this area. To them, objects in the spirit have both physical dimension *and* weight. For Jen, if there was an angel standing in front of her and she tried to walk forward she would most likely bump into it, whereas I have walked straight through that same pocket of air with no problem. Mind you, I might see the same angel in my mind's eye, but I can move through it, where she can't see it but usually can feel it easily.

The 6th sense I mentioned is perception. This perception is an internal "knowing" about something. How do I know what I know? I don't have a clue. When it happens, I just know that I know that I know. Oftentimes when it happens to me I have a vision that only lasts for a second, much like taking a snapshot with a camera. When I have this type of vision it is usually unclear, but I end up perceiving so much it like the thousand words came with the picture! This perception-download can accompany the other five senses or it can operate on its own, but if another sense is the delivery mechanism for this perception, do not worry if the other sense is not clearly defined, such as an unclear picture or hard-to-place smell or taste, because in this instance the information itself is the important part.

This sums up what I consider the "basics" of discernment although it is one of those topics that is so broad there's always more to learn about things of the spirit. The gift of discernment is a gift of information--it tells us about spiritual activity, but it does not actually do anything to move, evict, or otherwise harm the spirits.

This is important to know because the gift of discernment of spirits is a form of spiritual reconnaissance whereas the armor and sword of the spirit are the weapons we use for spiritual combat.

When dealing with demons it is important to know that demons, like in-game mobs, have levels of power. There are extremely weak ones and others that are spiritually very strong, and at times far stronger than an individual person. In Christian circles these are often referred to as Principalities, and as a general whole, it is best to leave them alone unless we have direction from God to do something about it. In certain circumstances we can take them on, but again it is not likely to be successful if on a solo mission regardless of who we are and how spiritual we think we are. It's sort of like trying to solo a Level 250 boss-monster with 100 times our Health and with damage-dealing capacity that is fifty times that of our level 30 character. In short, we will lose. What is more likely to happen is that if we are still alive after the fact (yes, people have died in Real Life as a result of this kind of spiritual combat), we will likely lose interest in most things spiritual for a length of time--months or probably years--until we recover enough from it to keep moving forward. Having had a similar experience myself, I will say that it does pay to be wise about what spirits we take on in battle. With that said, I will also say that I'm not a fan of shrinking back in fear. Certainly if we are trying to take on a regional principality on our own that is probably foolish, but if we are delivering someone from demons than I have a "bring it on" kind of attitude and am more willing to take the risk of whatever comes with it. I find individual people to be of greater value than the spiritual space in a region, although I do understand the effects of controlling an atmosphere as discussed in a previous chapter.

Demons have personalities. All spirits do, in fact. They're not mindless robot-drones that simply perform autonomously from a program, but are reasoning and thinking beings. Some are more timid or nervous, while others are arrogant or belligerent. They have as many personalities and personality traits as humans do. Discovering the personality of the demon one is working with at that moment can help set the person free. I have a friend who approaches deliverance from the perspective of an interrogator. His view is that the demon *will* submit to his control, and he will pump information out of that spirit all day long if it means getting the person free. He will at times get the demon to tell him who the main spirit in charge of the cluster is (most demons operate in clusters with one spirit ruling over the rest), allowing him to root out the strongman and not just the peons. Some demons are so full of themselves that if you butter them up in conversation, they'll spill the beans out of pride, showing you just how superior they are while in fact telling you everything you wanted to know about their operation.

After this friend shared his perspective with me, I decided to give it a try. I was working with another friend and delivering them from some issues that came up around a séance they had attended years before as a kid. They were a believer at the time and knew séances weren't godly, but their friends sprung it on them so quickly they barely realized what was happening until the séance was in full swing, and they ended up kicking the spirit out, but not without getting influenced by it. When we did deliverance, I got the spirit to start communicating with me, but after it started telling me information the other spirits kicked it out of her so it wouldn't rat them out any further. Demons have their own unique hierarchies and infighting amongst themselves. Sometimes demons will be more afraid of the ruling demon over them than they are of you, and at those times you aren't likely to get them to talk--unless you can make them more afraid of you. Angels can help with that. Have an angel stick them with a sword a couple thirty times or so and they might loosen their tongue a bit.

There is always more to learn on this topic, and how we can fight against demons to set people free. While this chapter has touched on the basics of spiritual warfare, it doesn't include the topic of inner healing, which will be addressed in the next chapter. There are many teachers who are known for their knowledge and understanding of deliverance, and some good books to further understanding of the topic. *They Shall Expel Demons* and *Spiritual Warfare* by Derek Prince are two I have found useful. There are many other books and resources on the topic as well, but the basics shared here should get us started as we engage and evict demons in ourselves and others.

Ding! A system message appears.

By performing a certain action you have gained the Dominating Aura skill:
+10 to Spiritual Attack
+5 to Defense

CHAPTER 17

HEALING

There's an old gamer saying that says, "A priest is only as good as his biggest heal." Well, maybe not--I *might* have just made that up, but there *should* be a saying like that because in a party setting, it's true. Healing is a significant part of team play and the healer can often make or break a party's effectiveness. While self-healing items such as potions exist, and a player can use the Bandaging skill to fix himself (but only when not in combat), often it is more effective to heal another using divine skills which can be used in any situation, whether in or out of combat.

The actual healing skills themselves vary in both level of ability and type of skill. For example, low level healers have skills with names like "Basic Heal" or "Hand of Restoration." As player level increases, higher level spells such as Party Restore, Major Healing, Recovery, and even Resurrect become available. The significance of these different levels cannot be understated. If a mob is removing 200 health per hit every 5 seconds and the player's Hand of Restoration skill can only replace his health by 150 every 10 seconds, he is as good as dead. When using a higher tier healing skill, that damage can easily be overcome, making the difference between life and death.

Each RPG game typically has a few classes that are able to use healing skills. The Cleric or Priest class is the main healing class, which focuses on divine healing, buffs, and overall party support, although the members of this class have Holy attacks that are especially effective against demons and the undead. Paladins are Holy Knights, dealing physical attacks as well as having some measure of divine protection and healing skills due to their religious affiliation. They are a bit of a hybrid class, but this allows them to party well with others and they come in handy if there is no dedicated healer around. Druids are more nature-based and tend to use healing spells that harness the natural energies around them, much like someone who performs energy medicine in Real Life. Finally the Alchemist, while technically a crafting class, has the ability to make potions, salves, and other items that can increase health and reverse negative status effects such as Poisoning and Disease.

In reality there is no single healing-related class that is better than another as all have their benefits and weak points, and Real Life is no different. The most obvious healers are the physical healers--those who work in the medical field such as Nurses, Chiropractors, Doctors of Oriental Medicine, Massage Therapists, Medical Doctors, and more. These could be likened to Alchemists and those who have the Bandaging skill. These practitioners use earthly knowledge to perform physical healing. Each form of medicine has its limitations and benefits, but each are based on techniques that act on the physical body and use knowledge of the body's physical systems.

Acupuncturists, Energy Healers, Homeopaths, and part of the work of Doctors of Oriental Medicine fall into the category of energetic healing, and as such are like druids, using nontangible means of healing that still fall within the laws of the Natural realm.

All of these specialties make use of the energy signatures and energy fields in the external world to bring not just physical healing, but also resolve old and unhelpful emotional patterns and energies that hold us back in life. These methods are less-useful during events like a heart attack, but in non-emergency situations the results are often longer-lasting and the healing can go much deeper than physical medicine, addressing multiple aspects of a person's health and increasing their overall vitality.

The final type is that of divine healer. In-game this healing comes from a Cleric, Priest, or Paladin, and the healing is done through a release of God-power into the person to bring about wholeness. In the Real World, while some would classify energy healers into this category, I separate energy healing as not quite the same thing. Energy healers use divine energy via a secondary source, similar to how one could view an image behind them due to light reflected off a mirror rather than directly looking at the image itself. Energy healers absorb and gather the life-energy (often called Ki, Prana, Chi, Qi, and Shakti) that makes up and fills the universe and apply it to people and situations to bring healing, whereas divine healers use God-energy directly from the source (God) instead of secondarily from the Universe around them. As I regularly use both methods of healing, I somewhat tell the difference between the two, and directly accessing divine power does not require the same internal effort on my part that working with universal energy requires; in fact, it is much easier to use although less under my control. However, both are very helpful and can be used quite effectively in different times and situations.

In Real Life, anyone can perform divine healing regardless of their class. There is no requirement that one have any special belief system to gain access to divine power for healing. There is no special moral code or righteousness that one must attain to in order to heal using divine power. In spite of this fact, those who have not accessed their righteousness through Jesus Christ will find that they have to do all sorts of righteous works in order to make themselves more holy, whereas those who follow Jesus simply *are* holy and the life that is within Him flows through them wherever they go. Healing through Jesus is a massive simplification of centuries of rules and laws, rituals, ceremonies, and sacrificial systems. After all, sacrifices were used to remove sin, thereby making one more holy, much like in-game removing all of a player's infamy would functionally increase their fame as the negative no longer offsets the positive. The end result of holiness? Demons cannot touch he who lives in full holiness as the light of heaven that surrounds the individual repels all darkness, and God hears his prayers and answers them.

Once, all followers of Jesus were filled with sin, separated from God, and only able to receive temporary appeasement of sin, but now in Jesus Christ they have free access through his righteousness to God. No longer separated, they can trust that if they pray for someone to be healed, God will release a measure healing to them no matter what does or doesn't visibly occur in that moment. In spite of this fact, healing does not always manifest immediately, or sometimes even at all. Thus, divine healers have learned many things about effective healing and the ways that different methods of divine healing function for best results--similar to the in-game experience.

In regards to healers using a variety of methods, it is important to note that certain skills work better than others at different times, and that they work in different ways. For example, using a healing skill while in battle heals damage, but there are some skills that are limited in that they cannot be used in certain situations. A First Aid or Bandaging skill typically cannot be used in combat. This is because the circumstances in battle are not conducive to stopping fighting, as the fighter would have to set down his weapon, pull out a package of bandages, and wrap the injury. If someone did that in Real Life he would be killed. Real Life, as expected, is the same as games. In some situations healing can be done through sheer magnitude of power, while in others, faith is the conduit through which Heaven invades the physical realm. In yet other situations it is neither power nor faith but use of authority that fixes the problem. Two other strong contributors to healing are truth and love. The final two are inner healing, closely linked with love and truth, and that of exorcism or casting out demons as discussed in the previous chapter. I call these various means the "Seven Facets of Healing."

THE SEVEN FACETS OF HEALING

POWER

Power is the most straightforward of the Facets and has a variety of uses. It can be used to cast out demons by force or literally regenerate damaged tissue or create missing body parts. Power can be used to force spiritual encounters for people to experience, which at times can give someone the perspective he needs to receive emotional healing in some area. Jesus was familiar with this method of healing. Luke 5:17 states, "One day Jesus was teaching, and Pharisees and teachers of the Law were sitting there. They had come from every village of Galilee and from Judea and Jerusalem. And the power of the Lord was with Jesus to heal the sick." Again Luke 6:19 says, "...and the people all tried to touch him, because power was coming from him and healing them all." Jesus knew, as we have learned, that directly accessing spiritual power is an effective way of fixing earthly injury, sickness, and disease. Amputees, those missing teeth, eyes, or other body parts, and those with organs or portions of organs surgically removed need some level of power to create the new body parts.

The Power-method of healing is usually the one church-goers are most familiar with. An altar call, where after preaching the speaker will call anyone in need of prayer to the front of the room, is common in many denominations. As a congregation usually has engaged Holy Spirit in worship prior to the preaching message, and the Bible promises that God confirms the word preached with signs accompanying it, the stage has been set for a display of power. When coming to the front for prayer, the angels have been equipped and God's people often receive a spiritual Power Buff, often referred to in charismatic circles as a "corporate anointing" where they tap into a larger flow of healing power than they might normally access on their own or in a different situation without an atmosphere of healing present. This is a great time to heal others and a great way to get results, but it is not the only method available and it is not foolproof.

The downside of operating in power is that it is not always reliable. Much in the same way that running out of mana ends the use of healing skills until more mana is regenerated, if something happens to cut off the flow of power to the healer, then healing will not manifest. If the situation does not line up just-so and there is no "power present to heal," it is quite probable that little to no healing will take place if power is the only way a person knows how to access healing. What, then, does one do if there is no big wave of power in the room or if he isn't in a church service with everything stacked in his favor? Simple. Operate out of authority.

AUTHORITY

Authority by definition is delegated power. While it might sound similar to power, I suggest they are different in their function. Power is raw energy whereas authority is based on a legal system.

Reputation and titles are probably the closest approximation to in-game authority as high reputation influences who will and will not obey a player; with the right title he could even command armies. For example, a policeman has authority given to him by the ruling authority over that region. As long as he is within his jurisdiction-- his sphere of influence--he has authority over the areas that have been released to his care. However, what happens if that cop is short, thin, has little muscle mass and gets into a fight with a 250 pound muscle-bound lawbreaker? That is a situation where power will be ineffective, yet there are times even in that type of situation where the policeman wins. Why is this? The lawbreaker may recognize his authority and surrender. Even if the lawbreaker does not surrender, the policeman may force him to give up not through the use of his own force, but by using his authority to command others to stop the lawbreaker.

A good example of this is in the Disney movie *Aladdin*. Early on in the movie, Aladdin the orphan is walking through the marketplace with Princess Jasmine who is disguised as a commoner. The city guards apprehend Aladdin and are about to arrest him. Three guards are present, all bigger than she, but that doesn't matter. She simply takes off her disguise and orders them as the Princess to let him go. In that situation Jasmine would have been easily overpowered by the guards, but they are required to listen to her. In an interesting twist, the guards tell her that her authority is no good in that situation for one reason alone--someone with greater authority than she gave the command to apprehend Aladdin. If this were a healing, even with Jasmine's use of authority the healing would have failed, which is why we must learn to operate from high levels of spiritual authority so that nothing else can contradict our commands.

Divine healers who are either not in places of influence in a church group and/or who do not have a wave of power ready at their disposal often use the authority method to heal others, especially when dealing with sicknesses that are demon-created. In Luke 4:33-36 Jesus dealt with one such situation. As the story relates:

> In the synagogue there was a man possessed by a demon, an impure spirit. He cried out at the top of his voice, 'Go away! What do you want with us, Jesus of Nazareth? Have you come to destroy us? I know who you are—the Holy One of God!' 'Be quiet!' Jesus said sternly. 'Come out of him!' Then the demon threw the man down before them all and came out without injuring him. All the people were amazed and said to each other, 'What words these are! With authority and power he gives orders to impure spirits and they come out!'

Jesus used this method of prayer often, and as the above passage suggests, he actually combined it *with* power for best results. There was one encounter in particular that Jesus had with a Roman centurion that surprised Jesus, but it was because the centurion was able to correlate what he understood about the military with how Jesus exercised heavenly authority. In Luke 7: 6-10 Luke writes:

> He was not far from the house when the centurion sent friends to say to him: 'Lord, don't trouble yourself, for I do not deserve to have you come under my roof. That is why I did not even consider myself worthy to come to you. But say the word, and my servant will be healed. For I myself am a man under authority, with soldiers under me. I tell this one, 'Go,' and he goes; and that one, 'Come,' and he comes. I say to my servant, 'Do this,' and he does it.'
>
> When Jesus heard this, he was amazed at him, and turning to the crowd following him, he said, 'I tell you, I have not found such great faith even in Israel.' Then the men who

had been sent returned to the house and found the servant well.

Jesus didn't have to use sheer quantity of power to heal--he knew that God had placed legions of angels under his command and that he was able to command healing to the desired location as the angels would bring the healing wherever instructed. Additionally, the words themselves that he spoke carried their own power to bring healing.

In fact, a week before writing this chapter I used the authority-method to heal a person somewhat randomly on my way to a meeting at work. I was walking down the street after parking my car and saw this woman walking with a cane. I thought to myself that I would like to know why she had the cane, and God shared the word "knee" with me in my mind. As she was walking in the direction I was headed, I struck up a short conversation with her about her cane, and it turned out she had arthritis in her left knee which made it difficult for her to walk. I was able to pray with her three times and each time her knee was progressively less painful until the last time she was able to stomp her left leg on the ground with no pain. When I prayed for her, I wasn't looking for some wave of power to show up and I didn't even touch her. I simply spoke a command, and as I did so the cells in her body, the arthritis, and even angels were responding to my command and carrying out what I decreed. That is how authority is used in prayer.

FAITH

Power and authority are useful and important Facets of Healing, but other factors influence healing and faith is a significant one. Probably one of the most-referenced and yet the most misused or misrepresented of the Facets of Healing, Jesus mentioned faith a number of times in the Gospels, usually to comment on the size or measure of someone's faith, whether great or little. Yet, there is far more to faith than just its size as faith is actually a creative force within us. In order to be effective in healing it is necessary to understand how faith works, as well as how it can be hindered and increased. Without this understanding it will be hard to make effective use of the faith we have been given.

First, as I mentioned above, faith is a force. It is something that we have and regularly release from within us. Oftentimes we exercise our faith without even thinking about it such as when we sit down in a chair or touch a light switch. Generally we don't spend time wondering whether the chair will hold us or whether the light will turn on--we simply expect that it will operate as it is supposed to and we act accordingly.

Many people believe that they have little faith at all, but what they don't realize is that the problem is rarely the quantity or size of their faith, but rather what they put their faith in. I will tell a story to illustrate this. My wife and I have occasional gatherings of believers at our house for a time of worship, hanging out, and generally just enjoying God and each other. Some of these times we have fun miracles happen and other times less-so, but there is minimal agenda as we try to let God orchestrate whatever He wants to do in the midst of us. I think most everyone who comes has an expectation that God is a God of Miracles and that He wants to show up in supernatural ways to bless and transform us all. At one meeting in particular, a group of probably eight of us were talking and I asked one man if he had ever stuck anything to the wall by faith before. As you can imagine, he hadn't. I got all excited as I have an absolute blast showing this to people as well as activating their faith to do it too. Grabbing a coin out of a bowl on our table, I had him feel that it wasn't sticky, and I made him do the same with the nearby wall. I then put the coin on the wall, held it for a moment, and let go.

I am guessing you are wondering if the coin stuck or if it fell according to the law of gravity. Well, it stuck, as I already knew it would. This man had never seen this before, so I had him try it. It worked!!! Then I had him try it on the door and halfway off the edge of the wall so only a portion of the coin was touching the wall. And on another wall just to show that I hadn't rigged the wall somehow beforehand. Next I did it with a glass bead to show that even glass could stick to the wall by faith.

[Author's Note: If you haven't tried this yet, stop reading and try it yourself! It's both fun AND educational, as well as a fantastic faith-builder.! Just press the coin lightly until you feel it adhere, then let go. For best results, hold it with your fingernail, not the pad of your finger as it will often stick just enough to your finger to knock it off the wall.]

Just after we did all this he turned to me and asked, "So then if I can stick things to the wall by faith, why can't I just put my hand here through the wall as well?"

"You definitely can," I said. So he tried it. And failed. Which, after my bold-sounding statement that he could and after working another miracle just moments before, would seem somewhat incongruous, does it not? Why wasn't he able to phase his hand through the wall? I can explain.

You see, I have done the sticky-object miracle many times over and already have a high level of faith for coins and some other things sticking to walls. As mentioned in a previous chapter I have done it with tableware, coins, playing cards, glass pebbles, and other random items. I have done it on doors, windows, walls, ceilings, and even hanging halfway off the edge of a wall or ceiling. In fact, I have a friend who works in construction who did it once with an entire sheet of plywood! I have a high level of faith for things sticking to walls due to my experiences. However, even though I know things can stick to the wall by faith, this same faith may not always translate over into other areas.

This is the tricky thing about faith: What we believe, deep down, is what we will release and manifest. The fact is that even though this man was actively a part of this gravity-defying miracle, he was unable to extend that faith further into another supernatural act. In fact, I suggest that everyone in that room, myself included, doubted that he would succeed in putting his hand through the wall. Now don't get me wrong, I would have been ecstatic if he had done so and would have shot my hand and then the rest of my body through it next if I was able to see him do it. But if we were honest with ourselves, even though we were performing miracles at that very time, none of us actually believed he would be able to put his hand through the wall. In all actuality we released a great deal of faith in that moment, but almost all of it in the wrong direction, in what is most commonly called "doubt."

Doubt isn't the opposite of faith, really, but rather it is faith in the negative. It is belief that the very thing we are looking at will *not* happen. To give an illustration, doubt is a little like a man who has a carriage and four horses. He attaches the front of the carriage to two horses, then sets the other two horses up as well--on the back end of the carriage facing the opposite direction. He climbs in the carriage and gives the command for the horses to begin pulling him. After all, he has places to be! After only a few moments he observes them going nowhere. He gives the command again and hears the clopping of hooves, but still feels no movement. Getting out, he gets angry with the horses and begins to whip them, urging them forward. As we all know, if at the end of the day the man doesn't change the way he ties his horses to the carriage, he will continue to get nowhere. This man needs to repent, which doesn't mean slinging snot and tears before some holy man or in some church or temple. That idea is incorrectly based off of the thought that repent comes from the French word *repentir* which means to be sorry for crimes and sins. Rather, the word used in the Bible is the Greek word *metanoia* which literally means to change one's mind. All the man would need to do is change his mind about how he manages his horses, line his actions up with that different thought by *moving* two of the horses, and he would get different results. Likewise, if I were to change my mind-- change my beliefs about what is and isn't possible, putting hands through a wall would be child's play for me as sticking coins to the wall already is.

Faith is essentially the force of belief or the power of belief. Hebrews 11:1 says, "Now faith is confidence in what we hope for and assurance about what we do not see." Faith is literally an unshakeable inner trust that something that hasn't even happened yet *will* happen. Have you ever said something with strong conviction, so much so that even though something hadn't happened yet that you simply knew that it was going to work out that way? That is a use of faith--declaring something that hasn't happened yet will be a certain way and it becomes so. God himself did this in creating the universe--he declared something that at that time was not in existence and as a result it began existing. God did this by faith by releasing the force of his expectation and will.

Knowing that doubt is actually a form of faith manifested in the negative helps us to understand how faith is hindered. The most common way that faith is hindered is through our own unbelief-- usually through the information that we feed ourselves in the external world and through our inner self-talk and our verbalized statements. In other words, we sow doubt into the field of our mind and then wonder why we reap a harvest of unbelief.

Knowing that faith can be hindered, let us look at how it can be increased and what the Bible says about that. Jesus taught the disciples about faith with multiple statements and parables. In Matthew 13:31-32 Jesus speaks of a mustard seed: "The kingdom of heaven is like a mustard seed, which a man took and planted in his field. Though it is the smallest of all seeds, yet when it grows, it is the largest of garden plants and becomes a tree, so that the birds come and perch in its branches." Later on, Jesus and the disciples encountered a boy who was demon-possessed and the disciples were unable to cast it out. Jesus referenced the mustard seed again at that time. Matthew 17:14-21 says:

> When they came to the crowd, a man approached Jesus and knelt before him. 'Lord, have mercy on my son,' he said. 'He has seizures and is suffering greatly. He often falls into the fire or into the water. I brought him to your disciples, but they could not heal him.
>
> You unbelieving and perverse generation,' Jesus replied, 'how long shall I stay with you? How long shall I put up with you? Bring the boy here to me.' Jesus rebuked the demon, and it came out of the boy, and he was healed at that moment.
>
> Then the disciples came to Jesus in private and asked, 'Why couldn't we drive it out?'
>
> He replied, 'Because you have so little faith. Truly I tell you, if you have faith as small as a mustard seed, you can say to this mountain, 'Move from here to there,' and it will move. Nothing will be impossible for you.'

If we look at the two events together, we see a bit of a picture forming. While a mustard seed starts out small, it ends up growing into a large tree. Thus, the original size of the faith is by no means a predictor of what it can grow up into given time. Likewise, when Jesus cast the demon out of the boy and he rebuked his disciples for their little faith, I believe something else was at work than meets the eye. When Jesus rebuked them, he didn't just say, "You screw-ups, why couldn't you make it happen?" He asked very specific questions, "How long shall I stay with you? How long shall I put up with you?"

What Jesus asked is a bit different than it sounds. Translated more accurately from the Greek that sentence says, "You unbelieving and distorted-in-your-thinking generation! How long will I be with you? How long will I sustain you and hold you up?" Jesus was challenging them on what they had failed to learn thus far under his tutelage. He wasn't telling them they were simply a burden, but that he was training them so he would no longer need to be the force undergirding them, but that as they were at that time it was clear they were not ready. When he spoke of their faith, he was trying to explain the power of the faith they already possessed. After all, he said they have little faith but then proceeded to tell that that faith as little as a mustard seed could let one cast a mountain into the sea. Based on what Jesus said, then in theory they should have been able to cast a mountain in the sea. Jesus was after *growth*, not just a complex esoteric concept of "faith."

Faith in many ways is quite simple. It begins with a change of mindset--which is synonymous with repentance. When we change our thinking we are able to believe differently. That difference in belief *is* the faith that is growing. As that faith grows, things that previously appeared impossible become not only probable but actual. What might have seemed an insurmountable barrier before is only a minor setback when faith is expanded. For example, long ago I never would have believed that things could stick to walls by faith. In doing so once, my paradigm of limitations had been stretched permanently and could no longer shrink back down to its previous size. A few years later when I witnessed gemstones literally fall from midair, my beliefs would no longer be able to shrink back to size yet again. Faith causes us to encounter life-changing experiences. Likewise, life-changing experiences cause our faith to increase, which is my favorite method of increasing faith.

Over the years I have gotten flak from other believers and even nonbelievers about this whole sticky-wall miracle thing. I have seen people find very mundane non-supernatural ways to make coins stick, including glue, adhesive paint, and I even saw one person posted a step by step how-to on social media by scoring the back of the coin to create a small metal shaving, allowing them to stick it to the wall like a pin to a cushion. Apparently it is much easier to mock real faith that gets results than it is to step out and try it oneself. It doesn't stop there. I have lost count of the number of times I have heard people say some variation of "People are dying of Aids/Starving/Homelessness/War/Pestilence and going to hell, and you're wasting your time sticking pennies to the wall?"

My first knee-jerk response, for good or ill, is to shoot down the stupidity of their accusation: "You know, sticking a penny to a wall only takes about eight seconds, which leaves lots of time left to heal people." I might point out that the same accusation can be made regarding *anything*. "People are dying and you're wasting your time washing your car/watching a movie/doing the dishes/going to your job/raking the leaves/shopping/etc." It's a completely ridiculous idea that doesn't actually match with common sense, or reality. However, there is more to this miracle than that. After pointing out the foolishness of the comment I usually expound on the following little-known fact: The first time I stuck a coin to a wall by faith it stuck to the wall for about five minutes before it fell. I literally felt the moment that it adhered to the wall and I could feel it pulling toward the wall and away from my finger, but that's not all. I also felt a bolt of energy shoot up my arm. From that time forward I noticed a permanent increase in the percentage of people who got healed when I prayed for them, and that increase has lasted and increased further *to this day.*

You see, supernatural encounters aren't just cool one-time happenings. They are belief-changing events that expand the Kingdom within us and grow our faith. For this reason I have in my own life actively sought out people who operate in unique miracles and experiences that I have not been exposed to before. As for the sticky-walls, what seems quite foolish on the outside has actually borne great fruit in my own life. I have even noted over time that the size and type of things that I can get to stick to the wall and the number of types of surfaces I can stick things to have increased. These things show a third way to grow faith: Exercise.

Exercise of faith does not occur in a vacuum. The regular and active use of faith is where growth happens and faith increases. In 1 Timothy 4:7-8 Paul said to Timothy, "Have nothing to do with godless myths and old wives' tales; rather, train yourself to be godly. For physical training is of some value, but godliness has value for all things, holding promise for both the present life and the life to come." It is really nice to know that we have muscles on our bodies, but if we never exercise those muscles they will not grow stronger. In time they will atrophy, which means to grow weaker. Likewise, faith must be exercised to be of much benefit. In the book *Divine Healing Made Simple* Praying Medic addresses this matter of exercising faith when he states:

> The strategy for growing your faith is to start with a generalized belief that God heals. From there, you simply lay hands on whomever you can and eventually, you'll see some of them healed. As you do, your weak, generalized faith will become more specific and stronger. As you continue in healing, you'll see different types of diseases and injuries healed. You'll develop more faith for specific conditions. If

you continue laying hands on people, the strong faith you have for a few things will broaden into a strong faith for many things. (74)

While exercising faith is a very good way to increase it, we can also increase our faith and reduce our unbelief by paying close attention to what we listen to and are exposed to by others. The saying "Whether you think you can or think you can't, you are probably right" applies here.

If we are constantly fed depressing music lyrics, watch daily misery-in-action on TV (also known as the news), read depressing books, and hang out with negative people, we will find ourselves speaking and believing those same depressing and negative ideas, and we will start declaring and confessing those things about ourselves and our lives. Our thoughts and words have ripple effects that literally alter the world around us to match the things we are saying and thinking, which is why the Bible says in Ephesians 3:20 that, "Now to him who is able to do exceedingly more than we can ask (speak) or think according to the power at work within us." We must choose wisely which power we will have at work within us, whether life or death, because it works both ways.

Those who listen to positive and uplifting messages, who surround themselves with people who think, speak, and act out of faith, hope, and positive beliefs, and who dare to believe for what many consider "impossible" will find that their faith grows and grows, and eventually nothing *is* impossible for them as long as they are willing to believe God.

TRUTH

Faith is a powerful and important Facet of Healing, but one of the contributors to healing, partly because it can contribute to faith is that of Truth. Truth in and of itself is fairly inert; it is mostly how truth is applied that makes it powerful and effective for healing. In any situation, what I believe about the situation will influence the end result. Quantum physics and the Observer Effect alone prove this is true on a quantum level, and all of life is made up of nothing if not uncountable measures of quantum particles. Thus, perception truly does become reality. What I believe about a sickness or injury will drive the results that I get when praying for the sick. If I believe that God gives both sickness and health, death and life, then it will be very difficult for me to have faith to believe that God actually *wants* to heal. It is for this reason in large part that I believe many denominations have very minimal results in healing.

Have you ever prayed like this? "Heavenly Father, I know that So-and-so is injured with a broken leg and they would really love to be healed. So if it is Your Will then please heal them, but if it is not Your Will then let them learn and grow through the sickness. Amen." Let me ask this: What do we call someone who takes their kid out back, breaks his leg, then refuses to take him to a doctor to operate and set the bone, all in the name of "teaching a life-lesson?" We call them a child-abuser, among a list of other choice names, and when we discover their behavior we have the parent arrested and put their child somewhere safe so they aren't abused again.

The idea that God gives sickness and injury is an erroneous belief, otherwise known as a falsehood, one that prevents people from being effective healers. When replaced with the truth, the fact that God does *not* give sickness or disease or injury or death, we can begin to have faith for healing where previously our faith was undermined by our doubt about God's will to heal. Perspective matters and truth makes all the difference.

In this particular case, the idea that God brings sickness and disease comes from the book of Job with an oft-quoted verse that says, "The Lord gave and the Lord has taken away. Blessed be the name of the Lord" (Job 1:21 *NASB*). Job's assumption was based out of a Hebraic belief system which says that God was responsible for everything, and thus if something happened to him, it was God's will. The Hebraic belief was that all spirits were agents of God, including Satan who is clearly portrayed as an enemy who stands opposed to God. Thus, the Hebraic view is that God brought the diseases on Job.

It has long been accepted in Exodus that God went through Egypt and killed the firstborn child of each household when in reality it was an attack of Satan, the enemy who steals, kills, and destroys. Due to the Hebraic mindset that says God inflicts both good and bad on people, the text says, "the Lord" instead of "Satan" or "The Angel of Death" when speaking about the one who went through Egypt and killed all the firstborn. Think about this: If God, considering he knew all the Hebrews lived in Goshen, wanted to not-kill the denizens of Goshen, all he would have had to do was simply not-kill them. Why would God need to warn his people against *His* acts of murder if God could simply have left the Hebrews entirely alone and chosen not to kill them? It's akin to taking a loaded gun and randomly shooting in a crowded room and telling everyone that they need to duck so they don't get hit instead of just unloading the gun and not shooting at anyone. Or better yet, instead of taking that loaded gun and aiming *just* at a shooter, randomly firing the gun in every direction to try to stop a shooter standing in front of you. The truth is that this deeply-entrenched version of reality is based on an understanding of God that is far inferior to the understanding we have now, and doesn't even make logical sense.

Jesus was clear there is a thief who steals and kills and destroys, and delineated that He, Jesus, brings abundant life. It is therefore impossible that death, loss, and destruction are the works of God when Jesus plainly stated they are not. Logically this means that everything that we experience in life is not "meant to be" and by corollary, we do not need to beg God as to whether it be His will to heal someone or if we are allowed to pray for them to be healed because we already know it *is* God's will to heal them.

A new perspective and understanding of reality really does have the power to transform our faith and our prayers, and ultimately the results we see and experience in everyday life. Truth is such a powerful transformative tool, and it is often used along with another Facet--that of Inner Healing.

INNER HEALING

Inner healing is sometimes viewed as some pansy emotional-thing that weak people need to go see a counselor for, but this view couldn't be further from the truth. Every single person on the planet has sustained inner hurts through his or her life experiences. My granddaughters are all under the age of eight and all of them have moments where they break down in tears over the littlest things-- whether because I accidentally stepped on a scrap of paper that in their mind was the most valuable treasure in the world or because I sent them to bed at bedtime.

There is a website called www.Reasonsmysoniscrying.com that is a massive compendium of silly and sometimes completely absurd reasons that children are crying or throwing temper tantrums. Regardless of how silly they are, in that moment, to that child, his inner wounding is real. It is possible he will rapidly heal emotionally from the fact that his parent threw out his dirty Band-Aid a month ago or wouldn't let him throw toys at his brother, but sometimes even with the smallest or silliest of things people don't heal. And whether it seems sensible or not, any unhealed emotional wound whether done on purpose or by sheer accident such as in the above examples, still creates a wound. As with physical wounds, when left unhealed over time will fester, grow, and bring death to surrounding tissue, emotional wounds work similarly. The problem is that emotional wounds can be hidden, pushed down, and ignored such that at times it is decades before someone realizes that he is hurt and gets healing, and many people go through their whole lives without ever being healed of deep inner hurts.

Sometimes the trauma is so deep that the soul fractures as a protective mechanism. I liken it to a gemstone that shatters into multiple fragments, with tiny chips here and there, creating one main gem with missing pieces. That gemstone could be likened to the core human soul or self, with the tiny chips next to it making up the various soul fragments. These fragments are what cause people to have multiple personalities, as the core soul moves all the painful memories into those pieces then fractures them off as a means of coping. This fragmentation happens most frequently when people are children as they lack the coping mechanisms and reasoning capacity that adults possess. I have become more and more convinced that everyone has soul fragments and not just those who visibly exhibit multiple personalities, but some people just have them better hidden than others. It is possible, through prayer, to heal these fragments and integrate them back into the core, creating a complete, vibrant gemstone without spot or blemish. Jesus had no soul fragmentation and it is his desire that we have this same experience.

Inner healing, while powerful all on its own, often resolving depression, anxiety, terror and fear, crippling grief and loss, and even mental disorders such as OCD, has the ability to heal physical maladies. The reason for this is that emotional injuries require some sort of outlet, and if they go untended with no outlet, they eventually will trickle down into the physical realm and cause physical diseases. I have heard stories of people who have forgiven someone and immediately were healed of their crippling arthritis or other bodily injury. It is no surprise, then, that current medical practices can literally medicate emotions away with pills, using physical medications to manage emotional conditions. Instead of taking medications for pains and conditions, would it not be much more sensible to get inner healing and have problems evaporate sometimes overnight? I am not suggesting that people randomly quit their meds, but if someone feels they have heard from God and they are receiving that inner healing they stop having symptoms of disease and choose to stop taking medications, that is an option available to them.

There are many different methods and ways of doing inner healing. There is the Theophostic Method, the Sozo Method, *The Healing Code* method with Dr. Alexander Lloyd, and Bach Flower Essence therapy for emotional healing. Elijahhouse.org has a series of teachings on Trauma that can be very powerful and effective, and there is a one-minute prayer found in those teachings that is extremely useful and simple to use in any emotionally charged situation.

I often use a short prayer when doing inner healing, which I have borrowed from my friend Praying Medic. First, identify the primary emotion or feeling that is bothering or afflicting you. Take that emotion and pray: "Father, I don't want this [name the negative emotion] anymore. Please take it from me and heal all of the wounds that caused it. I ask that you give me [state opposite positive emotions] in place of the [negative emotion]." See if you feel that emotion associated with that situation anymore. If you do, pray again. If you don't, identify the next problem-emotion. Repeat these steps as needed until all of the negative emotions surrounding that situation are gone. This is a simple way to address emotions, but it is not foolproof and sometimes it won't work due to a complex series of underlying issues. I personally use this first and only pursue further if this is ineffective.

I have provided a short list of what *could* include hundreds of other therapies and methods that can be used to assist with inner healing. While there are some methods which are better than others, it really doesn't matter to some extent how we do it so long as healing occurs. Different things work better for different people, so whatever works, go with it. In truth there is no one method that does it the "right way." I don't recall reading a single scripture where Jesus taught a specific method on how to heal physically, and emotional healing is no different. In the end there is one major factor that underlies most inner healing and that is Love, the next Facet of Healing.

LOVE

Love seems like such a simplistic concept, but it is the one thing all of us want and need more of and often find so difficult to obtain. Love is in part a feeling, but it is also an energy, a knowing, and a deep inner sense. Love is meant to be experienced, but it is also an abiding presence, especially when it comes from God. Love looks like a lot of things and all of them are life-giving; none of them bring death. In every place where we have experienced death in the form of inner hurts, injury, or sickness, we need to exchange it with life by receiving healing. Healing is in and of itself a manifestation of God's love--a love that is so strong and powerful that it can bring life and restoration every time there is injury or death working itself in our bodies. In other words, all healing is Divine Love in action, so it is impossible to separate healing from love.

When we are loved perfectly and fully, all of our emotional needs are met. As a result we don't attempt to take energy from others to replace our deficit by hurting them physically or emotionally. In the book *The Celestine Prophecy* James Redfield explains this energy-stealing:

Everyone manipulates for energy either aggressively, directly forcing people to pay attention to them, or passively, playing on peoples' sympathy or curiosity to gain attention (128)....Once humans understand their struggle [to obtain energy by stealing from one another]... we would immediately begin to transcend this conflict. We would begin to break free from the competition of mere human energy because we would finally be able to receive our energy from another source. (89-90)

When our needs are met by the "another source," also known as God, we are able to give His love freely to others to help fill the love-void in their hearts.

Have you ever really thought about the emotional struggles that you go through in your own life and then think about all of the people around you that must be going through similar things? I am sitting in a library as I type this and from here I can see over thirty people--all of whom have their own struggles and problems and trials. What would happen if someone could love them so absolutely that their problems melted away? That their fears and worries stopped galvanizing their thoughts and actions? After all, there is a reason that perfect love casts out fear; when one is full of love there is no room for fear to remain.

We have all had moments in our lives where we wanted more love from someone and didn't get it--a parent, a spouse, a friend, a child, a teacher or religious leader, a coworker, or a supervisor. Someone somewhere failed in the task to love us just as Jesus Christ loves us--completely. We all need love but we are all love-starved and there is the only way we can meet that need is from God. To truly begin to heal, whether physically or emotionally, it requires God-love.

While that sounds really simple when written on a page like it is here, the first thing I think when reading something like that is "Okay, that's great advice but *how* do I do that?" There are many ways to get inner healing, but here is one exercise you can use and adapt however you see fit.

Read this through slowly. Next, close your eyes and try it out:

> Take ten slow deep breaths in and out, and as you do this imagine yourself walking down a set of stairs, one stair per step. At the bottom is a door. Open that door and on the other side see yourself in this bright place of liquid, cloudy, thick substance. That is love in tangible form. As you stand in this place of tangible love, see yourself absorbing it, flowing into you, filling you. Let it fill you until you can't take any more and it starts overflowing like a fountain.
>
> Once the love is overflowing from within you in this bright place, continue to absorb that love and release it like a fountain for a few minutes. As you do this you are letting yourself not just be filled with love but are being *washed* by that love. It is literally cleansing you from within. Let yourself *feel* that love. Even place a hand on your physical heart as you do this--it will help you to let yourself experience that love within your body and soul. Whenever you are ready to finish, turn around and walk through the doorway and back up the steps, one breath per step, then open your eyes. You should not only feel more peaceful and calm, but there may be a feeling of fullness within you that was not there before. (This visualization was adapted from Kirby DeLanerolle with WOW Ministries in Sri Lanka.)

This is a simple visualization exercise that can be done almost anywhere, and while closing one's eyes is helpful, it is not required for the visualization to be effective.

There are a few final things to note about healing that didn't quite fit into any other part of the chapter but which I feel are important to know before moving to other topics. This deals a bit more with the practical aspects of healing, and that has to do with how to know when you are healed.

In-game each RPG player has what is called a Health bar or HP bar. This basically measures the player's level of health either as a fraction of a total number (345/2000) or as a percentage (17.25%). Unfortunately for us, Real Life doesn't have HP bars and doesn't allow us to "diagnose" how far along in the healing process we are in such an objective format. As a nurse, I have found it simple to use the typical hospital pain scale from 0-10 as a guide (with 0 being no pain and 10 meaning extreme pain). I also look at other signs and symptoms such as mobility, what something feels like when touched, etc. Although I am a registered nurse, special training is not required to be able to heal in the manner I am sharing here, and basic observation yields a lot of information. Anyone can see how one side of the body looks compared to the other side and observe for changes. Asking pain level and seeing if it increased, decreased or remained the same, and comparing pre-/post- abilities (for example using something across a room when praying for eyes to be healed, then comparing post-prayer vision to pre-prayer) are all methods I use to test for effectiveness. After all, if I believe God is going to heal the person because of something Jesus already did, there's no reason why it can't happen right now while I am praying, and often it does. After praying I have the person test out whatever the ailment was if possible, and using the results he or she gives me, I decide what to do from there.

If it is better I usually clarify. I ask, "Is it *all* better or *some* better?" Oftentimes people get minimal results and say "It's better," but I want to know if it is completely or only partially healed because they require different actions. If it is only partially healed I pray again, whereas full recovery needs no further action. If using a pain scale and the prayer recipient gives me a number that is more than zero, I pray again. I also encourage him at that time that Jesus did not die for him to get healed only partway, and remind him that with the evidence of the change in pain or mobility that God is healing him at that moment. This helps build faith and encourages him to let me pray until the body part is healed instead of stopping me partway through the process, as many tend to do.

If the pain gets worse or if it moves to another part of their body I know at least some if not all of what I am dealing with is a demon, and I address that accordingly. Oftentimes in public I will not tell someone I am casting out a demon and I say something like, "Every hindrance to this healing must go now in Jesus name." It's a way to pray that keeps the person I am praying for from getting even more weirded-out than they sometimes already are. Let me tell you that when people who have no grid for healing get healed through prayer they can get *very* freaked out, so I try to normalize things and remain calm during the process. If I started spouting stuff about demons to a random person I have no previous relationship with, he is liable to lump me in with the crazies and dash off instead of letting me continue to heal and deliver him. And yes, while I *am* casting out demons, there are times where the less he knows the better.

It is pretty common for people to be uncomfortable with receiving healing prayer, especially when it is done in public. It is easy to spot the signs of discomfort if you are observant. The most obvious signs are people getting fidgety, glancing at their watch, or continually making eye contact with a friend who is with them-- a silent plea to "rescue" them. Talking with the person for a few moments to introduce yourself or asking about their condition or even something random about them can help create a brief amount of rapport with them relationally so they are willing to stick with you to the end. While this might seem manipulative, it's a fact of life that people are relational and are willing to put up with more if they feel some sort of buy-in, and developing even a brief amount of relationship with that person will help this.

This might seem silly to some but it is actually quite important. I cannot tell you the number of people I have prayed for that got partially healed and then walked away and went on with their lives before their healing was complete. Whether it was that they thought it was strange, were busy, uncomfortable, or just happy with a reduction in their problem instead of a solution, it has always struck me as a real shame, and I am not alone in my experiences. It is common among healers to have the person to whom we are offering healing partially or fully reject what we offer, and the relationship that we build with them helps to bridge the gap of their discomfort.

One thing to be aware of when praying for others for healing is that we should *never* touch someone without their permission, whether in church or in public. We don't need some special contract or permission slip for them to sign, but ask first. The *only* people I don't ask first are very close friends and family whom I already know I have permission with--and even then I sometimes still ask! Especially when out in public, it can freak people out when we start touching them without asking, and it opens us up to accusations of assault. Asking first avoids all of these problems. With that said, be prepared they may sometimes decline for us to touch them. I am a very touchy-feely person and I like to hug everyone but my wife is the opposite. She is very picky about who touches and hugs her in any situation but especially with prayer. Everyone operates differently and we have to respect that. Besides, the truth is that touch is rarely required for healing. I have prayed for people over the phone for healing and they have been healed either instantly or gradually, and it works just as well when not in physical proximity, since faith and authority don't function based on proximity. While there are things touch does accomplish, it usually just helps our faith because we have an erroneous belief that touching someone is correlated with effectiveness, when that's simply not how it works.

Finally, don't let yourself or the other person get discouraged if nothing happens or if they only get partially healed and that is all you can manage. There are lots of times I have prayed for people and there was no change. While with many people praying a second or third time is the difference between nothing and something happening, in these moments there was literally no result at all regardless of how many times I prayed. I once prayed for someone over twenty times and nothing happened. This is where the uninformed start to blame, and many a person has been emotionally injured by being told that it was "their lack of faith" as to why they couldn't get healed. The problem is that kind of language and thinking is almost always harmful not helpful. I *never* blame another person for a lack of faith for healing. It doesn't matter if I feel deep down in my spirit that their lack of faith *is* the reason or not, I will not say that to them. I am the healer. I am the one carrying the life of Christ within me. It is *my* responsibility as the one praying for them to release the healing, to deal with the demons, to manifest the results. If they felt they could do it on their own, they wouldn't need someone else praying for them. Even if their faith *is* hindering it, I can't and am not responsible for managing their internal atmosphere. I am only able to be responsible for managing my own faith level, authority, power, love, truth, and inner healing to get the best results possible for others.

If the person really truly doesn't have any results at all, pray a number of times and then encourage them with something positive. Don't leave them on a low note of disappointment if at all possible.

268

Ask God for a word of encouragement to give them so they walk away with something uplifting instead of defeating. And then let that failure remind you of why we must walk in such a way as to be effective vessels of God's Divine Life and let it fuel you toward the next successful healing.

It is my ardent hope that as you have read through this chapter, that God has enlightened you with new understanding in the realm of healing and how it applies to our lives in the here-and-now. There is not a single person on this planet who cannot benefit from the information contained in this section as everyone has at one time suffered from sickness or injury. It is my hope and belief that as we put these principles into action and learn and grow in their use that we will not only live healthy and abundant lives ourselves but will spread that healing to those around us!

CHAPTER 18

END CREDITS

Ding! A system message appears.

> Congratulations Player! You have reached THE END!
> By performing a specific action you have gained the
> Bookworm skill.
> For reaching the End of the Book you receive:
> +2 Wisdom
> +2 Intellect
> +200 Fame
> You have gained a level!

I wish it was really that easy--that all we had to do was read a book and gain some stats, a level or two, and maybe even a skill. Fortunately or unfortunately, life is not usually that easy. It can, however, be that fun. While life doesn't always seem to be as interesting as a game, it becomes much more fascinating as we learn to engage the realm of heaven around and within us. What we used to consider random coincidences are now recognized as the Language of the Spirit--God speaking to us through our circumstances and "chance" encounters. What before might have been a boring bus ride home can now be an opportunity to release Kingdom life on those around us and to practice seeing in the spirit. Where once we were powerless in the face of sickness and injury, we can now become the solution to the pain in the world around us.

I want to encourage you that the information and revelation contained in this book, while fairly comprehensive is by no means complete, and is designed to give a glimpse into a broad range of areas pertaining to the Kingdom of God and living as followers of Jesus. My prayer is that you take this information and run with it, but even more than that I want to leave you with the understanding of just how limited our grasp of the Kingdom really is.

It has taken us hundreds of years since the Protestant Reformation, where Martin Luther began preaching that it is by grace alone that we are saved from sin and death, to gain successive levels and realms of revelation, including most recently the reemergence of the prophetic, healing on a worldwide scale, and the work of the Kingdom becoming much more broadly spread among those in so-called secular jobs as compared to it falling on those viewed as "men of the cloth." Even more recently God has been bringing a better understanding of what he means by "everlasting life" with the revelation of immortality.

The Bible has a great many promises, and a good number of them we have relegated to the far-off time when we all live happily ever after in heaven, but that is not the message that I see God giving us through the Bible. Rather, I see Him encouraging and empowering us to overcome in every area of life and to live out a life of victory instead of trying to hide from the world. After all, if all we do is expect that we are eventually going to lose anyway and then God is going to sweep in and save us, just barely, at the end, what kind of abundant life and what promise of a hope and a future is that?

Whatever you do and however you apply the contents of this book, please realize that God has far more for you than you can ask or think, and the moment you think of something really grand, recognize God has far more than even that planned. If you think you can have superpowers, then think bigger because God has more for you. If you want to glow in the dark, then think bigger because people have already done it. The only limitations that exist in life are those that the enemy tries to throw at us and those we place on ourselves. Be free to believe, free to dream, and free to live your life to the fullest, in confidence and without fear, knowing that God's ability to keep you is and has always been greater than the enemy's ability to draw you away and deceive you. In closing, as adapted from Philippians 4:7, May the peace of God that passes all understanding guard your heart and mind in Christ Jesus. Be well, be whole, live in the blessing of Heaven, and most of all, remember to level up!

GLOSSARY

AOE - Area of Effect - usually referring to the effects of a skill or spell that influence over a broad area instead of just effecting one individual. An example would be that of a meteor shower that hits a thirty-foot radius or a healing spell that heals everyone within ten feet of the caster.

Boss – any named character who is a higher level and stronger than the mobs around him, and who usually is in control of the mobs nearby.

Buff - an action (skill, potion, etc.) that temporarily enhances a player's stats or other attributes. Other words used to describe this effect would be amplification or augmentation. It is the positive form of a *status effect*, the opposite of which is a debuff. Example: A player is prayed for by a priest (in-game) that causes the player to have their health regenerate 5% faster for six hours.

Debuff - an action (skill, potion, etc. that temporarily decreases a player's stats or other attributes. Another word to describe this effect would be downgrade. It is the negative form of a *status effect*, the opposite of which is a buff. Example: A player is cursed by a witch (in-game) that causes the player's defense to decrease by 4% for thirty minutes, causing them to be more easily damaged by mobs.

DPS - Damage Per Second -- a calculation of how much injury/damage a player can do based on their skills, weapons, stats, and any other modifiers.

Drops – the items that are left behind after killing a mob

Game Master (GM) - The developers and/or administrators of the game. In pen-and-paper games this person is known as the Dungeon Master & both terms essentially represent the person in charge.

Guild – an organization in-game made up of players, usually with some broad common goal and/or people who are looking for a sense of camaraderie during the gameplay process. Being a guild member offers additional player benefits.

Guild Leader/Guild Officer – the person in charge of the guild and his ruling subordinates. Most guilds have one leader and multiple appointed officers to manage all guild business.

Mob – any bad guy, although it usually refers to a group of bad guys

Noob – a new player.

Usually noobs are known for asking simple questions, doing lots of silly things, and having poorly built characters. They haven't figured out the game enough to have a good understanding of how to make it work for them instead of against them. They die a lot & I mean a LOT.

Party – a group of people who all agree to play together. This typically involves some computer-automated functions such as shared experience and automatic sharing of item drops. These settings can sometimes be changed by the party leader.

Party leader – the person who sets up the party and invites everyone else to join it.

Player – any person playing the game

Plevel – Push-level – where one person of a low level forms a party with someone of a higher level to rapidly gain items, gold & experience

Non-player character (NPC) – a game-generated character who performs some sort of task or service in the game but doesn't have autonomy as a player

Respawn/Respawning - The act of in-game resurrection, whether by a player or by a mob.

Role Play Game (RPG) - A game where the player immerses himself in an imaginative world AS the character.

Tabletop RPG - A role play game done in a traditional non-electronic style that uses paper and pencil and a human storyteller to direct gameplay.

Tank - A player in a party who has a high defense and large pool of health. The tank usually acts as a decoy to draw the attacks from mobs while the other players attack freely due to the tank drawing the enemy attention.

WORKS CITED AND CONSULTED

Braden, Gregg. *Fractal Time*. Carlsbad, CA: Hay House, 2009.

---. *The Divine Matrix*. Carlsbad, CA: Hay House, 2007.

Clayton, Ian. "Transrelocation." Son of Thunder. Web. 2007. MP3.

Crombie, Ogilvie R. *Encounters with Pan and the Elemental Kingdom*. Findhorn
        Foundation: Findhorn Press, 2009. CD.

DuPlantis, Jessie. *Close Encounters of the God Kind*. www.JDM.org. 1996.
        DVD.

Hawken, Paul. *The Magic of Findhorn*. New York: Harper & Row, 1975.
        Print.

Johnson, Bill. "Spirit of Revelation." Redding, CA: Bethel Church, 2005.
        CD.

Living, Faith. "My Awesome Broadsword." *Faith Living Now*.
        FaithLivingNow.com Web. 11 Mar. 2014. Blog.

Mulinde, John. "How Satan Steals Our Prayers: Combat in the Heavenly
        Realms." www.divinerevelations.info Nov. 2000. MP3

Medic, Praying. *Divine Healing Made Simple*. Gilbert, AZ: Inkity Press, 2013.
        Print.

Prince, Derek. *They Shall Expel Demons*. Bloomington, MN: Chosen Books,
        1998. Print.

---. *Spiritual Warfare*. Charlotte, NC: Derek Prince Ministries, 1987. Print.

Redfield, James. *The Celestine Prophecy; An Adventure*. New York: Warner Books, 1993. Print.

Ranganathan VK et al. "From mental power to muscle power--gaining strength by using the mind." Neuropsychologia. 42.7 (2004): 944-56. PubMed Online 20 Sept. 2015.

Shackell, Erin M. and Lionel G. Standing. "Mind Over Matter Mental Training Increases Physical Strength." *North American Journal of Psychology* 9.1 (2007): 189-200.

Strong, James. *Strong's Exhaustive Concordance of the Bible*. Peabody, MA: Hendrickson Publishers, n.d. Print.

Tan, Peter. *The Spiritual World.* Peter Tan Evangelism: Canberra, AU 2007. PDF.

ADDITIONAL RECOMMENDED RESOURCES

Bickle, Mike. *Growing in the Prophetic*. Lake Mary, FL: Creation House, 1996. Print.

Gardner, Thom. *Alters of the Heart*. Shippensburg, PA, Destiny Image, 2003. Print.

Goll, James W and Michal Ann. *Dream Language*. Shippensburg, PA, Destiny Image, 2006.

Goll, James. *The Seer*. Shippensburg, PA, Destiny Image, 2004. Print.

Grubb, Norman. *Rees Howells, Intercessor*. Fort Washington, PA: CLC Publications, 1952. Print.

Heflin, Ruth Ward. *Glory; Experiencing the Atmosphere of Heaven*. Hagerstown, MD: McDougal Publishing Company, 1990. Print.

---. *Golden Glory; the New Wave of Signs and Wonders*. Hagerstown, MD: McDougal Publishing Company, 2000. Print.

Hinn, Benny. *Good Morning Holy Spirit*. Nashville, TN: Thomas Nelson Publishers, 1990. Print.

---. *The Anointing*. Nashville, TN: Thomas Nelson Publishers, 1992. Print.

Johnson, Tyler. *How To Raise The Dead*. San Bernardino, CA: Create Space, 2010. Print.

Sandford, John A. *Dreams; God's Forgotten Language.* San Francisco, CA:
    Harper & Row, 1968. Print.

Sanford, Paula & John. *The Elijah Task; A Call to Today's Prophets.*
    Plainfield, NJ: Logos INTL, 1977. Print.

Sheets, Dutch. *Intercessory Prayer.* Ventura, CA: Regal Books, 1996. Print.

Smith, Alice. *Beyond the Veil; entering into intimacy with God through prayer.*
    Ventura, CA: Regal Books, 1996. Print.

APPENDIX I:

EXCERPTS FROM THE GAMER'S STANDARD BIBLE*

The following are a series of Bible verses that have been transliterated into Gamer-language partially for fun but also to demonstrate the concepts in this book and how they might be applied in scripture. Much like other paraphrase-transliterations of the Bible, the goal here is to put verses in language that appeal to a certain audience for any benefit they may obtain from it. As a disclaimer, this is not meant to keep in close keeping with the Aramaic, Greek, or Hebrew, but with what I believe the underlying heart of the verses to be expressing in Gamer-style. Enjoy!

2 KINGS 4:1-37

The wife of a man from the Guild "Company of Prophets" called to Elisha "Your servant my husband is dead and you know he revered the LORD. But now his creditor is coming to take my two boys as his Pets."

Elisha replied to her, "How can my skills help you? Tell me, what do you have in your Storage Locker?"

"I have nothing there at all," she said, "except a small potion of olive oil."

Elisha said, "Go around and ask all your neighbors for empty potion bottles. Don't ask for just a few. Then go inside and shut the door behind you and your sons. Pour oil into all the bottles, and as each is filled, put it to one side."

She left him and shut the door behind her and her sons. They brought the containers to her and she kept pouring. When all the bottles were full, she said to her son, "Bring me another one."

But he replied, "There are none left." Then the oil stopped flowing.

She went and told Elisha, and he said, "Go, sell the oil and pay your debts. You and your sons can live on what is left."

One day Elisha went to Shunem. And a Noblewoman NPC was there, who urged him to stay for a meal she made with her Intermediate Cooking Skill. So whenever he came by, he stopped there to eat. She said to her husband, "I know that this man who often comes our way is a Prophet Class player of God. [10] Let's make a small room on the roof and put in it a bed and a table, a chair and a lamp for him. Then he can stay there to Rest and regenerate his HP and MP whenever he comes to us."

One day when Elisha came, he went up to his room and lay down there. He said to his servant Gehazi, "Call the Shunammite Noblewoman." So he called her, and she stood before him. Elisha said to him, "Tell her, 'You have gone to all this trouble for us. Now what can be done for you? Can we speak on your behalf to the king or the commander of the army?'"

She replied, "I have a home among my own people."

"How can I use my skills to do something for her?" Elisha asked.

Gehazi said, "She has no son, and her husband is old."

Then Elisha said, "Call her." So he called her, and she stood in the doorway to the Room of Rest. "About this time next year," Elisha said, "you will hold a son in your arms."

"No, my lord!" she objected. "Please, Prophet, don't mislead me!"

But the woman became pregnant, and the next year about that same time she gave birth to a son, just as Elisha had told her.

The child grew in age and level, and one day he went out to his father, who was with the reapers in the field harvesting the crops. [19] He said to his father, "My head! My head!"

His father told a servant, "Carry him to his mother." After the servant had lifted him up and carried him to his mother, the boy sat on her lap until noon, and then he died. She went up and laid him on the bed of the Prophet, then shut the door and went out.

She called her husband and said, "Please send me one of the servants and a donkey so I can use my Riding skill to go to the man of God quickly, then return using my Home Portal Stone."

"Why go to him today?" he asked. "It's not the Monthly Event or Server Reset."

"That's all right," she said.

She saddled the donkey and said to her servant, "Lead on; don't slow down for me unless my Stamina bar is empty." So she set out and came to the Prophet Elisha at Mount Carmel.

When he saw her in the distance with his Vision skill, the man of God said to his servant Gehazi, "Look! There's the Shunammite! Activate your Running skill to meet her and ask her, 'Are you all right? Is your husband all right? Is your child all right?'"

"Everything is all right," she said.

When she reached the Prophet at the mountain, she took hold of his feet. Gehazi came over to push her away, but Elisha said, "Leave her alone! She is in bitter distress, but I am still under the Cooldown for my Foresight skill so I don't know why."

"Did I ask you for a son, my lord?" she said. "Didn't I tell you, 'Don't raise my hopes'?"

Elisha said to Gehazi, "Tuck your Cloak of Comfort (+3 to Vitality) into your belt (+12 durability), take my Staff of the Prophet (+1 level to all skills) in your hand and use your Running skill. Don't greet anyone you meet, and if anyone greets you, do not answer. Lay my staff on the boy's face."

But the child's mother said, "As surely as the LORD lives and as you live, I will not leave you." So he got up and followed her.

Gehazi went on ahead and laid the Staff of the Prophet on the boy's face, but there was no sound or response. So Gehazi went back to meet Elisha and told him, "The boy has not awakened."

When Elisha reached the house, there was the corpse of the boy lying on his couch. He went in, shut the door on the two of them and prayed to the LORD. Then he got on the bed and lay on the boy, mouth to mouth, eyes to eyes, hands to hands. As he stretched himself out on the boy, activated his Resurrection skill, and the boy's body grew warm. [35] Elisha turned away and walked back and forth in the room and then got on the bed and stretched out on him once more, casting Total Heal. The boy sneezed seven times and opened his eyes.

Elisha summoned Gehazi and said, "Call the Shunammite." And he did. When she came, he said, "Take your son." She came in, fell at his feet and bowed to the ground. Then she took her son and went out.

ISAIAH 61:1-7

The Server Time of the Sovereign Lord is upon me because the Lord has anointed me to preach good news to the poor. He has sent me to use the Bandaging skill on the brokenhearted, to proclaim freedom for the captives and release from darkness for the prisoners. He has sent me to declare the Event "The Favorable Day of the Lord" and "The Day of Vengeance of Our God". To bestow upon them a Crown of Beauty (+10 Charisma) instead of ashes, the potion "Oil of Joy" (removes all debuffs) instead of the *debuff of Mourning,* and a Garment of Praise (+6% chance to negate darkness-based attacks) instead of a spirit of despair. They will be given the Title "Oaks of Righteousness," a planting of the Lord for the display of His splendor.

They will rebuild the Ancient Ruins and restore places long devastated; they will renew the ruined cities that have been devastated for generations. NPCs will shepherd your flocks; other Players will work your fields and vineyards. And you will dual-class as a Priest of the Lord, a Cleric of our God. You will feed on the gold of nations and in their treasuries and Contribution Points you will boast. Instead of the *Shame debuff* you will receive the status *Double Portion,* and instead of disgrace you will rejoice in your inheritance. And so you will inherit a double portion in your land and the permanent title "Joy" will be yours.

LUKE 2:52

"And Jesus increased his Wisdom stat and leveled up and increased his Fame with God and men."

Hebrews 10:32-36

"Remember those days after you had created your character, when you were low-leveled, when you endured great suffering while grinding. Sometimes as a complete noob your entire group got wiped, and other times you stood there right by other noobs who got wiped. You suffered along with those others who had their gear stolen and corpses looted because you knew that you had other indestructible items that were player-bound and leveled up alongside you. So do not throw away your confidence; it will be richly rewarded. Do not stop holding your warrior stance, which has great rage boosts, but patiently Tank the damage, for after the guild master's mom lets him play again, he will come and distribute the chests.

*This is a Gamer-version of certain Bible verses as transliterated by the Author and is covered by Copyright.

Thank you for reading THE GAMER'S GUIDE TO THE KINGDOM OF GOD. If you enjoyed this book, you can find more free content at www.thekingsofeden.com. Please consider leaving a review on Amazon.com so others can find this book more easily. Feedback is also welcomed by the author at thekingsofeden@gmail.com.

Other titles by Michael King include:

Gemstones From Heaven (Book 1 of the God Signs Series)

Upcoming Books:

The End of Revival

God Signs Series
> *Gold Dust from Heaven*
> *Oil from Heaven*
> *Manna from Heaven*
> *Feathers from Heaven*

About the Author

Michael King is a prolific writer by day and a Registered Nurse by night. He hungrily explores all things spiritual and has a love for signs, wonders, miracles, and all sorts of strange phenomena. Michael is married to a beautiful wife who also doubles as his professional editor. His blog, thekingsofeden.com focuses on spirituality with a hint of health-related topics along with a dash of fiction/fantasy writing.